The
Urban Housing
Crisis

**Recent Titles in
Contributions in Sociology**

Homelessness in the United States: State Surveys (Volume I)
Jamshid A. Momeni, editor

Explorations in the Understanding of Landscape: A Cultural Geography
William Norton

Postmodern Social Analysis and Criticism
John W. Murphy

Suburbia Re-examined
Barbara M. Kelly, editor

Impossible Organizations: Self-Management and Organizational Reproduction
Yohanan Stryjan

Religious Politics in Global and Comparative Perspective
William H. Swatos, Jr., editor

Invisible Victims: White Males and the Crisis of Affirmative Action
Frederick R. Lynch

Theories of Ethnicity: A Critical Appraisal
Richard H. Thompson

Population and Community in Rural America
Lorraine Garkovich

Divided We Stand: Class Structure in Israel from 1948 to the 1980s
Amir Ben-Porat

A Fragile Movement: The Struggle for Neighborhood Stabilization
Juliet Saltman

The Sociology of Agriculture
Frederick H. Buttel, Olaf F. Larson, and Gilbert W. Gillespie Jr.

THE
URBAN HOUSING
CRISIS

Social, Economic, and Legal Issues and Proposals

ARLENE ZAREMBKA

Contributions in Sociology, Number 90

GREENWOOD PRESS

New York • Westport, Connecticut • London

Library of Congress Cataloging-in-Publication Data

Zarembka, Arlene.
  The urban housing crisis : social, economic, and legal issues and
proposals / Arlene Zarembka.
    p.   cm. — (Contributions in sociology, ISSN 0084-9278 ; no.
90)
  Includes bibliographical references.
  ISBN 0-313-26691-3 (lib. bdg. : alk. paper)
  1. Poor—Housing—United States.   2. Housing policy—United
States.   3. Housing—Law and legislation—United States.   I. Title.
II. Series.
HD7287.96.U6Z37   1990
363.5'8'0973—dc20   89-38226

British Library Cataloguing in Publication Data is available.

Library of Congress Catalog Card Number: 89-38226
ISBN: 0-313-26691-3
ISSN: 0084-9278

First published in 1990

Greenwood Press, Inc.
88 Post Road West, Westport, Connecticut 06881

Printed in the United States of America

The paper used in this book complies with the
Permanent Paper Standard issued by the National
Information Standards Organization (Z39.48-1984).

10 9 8 7 6 5 4 3 2 1

To my parents,
Richard and Helen Jane Zarembka,
and to the memory of
Jane Dundon (Cummins) Barni and Gregory A. Courtney

Contents

Figures and Table

Preface

I began writing this book after working as an attorney in the Housing Unit of Legal Services for Eastern Missouri from 1976 to 1980. During that time, I represented persons being displaced by urban redevelopment corporations and dealt with issues of racial discrimination. My interest in housing started, however, long before that. When I was a law student in 1973, the neighborhood in which I lived became targeted for redevelopment, and I observed first-hand the gentrification and displacement process, as well as the ideology used to justify it.

Initially, this book began with a focus on displacement. Quickly, it became clear that displacement was too narrow a focus. Accordingly, the book now covers issues of financing, production, and discrimination as well.

Thus, the book, which began as an analysis of displacement, has become a proposal for a housing platform. It starts with a summary of the current housing crisis, which affects primarily lower-income and minority households, but which also affects middle-class people. It then proceeds with a discussion of the issues facing a society in developing an equitable housing system that will ensure decent, affordable, and handicapped-accessible housing for all members of society. After an overview of the housing platform in Chapter 3, the remainder of the book provides a detailed discussion of the existing housing system in the United States, summaries of relevant housing policies in several other countries, and concrete proposals for changes in the areas of financing, production and preservation, discrimination, and displacement. Because of my legal background, the book includes a discussion, in lay terms, of those court decisions that are particularly relevant to the issues discussed in the book.

This book was in press before the passage of the Financial Institution Reform, Recovery and Enforcement Act, P.L. 101–73, the "savings and loan bailout" act, and therefore does not discuss the provisions of the act. The act does not affect in any significant way the materials presented in this book, although some of its provisions are relevant to a few of the proposals made in this book.

Writing this book has been a process of several years, and many people have provided their help along the way. First and foremost, I wish to thank my family. My mother, Helen Jane Zarembka, read several drafts of the book and provided many helpful suggestions on writing style, grammar, and contents. My brother Paul Zarembka provided me with much support and help with the structure and organization of the book, as well as with suggestions regarding some of the economic analysis. My friend and partner, Zuleyma Tang Halpin, made useful suggestions throughout the writing of the book; she also endured many years of my work on the book and missed many weekends of bird-watching in the process. My father, Richard Zarembka, my brother, David Zarembka, my sister, Elaine Z. Belmaker, and my sister-in-law, Beata Banas', all made helpful comments on earlier drafts of the book.

I also wish to thank Aynsley Baur, who did the illustrations, typed various versions of the manuscript, figured out how to use the marvels of WordPerfect to make it all fit together, and made helpful suggestions along the way.

I also thank Kate Robinson and Judy Freiberg for their comments, and Bob Petrucci, Mike Blaney, and Kate Steane, all of whom sent useful information. Finally, I wish to thank Laurie Dyche for providing the spark that led to the writing of this book, and Susan Harris, Janet Kourik, Paulette Salfen, and Helan Page for their encouragement along the way.

Chapter 1

The Present Crisis in Urban Housing

Shelter: A fundamental human need. Yet millions of Americans cannot afford decent housing, and an increasing number have no shelter whatsoever. Millions more people in their thirties who, less than fifteen years ago, would have been able to buy a first home, are forced to rent. Other families, who bought houses ten, twenty, or thirty years ago, and thought themselves secure, are being forced out of their homes by urban redevelopment, rising utility costs and taxes, or unemployment. Urban areas are as segregated as they were twenty years ago. Something is wrong. Something needs to be done.

After summarizing the basic parameters of the present housing crisis for the poor, tenants, and homeowners, this chapter discusses the response of the government to the crisis. The balance of the book develops a comprehensive platform for altering our housing system, to resolve the current crisis and prevent future ones.

THE PRESENT CRISIS

The housing crisis hits the poor the hardest, of course. The acute shortage of affordable housing for the poor is reflected in several figures. Between two-thirds and three-fourths of the 7.5 to 8.1 million tenant households with incomes below the poverty line in 1985 neither lived in public housing nor received any housing subsidies,[1] and virtually none of the 5 million homeowner households below the poverty level received any significant housing subsidy.[2] As of 1985, almost 9.9 million households nationwide could not afford to pay anything for housing and still pay for their other basic necessities.[3] More than a half million families may be on the waiting list nationwide for public housing, although there are only 1.3 million, mostly occupied, public housing units in the entire country; the waiting list normally is several years long.[4] The waiting list for subsidized housing is closed in many cities.[5] The homeless population continues to grow. Even the middle class has been affected by the housing crisis. The homeownership rate has begun dropping for the first time since 1940, as rising home prices and interest rates drove homeownership out of the reach of millions.

Tenants

Tenants face both a decreasing supply of affordable housing, as well as increasing problems of overcrowded and substandard housing. The crisis is affecting not merely tenants who rent from private landlords but those in subsidized as well as public housing.

Lack of Affordable Housing. From 1974 to 1983, the number of units renting for less than $300 per month decreased by almost 1 million.[6] Between 1970 and 1983, over 310,000 units of low-income housing in New York City alone were lost to abandonment and demolition.[7] During this same period, nationally, median monthly rents in central cities rose 188 percent, over twice as much as median tenant income, which rose only 89 percent. The worst relative increase was in the central cities of the northeast, where median rent increased 185 percent, while median tenant income increased only 70 percent. Nationwide, in central cities, median rent as a percentage of median income increased from 21 percent in 1970 to 31 percent in 1983.[8] As of 1985, approximately one-fifth of all renters paid more than 50 percent of their income on housing costs, and over 3 million poverty-level renter households paid more than 70 percent of their income for rent.[9]

Two groups of tenants—those in rent-controlled units and those in public housing—that might be expected to be immune from rent increases, have not been so shielded. Tenants living in units covered by rent-control laws have faced rent increases, although the degree of increase depends on the type of rent control in effect. Most of the over 200 cities with rent control have moderate rent control, usually guaranteeing annual increases, lifting rent control when the unit is vacated (vacancy decontrol), and exempting new construction. Rent increases have occurred at about the same rate in both cities with moderate rent control and those without rent control. Strong rent control does, by contrast, make a difference. Strong rent control laws typically restrict rent increases to substantially less than increases in the Consumer Price Index (CPI), prohibit vacancy decontrol, and provide for well-funded

rent control boards. In cities with strong rent control, rent increases have been smaller, though they do still occur.[10] While strong rent control thus does provide some protection to tenants, fourteen states have passed laws, owing to lobbying by landlord groups, that preempt cities from passing local rent control laws.[11] Public housing tenants also have not been immune from rent increases. In 1981, the limit on rent to 25 percent of the tenant's income that had been set in 1969 was raised, to permit rent to increase to 30 percent of the tenant's income by 1986.[12])

Yet most renters cannot afford to pay even 25 percent of their income on housing and still have enough money left over to feed and clothe their families, as well as take care of other necessities, such as heating, medical care, and transportation. Michael Stone has calculated that, in 1980, a family of four with a gross income of $17,500 could not afford to spend 25 percent of its income on housing and have enough money left to pay for all its other needs, even at the Lower Budget figures developed by the Bureau of Labor Statistics. If the family had only $11,000 in income, it could not afford to pay anything on rent.[13] Yet two-thirds of all tenant households at that time had incomes below $15,000.[14] For blacks and Hispanics, the situation is even grimmer: in 1983 black tenants had a median income of only $8,900, and Hispanic tenants $11,100.[15]

Compounding the housing crisis for tenants is the destruction and conversion of lower-priced housing units. From 1973 to 1979, 91 percent of the 973,000 central city rental units demolished or abandoned had rented for $200 per month or less.[16] About 1 million single room occupancy units were converted to condominiums or destroyed from 1970 to 1980.[17] Every year about a half-million units of housing are lost to lower-income people because of abandonment, conversion, demolition, or privatization of federally subsidized housing projects.[18] Despite the shortage of housing for tenants, public housing units have been demolished, sold, or allowed to deteriorate, with very little new public housing being built. From 1979 to 1988, there was a net increase of only 221,600 public housing units; during this same period, the number of poor people increased by 7 million.[19]

Substandard and Overcrowded Housing. In addition to the loss of affordable housing units is the problem of the quality of housing. It certainly is true that the overall quality of housing has improved considerably since the end of World War II. The percent of housing lacking some or all plumbing decreased from 55.4 percent in 1940 to only 2.6 percent in 1980, while the percentage of units having more than 1 person per room (the definition of crowded) decreased from 20.0 percent to 5.0 percent. The percentage of housing units needing major repair also decreased substantially.[20]

These improvements, however, mask the disproportionate burden of substandard housing borne at the present time by tenants, low-income, and minority families. (See Figure 1.) In 1985, of a total of 7.4 million occupied housing units with severe or moderate problems, 5.3 million were in central cities or suburbs.[21] Public housing tenants are not immune to poor quality apartments. At the present time, public housing needs $9 billion worth of repairs and a total of $20 billion for modernization.[22]

Not only do many tenants still live in substandard housing, but crowding continues to be a significant problem. Among tenants, crowding actually has been *increasing*, which is likely to cause further deterioration of the quality of tenant housing. In 1975, 1,157,000 renter households lived in crowded units; by 1985, the number increased to 1,516,000.[23] Doubling-up also has been increasing. In the ten-year period from 1976 to 1986, the number of related subfamilies that were doubling up increased from 1,190,000 to 2,256,000, and the number of unrelated subfamilies increased from 189,000 to 505,000.[24] (Not all of the unrelated subfamilies were, of course, doubling up from economic necessity; some are families of persons unrelated in the eyes of the law who have chosen to live together.) Overcrowding is a particular problem for racial and ethnic minorities, both renters and homeowners. (See Figure 2.)

Women with Children. Those tenants hardest hit by the combination of decreasing adequate rental units and rising rents are single women with children. Women earn less than men, so that their ability to pay for housing is, on the average, less than that of men; a much greater percentage of their income goes to rent than is the case in households where a man is present. In 1983, less than half of married couples with children, but over three-fourths of single women with children spent 25 percent or more of their income on rent.[25] Discrimination by landlords against women with children exacerbates the housing crisis faced by single women. Until recently, many rental advertisements contained explicit prohibitions against children.[26] Thus, even if a woman is lucky enough to have sufficient monthly income to rent an apartment, she will find an additional barrier to renting the apartment that those without children do not face. Finally, women with children also face the reality that the rental units being removed from the housing stock at the fastest rate are precisely those larger units best suited to their needs. In the three-year period from 1973 to 1976, for example, 6.6 percent of renter-occupied units of seven rooms or more were removed from the housing stock of central cities.[27] The special problems faced by women with children can lead to two unintended, though often devastating, consequences. First, because of the shortage of housing, the difficulty of finding a landlord willing to rent to children, and most women's limited financial resources, a woman living with a man who abuses her or her children is often forced by these circumstances to live with the violent man, in fear for

Figure 1
Percentage of Housing Units with Moderate or Severe Physical Problems, 1985

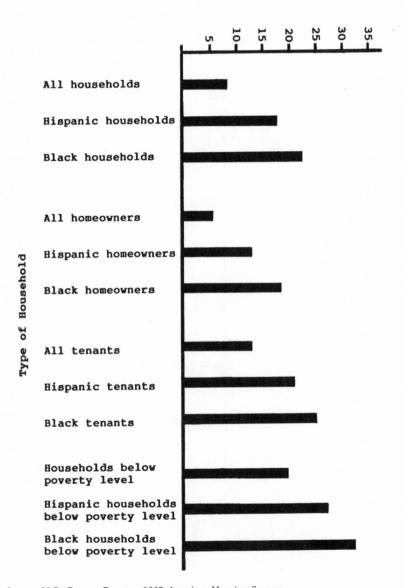

Source: U.S. Census Bureau, *1985 American Housing Survey.*

Figure 2
Degree of Crowding—by Ethnic Group, 1980

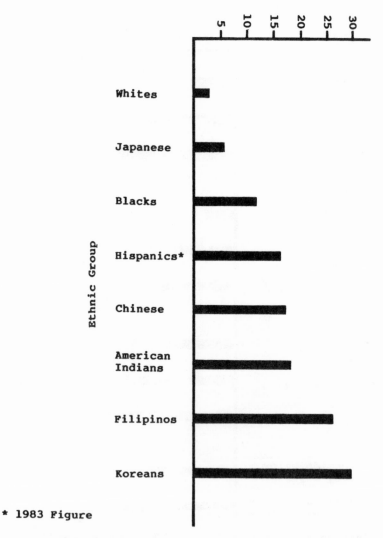

Source: C. Matthew Snipp and Alan L. Sorkin, "American Indian Housing," in *Race, Ethnicity and Minority Housing in the United States,* ed. Jamshid A. Momeni, p. 156; Julia Hansen, "Housing Problems of Asian Americans," in ibid., p. 179; and Cushing N. Dolbeare and Judith A. Canales, *The Hispanic Housing Crisis,* p. 12.

her safety and that of her children. Shelters for battered women are inadequately funded to provide the refuge needed by these women and children. Second, women who live in deteriorated apartments with their children because they cannot find a decent affordable apartment may find themselves cited for child neglect. The state may then take their children away from them and place them in foster homes, while telling the mother that she cannot have her children back until she finds a better place to live. If the mother was receiving Aid for Dependent Children from the state, she loses this aid once her children are taken away and therefore does not have money to find housing so that she can regain custody of her children.[28]

The Homeless

Those unable to find adequate housing are forced onto the streets if they cannot find a friend or relative willing to put them up. These are the homeless, those who carry all their worldly possessions with them by day and sleep in doorways, bus stations, cars, and emergency shelters by night. The homeless include not only those who are on the streets more or less permanently but also those who move in and out of homelessness. It is estimated that, while at least 735,000 persons are homeless on any one night, 1.3 million to 2.0 million persons are homeless at one time or another during a year.[29] The National Coalition for the Homeless estimates an even higher figure, 3 million, for the number of homeless.[30] Emergency shelters in city after city report that rising numbers of people are flocking into their overcrowded shelters for relief. A 23-city survey conducted by the National Coalition for the Homeless in 1987 revealed that the number of homeless persons increased by 25 percent from 1986 to 1987. As of 1987, New York City had an estimated 70,000 to 90,000 homeless persons, many of them children, while Los Angeles had 50,000 and Chicago 25,000 to 30,000.[31] Between 220,000 and 800,000 school-age children are homeless.[32]

Those forced to double up because of the unavailability of housing should be included in the homeless statistics as well; many are only a step away from homelessness—a disagreement in the household can lead to the streets for one or more members of the household. Also not counted in the statistics are those battered women who, but for their lack of money, would move out on their abusers.

While many of the homeless are mentally ill, resulting from earlier policies of deinstitutionalization of mental patients without adequate support services, substantial numbers are those who have lost their jobs and their apartments, those who are fleeing abusive homes, and those displaced by redevelopment and gentrification.[33] Indeed, about 20 to 30 percent of the homeless are employed, and about one-third to two-fifths are families with children.[34] A 1988 study estimated that, nationally, at least 100,000 out of the 735,000 that are homeless each night are children.[35] Racial and ethnic minorities also predominate among the homeless.[36]

Homeowners

The housing crisis is not limited to tenants, although it strikes them the hardest. Homeownership rates have begun to decline, particularly among those in the prime years of new household formation (below age 35), for lower-income households, and for Hispanic households.

The percentage of households that own homes has, of course, always been correlated with income and ethnic origin. (See Figures 3 and 4.) But for the first time since 1940, the homeownership rate in the population as a whole has begun to decrease. From a high of 65.6 percent for the population as a whole in 1980, the percentage of families buying their own homes had decreased to 63.8 percent by 1986. The largest decrease in homeownership between 1981 and 1986 occurred among families where the age of the head of household was under 35. Yet homeownership rates decreased for *every* age group during this period, except households where the age of the head was between 50 and 55 years and those where the head was 65 years of age or over. (See Figure 5.) It should be noted, moreover, that the rate of homeownership in the portion of the population receiving the lowest fifth of income has been decreasing since at least 1960: between 1960 and 1983, the percentage of such persons owning homes decreased from 51.0 percent to 43.4 percent.[37] Likewise, for Hispanics, the homeownership rate began dropping in the 1970s, falling from 46.2 percent in 1970, to 43.3 percent in 1980, to 39.6 percent in 1985.[38]

The declining homeownership rate is due, in large part, to rapid increases in both mortgage interest rates and home prices. Real mortgage interest rates jumped from a postwar average of about 3 percent to a high of 8 to 9 percent in the early 1980s, and remained over 7 percent in 1984.[39] Nominal interest rates for fixed rate mortgages rose from less than 5 percent in the early 1950s to 7.5 percent at the end of the 1960s and jumped to 17.5 percent for a period in 1981. Even though nominal rates dropped after 1981 and dipped to about 9 percent in 1987, they rose to between 10 and 11 percent in 1989.[40] It is estimated that for every one percentage point rise in mortgage interest rates, between 1 and 2 million fewer households are able to afford a home.[41] As inflation took off in the 1970s and early 1980s, housing prices shot up, increasing at a higher rate than inflation. Between 1970 and 1985, median sales prices for new single-family homes rose 259 percent, and the median sales price for existing single-family homes rose 227 percent, while the CPI increased 177 percent.[42]

Figure 3
Homeownership Rate—By Income Quintile, 1980

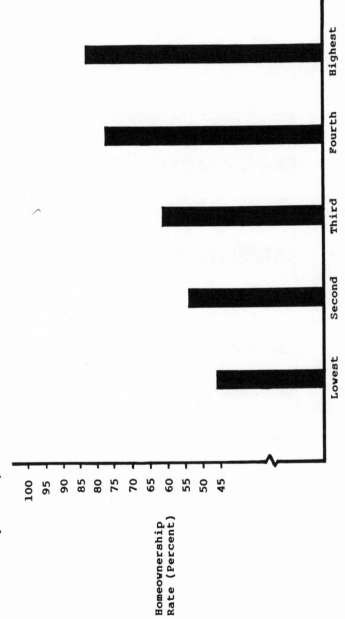

Source: Mortgage Bankers, "A Report on National Housing Policy," in *A New National Housing Policy*, Exhibit V-2.

Figure 4
Homeownership Rate—By Ethnic Group, 1980

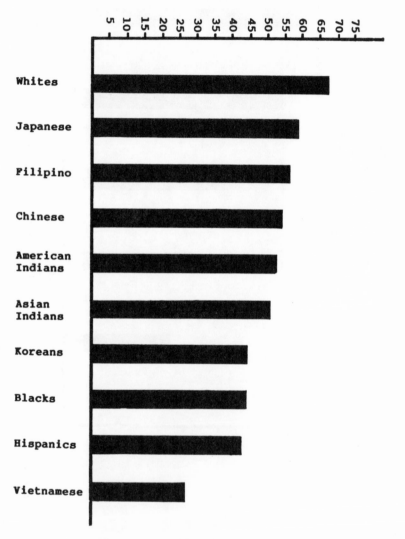

Source: Robert D. Bullard, "Blacks and the American Dream of Housing," in *Race, Ethnicity and Minority Housing in the United States*, ed. Jamshid A. Momeni, p. 59; Manuel Mariano Lopez, "Su casa no es mi casa: Hispanic Housing Conditions in Contemporary America, 1949–1980," in ibid., p. 130; C. Matthew Snipp and Alan L. Sorkin, "American Indian Housing: An Overview of Conditions and Public Policy," in ibid., p. 150; and Julia L. Hansen, "Housing Problems of Asian Americans," in ibid., p. 181.

Figure 5
Change in Homeownership Rate—By Age of Head of Household, 1981 to 1986

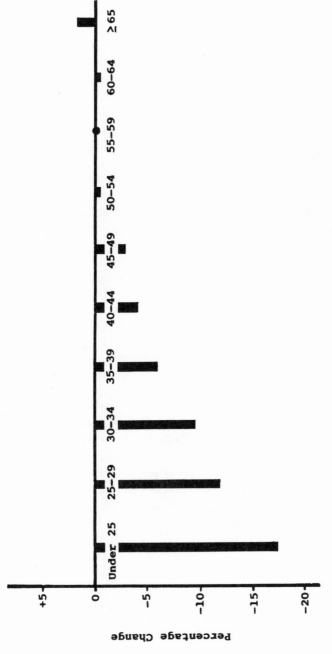

Source: Mortgage Bankers, "A Report on National Housing Policy," in *A New National Housing Policy*, Exhibit II-4.

11

The combination of interest rate and price increases meant that, by 1981, a buyer purchasing a home had to pay, on the average, over 200 percent more for monthly mortgage payments than an average buyer just five years before.[43] The rise in interest rates and sale prices put homes out of reach for many Americans. Whereas in the 1950s about two-thirds of all American families could afford to buy a *new* home, by 1970 only half could afford to do so, and by 1981 only one-tenth could.[44] The median sales price of existing houses increased from $23,400 in 1970 to $64,600 in 1980, almost a threefold increase.[45] Yet median family income during this same period just slightly more than doubled.[46] Despite the tax benefits of homeownership (deductibility of mortgage interest and real estate taxes), after-tax costs of homeownership[47] increased from 21.9 percent of median family income in 1970 to 37.4 percent in 1982. While mortgage interest rates have decreased and home prices have risen less slowly than median family income since 1981, resulting in the after-tax cash costs of homeownership dropping back to 30.4 percent of median family income by 1986, this is still substantially higher than the 1970 figure of 21.9 percent.[48]

While rising home prices and mortgage interest rates certainly have played a role in the decreasing percentage of homeownership, foreclosures undoubtedly also have played a role. Unemployment and expenses of homeownership can force a homebuyer into default. The average duration of unemployment grew from 11.9 weeks in 1978 to 14.5 weeks in 1987, while the number of those unemployed more than six months grew by more than 60 percent. Yet the percentage of unemployed persons receiving unemployment insurance benefits dropped to a record low of only 31.5 percent in 1987.[49] At the same time, inflation caused monthly housing expenses to rise. For example, while the overall CPI rose 177 percent from 1970 to 1985, utility rates rose much more substantially, with the CPI for fuel oil and coal rising 463 percent during that same period, and gas and electricity increasing 322 percent.[50] By the beginning of 1985, over 6 percent of home mortgage loans were at least 30 days overdue, the highest rate since 1953. While the delinquency percentage decreased thereafter, it began rising again in late 1988.[51]

Displacement

Rising rents, increased housing expenses, increases in the poverty rate, and shrinking supply have forced many poor and working class residents, both tenants and homeowners, out of their homes. Of the variety of causes of displacement, the most common immediate causes are rent increases, destruction of single-room occupancy hotels, and private and public "revitalization"[52] (which may also lead to rent increases), aided at times by the use of eminent domain.[53] Moreover, the homeowner affordability crisis discussed in the previous section has exacerbated the housing shortage faced by central city poor and working-class families. Young middle-class persons who formerly would have bought homes, but who have been squeezed out of the housing market, as well as those forced out by foreclosure, now look for places to rent, putting further pressure on the limited rental market. Virtually none of this displacement is covered by the federal Uniform Relocation Act: those displaced therefore rarely receive assistance. (See Chapter 7.)

Redevelopment normally does not occur unless factors exist that make a neighborhood potentially attractive to middle- and upper-class persons (for example, proximity to a revitalized downtown business district that contains many jobs for professionals). But where it does occur, tenants and sometimes working-class homeowners face eviction. This redevelopment cannot be financially successful without the commitment of financial institutions to lend money not only to the redevelopers but also to the persons who will buy the new or refurbished houses. Financial institutions, often formerly unwilling to lend money in the neighborhood, may become willing to lend money to the real estate investors and new urban rehabbers, in many cases because the local government has thrown its political and financial support behind the redevelopment. Real estate developers move into the rehabilitation business, which, with the prospect of high-income in-movers, becomes profitable. The developers make their profits not only because they can charge higher rents to the in-movers but also because the very fact that they can charge higher rents makes the property more valuable (since the market value of rental property is determined in large part by the amount of rents collected). Therefore, when the developer sells an apartment building to a landlord he or she can command a higher price.

In tandem with such real estate activity, or sometimes separate from it, middle- and upper-class rehabbers move into the neighborhoods and evict the existing tenants so that they can convert the buildings into single-family residences. With the rehabilitation, redevelopment, and movement of middle- and upper-class persons into the neighborhood come rent increases and the expulsion of the former residents. Where private real estate and market activity is not enough to "turn the neighborhood around" (read: make it acceptable to middle- and upper-class whites), government-sponsored redevelopment may use eminent domain to displace both tenants and homeowners. Those displaced seek housing elsewhere, thereby increasing demand in the areas to which they move, precipitating further rent increases in those areas.

The costs of displacement are born primarily by those households that are dislocated, rather than by the redevelopers, rehabbers, and in-movers. It is ironic that a working class community that improves its neighborhood may also find that its reinvestment in the neighborhood attracts middle- and upper-class persons, who may proceed to displace members of the neighborhood as they buy up properties and convert them into chic upscale housing.

Those displaced come from every class and race. Most of those displaced, however, tend to be whites who work in blue-collar or lower-status white-collar occupations. When blacks live in white neighborhoods undergoing redevelopment or gentrification,[54] blacks are disproportionately displaced compared to whites. Those who take over the housing formerly occupied by the working class tend to be young, middle- and upper-income whites in professional, managerial, or white-collar sales and clerical positions. They typically do not have children and have moved from another section of the city. The in-movers tend to be opposed to class integration and expect the neighborhood to become all white within five years.[55]

It is impossible to know accurately the extent of the displacement that is occurring, for no one keeps records. Because of a lack of accurate data, those who have studied displacement have not been able to agree on the exact numbers forced out; yet most do agree that displacement is a growing problem. One of the most thorough analyses of the problem, done by Richard LeGates and Chester Hartman in 1981, estimated that about 2.5 million persons are *forced* to move involuntarily each year in the United States, with the heart of the problem being in the central cities.[56] This figure may be an underestimate of the extent of annual displacement. The 1985 American Housing Survey reported that of the 17,103,000 households that had moved during the previous year, 735,000 attributed their move to private displacement (other than the owner moving into the unit), 173,000 attributed their move to government displacement (including a unit being unfit for occupancy), and 1,240,000 wanted lower rent or housing expenses.[57] Since there are about 2.9 persons per household,[58] the number of persons who move each year due to such private or government displacement, or for financial reasons, may be over 6 million persons. Among central city tenants who had moved, 15.8 percent of the households (859,000 households, or approximately 1,975,700 persons) attributed their move to such private or government displacement or the search for lower rent.[59] Even assuming that some of the answers given by respondents in the survey overlap (for example, that the respondent listed both private displacement and the desire for lower rent or housing costs as the reason for the move), the number of annual moves that are involuntary or due to the need for cheaper accommodations is staggering.

Demographics

To be sure, demographic changes in the American population have contributed to the housing crisis. New household formation has increased faster than the population since 1960. The largest discrepancy between the two occurred during the period from 1975 to 1980, when new households grew at an annual rate of 2.5 percent, while population growth occurred at an annual rate of only 1.1 percent. From 1970 to 1980, almost half (48.6 percent) of the increase in the population occurred in the age group from 25 to 34, the prime group for household formation. Yet from 1981 to 1985, the percentage of new households that purchased homes, rather than renting apartments, dropped dramatically compared to the 1970s. From 1981 to 1985, only 41.1 percent of new households purchased homes, compared to 67.9 percent of new households from 1971 to 1975, and 72.9 percent from 1976 to 1980. Thus, from 1981 to 1985, 58.9 percent of new households were renters, putting a great deal of pressure on the rental market.[60]

The projected demographic trends for the 1990s, combined with the other trends in housing discussed in this chapter, are likely to cause the housing crisis to worsen as we move through the nineties. Single-parent, female-headed households, and "old elderly" households (i.e., those over 75 years of age) are expected to increase sharply in numbers, as are those in their prime homebuying years (ages 30–45). Yet housing construction recently has consisted primarily of larger homes, at higher prices (the "trade-up" market). Moreover, financial institutions have been demanding higher percentage down payments for all types of homes. None of these population groups will be served well by such trends.[61]

Racial and Ethnic Segregation

The housing crisis in most people's minds is the one involving homelessness, deterioration, high home prices, and high interest rates. But there is another crisis that has existed for so many years that it fails to draw the media's attention: the persistence of widespread racial segregation and discrimination.

The Fair Housing Act was passed in 1968. Nevertheless, twenty years later, although segregation has decreased slightly, racial and ethnic segregation is widespread in urban areas. Of all the racial and ethnic minorities, blacks by far are the most segregated, with a disproportionate percentage of blacks residing in central cities. In 1985, 48 percent of the non-Hispanic white population lived in suburbs, yet only 25 percent of blacks did so; 60 percent of blacks lived in central cities while only 28 percent of non-Hispanic whites did so.[62] According to an analysis of 1980 census data in 59 metropolitan areas, the large majority of central cities in the metropolitan areas have a high degree of segregation (dissimilarity index of .600 or more) between blacks and non-Hispanic whites. Even though the degree of segregation decreases in suburban areas, 40 percent of the metropolitan areas had a high degree of segregation in their suburbs, and the vast majority of those in the moderate range of segregation (.300 to .600) were at the high end of that range. Black segregation in the suburbs is particularly pronounced in metropolitan areas where there are large black populations. Overall, the black-Anglo dissimilarity index in 1980 was .691 in the central cities and .573 in the suburbs of 59 metropolitan areas. None of the 59 metropolitan areas had a low degree of black-non-Hispanic white segregation (0.000 to 0.300). While Hispanics are significantly less segregated than blacks, there still is moderate segregation of Hispanics in central cities, with the dissimilarity index for 59 metropolitan areas being .450 in the central city; in suburbs, Hispanic segregation is reduced to .379 but still is in the moderate range. Among Asian-Americans, there is a moderate degree of segregation in both central cities and suburbs (dissimilarity indexes of .413 and .376, respectively, in 1980), with the range of segregation varying quite a bit from area to area. Of the three ethnic groups, Asian-Americans are the most suburbanized and the least segregated.[63]

The persistence of segregation is a reflection of the degree of discrimination in our society and is not merely a result of income differences between ethnic groups, nor minority group preference. Compared to non-Hispanic whites, racial and ethnic minorities tend to have lower rates of homeownership, poorer housing quality, and more crowded living conditions, even when the socioeconomic status of the minority is greater than that of whites (for example, most Asian-American ethnic minorities).[64]

The generally lower income of blacks is not a sufficient explanation for the degree of black segregation. Low-income whites live in suburbs to a much greater degree than do low-income blacks. When family type and size, age of the head of household, and household income are controlled for, black segregation is still far greater than it would be if there were not discrimination. Moreover, black preference is not the explanation for the persistence of high degrees of segregation. Black segregation is far greater than that of any immigrant groups in the past, and blacks consistently express a preference for living in mixed, rather than all-black, neighborhoods.[65] Racial discrimination thus is still an extremely important factor in the persisting patterns of segregation. While the vast majority of whites (88 percent in 1976) state that they support the right of blacks to live wherever they can afford to, only 46 percent of whites (1983 figure) have supported an open housing ordinance. Thus, there is a substantial discrepancy between the principles that whites say they hold regarding integration, and their willingness to support laws to combat housing discrimination.[66] HUD's Housing Market Practices Survey in the 1970s confirmed the persistence of discrimination against blacks in housing. It found that their black auditors (i.e., testers) received less information about the availability of rental housing than did their white auditors 27 percent of the time, and less information on the availability of for-sale housing than did whites 15 percent of the time. This study undoubtedly revealed less discrimination than in fact exists, because it focused only on the initial inquiries about housing; the study did not look at different treatment of blacks and whites at later stages of the search for housing (e.g., security deposit or financing requirements), nor did it study steering by real estate agents.[67] Other studies of discrimination have found even higher degrees of discrimination. A 1983 study of Boston found that whites were shown 81 percent more rental units than nonwhites. A 1983 survey in Evanston, Illinois, found that 75 percent of whites, but only 12 percent of blacks, were shown homes in largely white areas.[68] A recent study of home mortgage loans in Atlanta concluded that race, rather than household income or home value, is the reason for the wide discrepancy between the ability of blacks and whites to obtain mortgage loans from banks and savings and loan institutions.[69]

While studies of housing discrimination against Hispanics have been few, those that do exist confirm discrimination against Hispanics. A study of Denver, Houston, and Phoenix indicated that housing discrimination was as great in Denver against Hispanics as against blacks, and that housing discrimination against Hispanics in all three cities has been increasing.[70] Another recent study revealed that Hispanics tend to pay higher interest rates on mortgage loans than do whites.[71]

In short, housing discrimination remains a continuing and substantial issue for minorities.

THE RESPONSE OF THE FEDERAL GOVERNMENT

At the very time when the crisis in housing was coming to a head, the response of the federal government was to cut back on housing programs that aid the poorer segment of the urban population, relying on private enterprise to solve the problem, and to shift responsibility to state and local governments. It also deregulated the mortgage industry, leading to the savings and loan crisis of the late 1980s. At the same time, the indirect subsidization of middle- and upper-class homeowners by the federal government through the tax system has mushroomed.

Cutbacks in Housing Programs for the Poor

Since 1980, there have been substantial reductions in the construction of new low-cost housing, cutbacks in direct subsidies to the poor, and a shift in emphasis to housing vouchers. Budget authority for non-Indian conventional public housing decreased from $4.2 billion in 1981 to $573 *million* in 1988; the number of new additional non-Indian public housing units decreased from 18,003 in 1981 to 3,109 in 1988. During the same period, budget authority for Section 8 new construction and substantial rehabilitation decreased from $10.2 billion to $1.5 billion, with the number of additional new construction/substantial rehab units decreasing from 141,530 in 1981 to 10,032 in 1988. While the budget authority for public housing, Section 8 new construction/substantial rehab, and Section 8 existing units all decreased substantially from 1981 to 1988 (from $20.2 billion to $2.9 billion), the housing voucher program, begun in 1984, had budget authority of $1.2 billion in 1988.[72]

At the same time that Congress has been cutting back on new low-income housing construction, tenants are facing the loss of subsidized housing built under the Section 221(d)(3), Section 236, and Section 8 New Construction programs. Owners of Section 221(d)(3) and 236 projects have begun to withdraw from the subsidy programs by prepaying their mortgages and thereby ending their contractual obligation to rent to low-income households. Owners of Section 8 projects have begun prepaying their mortgages and terminating their contracts, and renting their units out at market rates. In response to the impending loss of subsidized housing, Congress passed the 1987 Emergency Low Income Housing Preservation Act of 1987, which imposed a two-year moratorium on conversion to market-rate housing of Section 8 New Construction, Section 221(d)(3), and Section 236 projects. (These matters are further discussed in Chapter 5.)

The only new program directed at low-income people in the past decade beside the housing voucher program is the 1987 McKinney Homeless Assistance Act. This law authorizes money for shelters, social services, education, health care, and job training for the homeless. It also requires that vacant and underused federal property be made available to provide shelter for the homeless. The Reagan administration resisted complying with the provisions of the law pertaining to federal property, forcing the U.S. District Court in Washington, D.C., to issue an injunction in 1988 to enforce federal compliance with the law.[73]

Increased Subsidies for the Middle and Upper Classes

While the federal government has been cutting back assistance to low- and moderate-income households, its support for middle- and upper-class housing has increased dramatically. From 1980 to 1988, lost tax revenues due to the mortgage interest and real estate tax deduction doubled, from $25 billion to $50 billion.[74] Because these tax deductions are available only to those who itemize their deductions, it is the affluent homeowner who primarily benefits from this indirect housing subsidy.

Financial Restructuring of the Mortgage Market

As for the mortgage crisis, the overall thrust of the government's response has been twofold: (1) to tie the mortgage system into the national capital markets, thereby forcing mortgages to compete with other investments, and (2) to deregulate financial institutions that provide mortgage loans. Thus, the direction of change has been toward a "free market" economy in housing, very similar to the sort of housing economy that existed before the reforms brought on by the Great Depression, but this time with government insurance programs to guarantee investors the safety of their investments in housing finance.

As the secondary mortgage market expanded in the 1960s and 1970s, this market became similar to the market for other bonds and securities and now must compete with these other investments for investors. In order to make mortgages easier to package and sell on the securities market, the Federal National Mortgage Association (FNMA) and the Federal Home Loan Mortgage Corporation (FHLMC) have worked together to standardize the mortgage instrument nationwide.[75] These developments are likely to cause financial institutions to be less willing to make mortgage loans that do not meet nationally developed standards, because unusual mortgages will be more difficult to sell on the secondary mortgage market. This, in turn, will make it more difficult for less expensive housing or housing located in less valuable neighborhoods to obtain mortgage financing.[76]

These results are beginning to be apparent. Down-payment requirements for home mortgage loans have increased, largely as a result of the underwriting requirements of the secondary mortgage markets: few conventional loans are now written for less than 10 percent down.[77] Moreover, with institutions other than the original lenders managing the loans, there has been an increase in the points and service fees charged when the property is purchased.[78] In addition, as mortgages increasingly are bought and sold on national markets, homebuyers are finding it more difficult to keep track of the person or institution that is handling their loan payments.[79]

Not only have mortgages become more linked to the secondary mortgage market but Congress has deregulated the financial industry. In 1980 Congress allowed thrifts, which had been required since the thirties to specialize in mortgage loans, to invest 20 percent of their assets in consumer loans, commercial paper, and long-term corporate debt.[80] It also increased the limit on federal deposit insurance from $40,000 to $100,000. This was followed in 1982 by the Garn–St. Germain Act, which allowed thrifts to invest up to 90 percent of their assets in nonresidential loans, which are riskier than mortgage loans.[81] This led to a rush of investments into risky construction and development projects, some of which collapsed, bringing the savings and loan institutions with them. The deregulation of interest rates authorized by the Garn–St. Germain Act and completed by 1986, allowed savings and loans that were speculating in risky investments to outbid more conservative savings and loans for deposits, by offering higher interest rates, thereby weakening more stable savings and loans. The savings and loan crisis that erupted in the late 1980s was a direct result of these policies, lack of oversight by regulators, and corruption.[82]

In 1982, Congress also permanently overrode all state usury laws that limited the interest rate that could be charged on mortgage loans, the rationale being that mortgage interest rates were not keeping up with prevailing interest rates, and therefore credit was moving out of mortgages.[83] At the same time, it also overrode the laws of 17 states that prohibited due-on-sale clauses (except for VA- or FHA-insured mortgage loans).[84] Due-on-sale clauses, provisions in deeds of trusts that allow the lender to declare the whole loan principal due and payable whenever the property is sold, allow lenders to prevent loan assumptions whenever there is a transfer of title to the property, thereby forcing a refinancing when the property is sold. The effect of these two actions by Congress is to permit lenders nationwide to accelerate loans whenever the property is sold, resulting in a new round of loan applications fees, points, and other fees to the purchaser, and, with usury laws invalidated, to charge higher interest rates if market conditions allow.[85]

Federal agencies took further steps toward deregulation in the eighties by completely deregulating the mortgage instrument. The result has been the development of several new types of mortgage loans, with the Adjustable Rate Mortgage (ARM) and home equity loans being the two most common variants. Under the ARM, the loan interest rate is adjusted periodically, usually once a year, based on market conditions, normally with a cap of no more than 2 percent increase in a year, and no more than 4½ to 6 percent over the life of the loan. If the interest rate increases very much, particularly in the early years of the loan, the result can be that the amount the borrower owes to the lender actually increases, as the interest charges outstrip the amount of payment. About 60 percent of new home mortgage loans, as of 1989, were ARMs. Home equity loans are loans on the equity in a purchaser's home, with interest rates usually floating rates at 1.5 percent above prime. Since the 1986 Tax Reform Act began the elimination of the deductibility of interest payments on consumer loans but allows interest on home equity loans to be deducted for certain types of loans, home equity loans have become quite popular. As of 1988, about 5.6 percent of homeowners had home equity lines of credit, totalling $75 billion of debt, with most of these accounts established since late 1985.[86] A third type of loan, a relatively recent addition that is aimed at elderly homeowners, is the reverse mortgage. Under this type of loan, a person can borrow money against the equity of his or her home, or be paid an annuity, with the lender being repaid with interest (and sometimes sharing in the appreciation in the value of the home) upon the owner's death, sale of home, or move out of the home.[87]

The result of the developments of the 1980s is to link the residential finance structure more closely to the national financial structure, and concomitantly, to make the national financial structure more dependent on the regular payment of mortgages.[88] That is, as mortgages are bought and sold on the national investment markets, a rash of loan defaults in one area will affect not simply that area, but investors nationwide. We can expect to see the cost of housing increasing, as credit for mortgages has to compete with other credit demands, and as the thrift industry no longer has protected status. Whether or not money is invested in housing increasingly will become dependent on the rate of return on housing investments compared to other investments.[89]

Shift of Responsibility to State and Local Governments

While cutting housing programs for lower-income housing in the 1980s, the federal government sought to shift the responsibility for housing to state and local governments. In a period of growing shortages of affordable housing, states responded by developing a variety of programs, the primary one being the sale of tax-exempt bonds. Under the tax-exempt mortgage revenue bond programs, states provide below-market-rate mortgages to low- and moderate-income (predominantly moderate-income) households for home purchases, and below-market financing for the production of rental units for low- and moderate-income households. From 1976 to 1985, such programs assisted 890,000 homeowner units and 637,000 rental units.[90] As of 1991, all new homeowner loans under such programs will be subject to recapture of some portion of the interest subsidy upon resale.[91]

The Tax Reform Act of 1986

In 1986, Congress did take steps to reduce the incentives for speculation in real estate. The 1986 Tax Reform Act lengthened the time period over which depreciation can be taken on property, limited severely the deductibility of "passive losses" (e.g., losses from property that investors do not actually manage), and eliminated the special tax status of capital gains. Although the act did include a tax credit for investors in low-income housing projects, the tax credit was limited to two years. While these measures are desirable in the long run, because they will reduce the speculative tendencies in rental housing (see Chapter 2), in the short run the changes in the tax law are expected to reduce investment in rental housing.[92]

Discrimination

In the area of housing discrimination, Congress took a major step forward in 1988 by amending the federal Fair Housing Act, effective March 1989, to strengthen the ability of the government and individuals to combat housing discrimination. This act will be further discussed in Chapter 6.

CONCLUSION

The present housing crisis has many causes. Some have already been touched on briefly—demolition of low-income housing, cut-backs in federal housing programs, poverty, discrimination, unemployment, inflation, condominium conversions, redevelopment. While some of these causes, such as poverty, unemployment, and inflation, reflect broader problems in the economic structure, the rest pertain directly to housing. The response of the 1980s to the housing crisis has been a cut-back in support for low-income federal housing programs, and an increased reliance on private enterprise to solve the problem. Yet, as discussed in Chapter 2, private enterprise by itself cannot provide adequate affordable housing for all Americans. The type and location of housing that is built by private enterprise is not based primarily on people's need for housing but rather primarily on its value as an investment. Because it is not profitable to build housing for lower-income persons, a purely capitalist system fails to provide an adequate supply of affordable, decent, safe, sanitary, and accessible housing for lower-income households. As long as housing production, pricing, and allocation are primarily left up to private enterprise capitalism, we will have a continuing crisis in housing and continuing problems of displacement. Moreover, the problems of racial segregation and discrimination cannot be solved by a laissez-faire approach, as racism is still quite alive in the United States.

It is beyond the scope of this book to examine the causes of the housing crisis that reflect broader economic problems. Instead, the book focuses on policies pertaining specifically to housing. Chapter 2 examines the difficulties involved in assuring an adequate and affordable supply of housing under capitalist and alternative models of housing production, pricing, and allocation, as well as issues involved in dealing with discrimination and displacement. The balance of the book presents a housing program for the United States.

Chapter 2 ⸺⸺⸺⸺⸺⸺⸺⸺⸺⸺⸺⸺⸺⸺⸺⸺

Issues in Devising a Housing System

It is in many ways easier to analyze the causes of housing problems than it is to develop solutions. Yet it is vitally important that we develop creative solutions that break out of old molds that have proven unsuccessful. The chapters that follow focus on the general issues of financing, production, and allocation, and explore alternatives in these areas that have been tried in this country and others. In addition, the particular problems of discrimination and displacement are examined, with special attention to the response of the legal system to these problems. In each of these areas, concrete proposals are made in an attempt to provide a comprehensive approach to the housing problem. This chapter starts the process by reviewing the general issues involved in developing an alternative to the present system of housing in the United States, without, at this point, proposing solutions to the problems raised. The proposed solutions are the subject of the remainder of the book.

But first certain terms must be defined. *Value* refers to the intrinsic worth of a dwelling unit. Thus, value consists of the various factors that make a dwelling unit more or less desirable to members of the population (e.g., location, size, light, amenities provided, and the surrounding neighborhood). *Cost*, on the other hand, refers to the amount of money it takes to build and maintain the dwelling unit. *Price* or *rent* will be used to mean the amount of money that purchasers or tenants pay for the dwelling unit. Thus, the value of a dwelling unit may or may not be the same as what it costs to build and maintain the unit, and what it costs to build and maintain the unit is not the same as the price charged to buyers or renters for the use of the dwelling unit. How these three units of measure compare for a given unit of housing depends on the housing system that is established in a country or locality.

Several facts about housing make it a consumer item that is quite different from other types of consumer goods: its high cost, the time needed to produce it, and its fixed location. The cost of new housing is high, and it cannot be paid for in one payment; therefore, in virtually all countries, housing is paid for over time, through some system of financing or renting. Maintenance of housing is likewise expensive, necessitating continuing and substantial expenditures after the original cost of producing the housing has been paid. Housing also takes a great deal of time to produce. Because of the time involved and the expense of housing, most housing occupied by people is used, rather than new. At any point, only about 3 percent of the housing stock is new.[1] Finally, with the exception of mobile homes, housing is fixed in location, so that consumers cannot move it with them. For this reason, the value of a particular dwelling unit depends in part on the value of the land where the unit is located. Even if all housing of the same size costs the same, housing located in a swamp would be less desirable, and therefore have lower value, than housing located in a drier area. In addition, because of the fixed location of housing, a society must have a mechanism that allows people to move and yet still have housing in their new location.

Regardless of the type of housing system, and regardless of how well a society houses its population, there may still be some sense in which a sufficient amount of adequate housing is lacking. Standards as to what is "decent, safe, and sanitary" change over time as societies advance economically. What is considered adequate housing in one century may be inadequate in the following one. For example, private indoor plumbing, while not a "necessity" of life in an absolute sense, certainly is one of the amenities of adequate urban housing that is expected in the United States today. In future decades or centuries, however, it is likely that current minimum standards for urban housing will be considered inadequate, and new standards will have been adopted. At that point, those persons living in housing that meets the old standards, but not the new ones, will be considered inadequately housed.

This points up one of the difficulties in devising alternative housing policies. Strategies that work in one locality might not work in another. For example, New York City has many high-rise tenements and apartment complexes, while St. Louis is much more spread out, with few high-rise apartment buildings. It is very possible that a high-rise housing production strategy would be acceptable in New York City but not in St. Louis, because of differing expectations of tenants, homeowners, and landlords in the two areas. Likewise, alternatives appropriate for a large urban area might be inappropriate for a smaller area.

A more fundamental problem with devising alternative housing policies is the fact that the housing crisis in the United States is not an isolated problem. The difficulty that people have in obtaining adequate housing is interrelated with unemployment, general economic and social conditions, and federal and state budget priorities. The housing crisis in this country cannot be solved without some fundamental changes in our economic structure and priorities. While an overall analysis of the U.S. economic system is beyond the scope of this book, the framework used in this book to analyze the housing crisis and develop solutions to it may well provide a model for analyses of other social problems.

Several assumptions and values guide my proposals on housing. First, I assume that housing is a scarce resource in any society, for the reason that housing quality differs, so that there is always a scarcity of "better" housing. At no time in the foreseeable future will housing be a "free" resource. At the same time, I believe that decent, safe, sanitary, and handicapped-accessible housing is a basic human right, and that providing a basic adequate level of housing for all people is a goal that we should fulfill in this society. The existing standards for decent, safe, sanitary, and handicapped-accessible housing in the United States, which have been established through various codes, are the minimal standards of housing that should be available for all persons in this country. Until these standards are reached, we cannot say that the housing crisis has been resolved. Yet ensuring a basic level of housing for all persons does not necessarily imply that all housing must be the same, nor that people should not or cannot have a choice.

Finally, nondiscrimination in the allocation of housing is an important goal. Yet discrimination can occur both in market-based housing systems as well as in administratively allocated systems (see "Allocation of Housing"). Establishing an equitable housing system is a very difficult task, involving the interaction of the systems of financing, production, and allocation. For example, a poor person in the United States, living in a system that gives priority to housing those who have money, experiences inequality, as does a single person or a gay or lesbian couple in an administrative allocation system that gives priority to those who are married. Likewise, a family with children cannot have equal access to adequate housing in a system that lacks housing units large enough to accommodate children.

The remainder of the chapter reviews methods of financing, producing, and allocating housing, focusing on a capitalist system and problems raised within that system. Alternatives to capitalist methods are explored, and their shortcomings are discussed. The chapter then raises issues involved in eliminating discrimination and displacement.

AFFORDABILITY

Pricing in a Capitalist Economy

Lack of affordability of housing is one of the aspects of the housing crisis facing the United States, as discussed in Chapter 1. In a market economy such as the United States, the price of a house or the rent charged for an apartment depends on a variety of factors: location, median housing prices in the locale, amenities, interest rates, housing supply relative to housing demand, household incomes, type of landlord (professional versus amateur), tax code treatment of real estate, and age of the property.[2] Unless market conditions have caused the real estate market to collapse in a particular area, the price usually will be higher than the cost of building and maintaining the property. This is so particularly when the property has been purchased and resold several times, each time at a higher price. Price will tend to be similar to value when the amount that people are willing to pay for a house or apartment reflects the value that people put on the property. Since housing is a necessity, however, when there is a shortage of decent housing, the price of homes or apartments may greatly exceed value as well as cost (unless there are nonmarket restrictions on price, such as resale price controls or rent control).

Real estate speculation can substantially and rapidly increase the differential between price and cost in the rental housing market, causing jumps in rents. A real estate speculator (as opposed to a landlord who is holding property as a long-term investment) buys rental property as a relatively short-term investment. He or she has a profit interest in providing minimal maintenance and reselling the property at an increase in price. A speculator can "milk" an apartment building by buying the property, holding onto it for several years, collecting rents while doing minimal repairs, and taking tax deductions for depreciation.[3] Since the speculator has done few, if any, repairs, upon resale of the building, he or she will likely recoup all or a substantial part of the initial investment. If property prices are rising in the area, the profits upon resale are much greater. If the building is sold to another speculator, then that new speculator engages in the same process (as do successive speculators).[4]

For a homebuyer under a capitalist system, if he or she has a fixed-rate mortgage, the monthly price that is paid for housing is set at the time of the house purchase, with the variable expenses being only maintenance, utilities, and taxes. Once the mortgage is paid off, the monthly price for housing drops. Thus, a homeowner's mortgage payments reflect the price of the house and the interest rates when he or she purchased it; the maintenance expenses equal the market prices for the repairs in the year in which particular repairs are made. For a purchaser with an adjustable rate mortgage, the monthly mortgage payment reflects the price of the house when it was purchased, plus the (approximately) current price of interest, which fluctuates. Purchasers under either fixed-rate or variable-rate mortgages receive the benefit of any increase in the market price of their property. This gain in value is not realized until the property is sold, however. If the homeowner wishes to buy another home after selling his or her first home, he or she will likely find that the prices of other comparable houses have also gone up. Therefore, the homeowner will have to use most or all of the gain made on the first home toward the purchase of another home. Would-be first-time homebuyers who do not have capital gain to use for their down payment bear the brunt of escalating housing prices, for they have no accumulated equity in a home to use toward a down payment; many are priced out of the market altogether.[5]

Methods to Control Prices

There are several systems that can be instituted to control housing prices, some involving renters, some involving purchasers: rent control, cost renting, subsidies, low-interest state bank loans, land price controls, and resale price controls. These are discussed briefly here, and in more detail in Chapter 4.

Rent Control. Three main approaches to rent control have been tried: (1) rent based on value, (2) "fair" rent standards, and (3) rent increases only upon petition. The first system sets rent according to the value that the rent control authority puts on the dwelling unit. The rent control board determines how much intrinsic worth the unit has as a dwelling unit, based on its size, location, amenities, and neighborhood, and sets rent accordingly. The second system tries to set a "fair" rent on property that guarantees landlords a certain rate of return. The third system freezes rents at current levels and allows rent increases only upon petition of the owners to the rent control board. So long as the society basically is capitalist, however, rent control will tend to cause landlords to get out of the landlord business, if they are able to obtain better profit margins in another field. A landlord can do this by converting the property to condominiums and selling it, by razing the building and selling the land to other developers (a viable tactic only if the land is in high demand), by converting the property to commercial uses, or simply by neglecting maintenance on the building until the building becomes uninhabitable. Without strong controls to prevent these landlord tactics, rent control is unlikely to provide a solution to the problem of housing prices in a society that is otherwise capitalist.

Cost Renting. Cost renting (also called rent pooling) is another approach to the problem of rental prices, used to some extent in Sweden and Britain. Under this system, all the costs of building and maintaining the housing that is controlled by one owner are pooled. The rent for each family is a proportionate share of that total cost. Tenants in newer buildings, which tend to have cost more to build and to be more modern, pay the same rent as tenants in older buildings, which tend to have cost less to build and to lack some modern amenities. Thus, tenants in older apartments in effect subsidize tenants in newer apartments: tenants in older apartments pay a higher amount of rent relative to value than do tenants in newer apartments.

Subsidies. Another way that housing can be made affordable to renters is through direct or indirect subsidies to renters or landlords. Direct subsidies can be of two types: (1) supplementing the family's income with a cash subsidy, so that the family can afford to pay the amount of rent that is being charged by the landlord; or (2) paying money to landlords to subsidize the rents. Indirect subsidies also take two forms: (1) tax deductions or credits for renters; or (2) tax deductions or credits for landlords that agree to limit rents.

Direct and indirect subsidies to tenants and direct rental subsidies to landlords accept the rents that are charged as legitimate, and landlords' profits are not controlled. Indeed, landlords as a class benefit from such subsidies for two reasons. First, such subsidies allow more people to be able to afford the prices that the landlords wish to charge for their apartments. Second, subsidies tend to have the effect of raising overall rent levels in an area, as the total amount of money available to pay rent increases. Indirect subsidies to landlords, although reducing the rent charged, accept rental profits as legitimate, and allow landlords to make their profits via the tax write-offs.

With regard to purchasers, governments have used several methods to subsidize the price that purchasers pay for housing: indirect tax subsidies, interest rate subsidies, and low-interest state bank loans. In the United States, the most substantial homeowner subsidies are indirect subsidies—the mortgage interest and real estate tax deductions, available only to homeowners who itemize their deductions on their federal tax returns. This system is inequitable to homeowners who have too few deductions to itemize their deductions, as well as to renters, who cannot deduct their rental payments. Moreover, allowing homebuyers to deduct their mortgage interest payments results in the government having no control over the amount of the subsidy to homebuyers; the subsidy increases whenever interest rates, and hence mortgage interest payments, rise.

With interest rate subsidies, the government pays part of the mortgage interest owed on the mortgage loan. Accordingly, the home purchaser pays a lower effective interest rate out of his or her own pocket. While this does decrease the price that the home purchaser pays each month for housing, it does not control housing interest rates in any way. Mortgage financiers continue to make the same rate of return on their loans, unless the government puts a cap on the rate of return that is allowed. However, in a capitalist economy, if a cap is put on the rate of return, then financial institutions will tend to withdraw their money from mortgage loans and invest their money in other types of loans that pay higher rates of interest.

A type of subsidy common in Eastern European countries is the provision of state bank loans at a low interest rate to home purchasers. Here the state bank subsidizes housing expenditures by charging a lower rate of interest on housing loans than on other loans. If the state bank is set up specially to provide housing loans, this has three advantages for consumers. It reduces monthly housing prices; it helps to assure a continual supply of housing credit; and it reduces the fluctuations in the quantity of housing production.

Land and Resale Price Controls. Governments have attempted to control housing costs in two other ways: through land price controls and resale price controls. Cuba has instituted a system of land price controls, by setting the same price for each square meter of land, regardless of where it is located. While this has the advantage of preventing land speculation, it amounts to a subsidy for those who reside in more desirable locations, since they pay the same amount per square meter of land as those residing in less desirable locations. Resale price controls, on the other hand, limit the amount of money that an owner can receive upon resale of property, whether land or the structures built on the land. Usually this is limited to the amount of investment the owner put into the property, plus an adjustment for inflation. Such a system would tend to stabilize housing prices. If it were not instituted nationwide, however, those living in jurisdictions with resale price controls may find it hard to accumulate the capital necessary to purchase a house in areas without such controls, where prices likely will be higher.

HOUSING PRODUCTION

Production under Capitalism

Housing is built in a pure capitalist society only if it is profitable for the builder. Moreover, the housing is built on a speculative basis. Typically a builder will build without first having a guaranteed buyer, in the expectation that he or she will be able to sell the completed house at a profit. The type and cost of housing constructed depends on builders' (and lenders') perceptions as to what will bring the highest rate of profit, which generally is higher-priced housing.

Since all people need housing, there is always a demand for a certain minimum amount of housing. The demand for housing in a particular locale varies, based on several factors. Population changes, whether owing to shifts in birth and death rates or to migration, clearly will affect housing demand. The demographics of the population in a locale will affect the quantity of each type of housing that is demanded, depending on household sizes. Cultural factors play a role in determining the type of amenities demanded, as does advertising and the state of development of consumer goods. (For example, the demand for microwaves, once they are invented, will depend at least in part on how they are advertised and marketed.) Neighborhood quality and school district reputation will affect demand for housing in a particular location.

The fact that there is demand for a particular type of housing does not, however, guarantee that it will be built, even if the existing supply of that type of housing is less than the need for it. Housing that is not profitable will not be built in a private enterprise system. Instead, the system relies on "filtering" for housing to reach lower-income families. As housing is built for higher-income consumers, the housing they previously occupied theoretically is freed up and filters down to consumers with less money, who are then able to move out of poorer-quality housing. Some economists use a "train" imagery: housing is a train, with the last cars being the worst quality. As new cars are added to the head of the train, those cars at the end of the train are taken off, and everyone moves up one car on the train.[6] (See Figure 6.) Thus, according to the filtering concept, everyone has benefited from the construction of new housing, and everyone's quality of housing has improved.

The capitalist system of housing production summarized above has, of course, been modified in the United States. The modification has occurred through various subsidy, loan guarantee, and public housing programs (see Chapter 5). While these programs have helped to increase production of housing for income groups that might not otherwise have had housing produced directly for them, they have been severely cut back in recent years. Thus, the United States presently retains a predominantly capitalist system of housing production.

The major advantage of a capitalist method of production is that production by the mechanism of supply and demand allows for a wide variety of housing types, with a range of amenities possible. This tends to assure choice for housing consumers who have money, provided that there is an adequate supply of available housing in the locale where the consumer wishes to reside.

There are, however, three major problems with a predominantly capitalist system of producing housing. It leads to great swings in housing production; a large percentage of the money spent on housing is tied up in finance charges, thereby reducing the money available for con-

Figure 6
Filtering

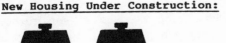

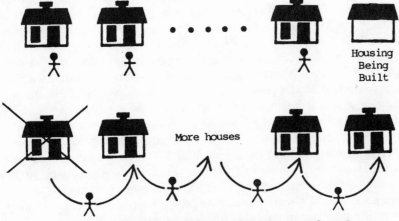

struction; and the filtering mechanism that is supposed to ensure that housing trickles down to the poor does not work very well.

Cyclical Nature of Housing Production. Turning to the first problem, the overall rate of new housing production is very reactive to the ebbs and flows of the national economy. In the United States, for example, residential construction is the most cyclical sector of the economy, exhibiting the most intense swings over the course of time. Annual housing starts have risen or fallen by as much as 700,000 units in a year.[7] Although residential construction accounts for only 4 to 5 percent of the GNP, during a recession as much as two-thirds of the overall contraction of the national economy may occur in the residential construction industry.[8]

The level of housing production is highly cyclical because of its dependency on interest rates and credit availability. A building is a large, bulky, expensive item. A builder almost never has the funds to pay out of his or her own pocket all the costs associated with building a house or an apartment building; therefore, he or she must borrow money or sell stock in the building corporation. Builders, for the most part based locally, rarely have a national market of investors on which to draw for funds to use in building. They therefore are dependent on loans and extensions of credit from financial institutions for their building activities. The availability of credit, as well as the interest rate that a builder must pay, hinges, to a large extent, on government monetary and fiscal policies and governmental policies in the secondary mortgage market, as well as on general economic conditions in the society.

When credit becomes less available or interest rates rise, construction activity drops, for two reasons. First, when the availability of credit decreases, builders are less able to borrow money from financial institutions. This results in builders having less cash on hand with which to pay suppliers and workers. A rise in interest rates has a similar effect, particularly when the interest rate on the construction loan is a fluctuating rate tied to the prime rate of interest. As the builder's interest costs rise, there is less money to spend for the actual bricks, mortar, and labor required to produce housing. Second, when credit availability decreases or interest rates rise, potential buyers of housing decrease. Fewer people are able to obtain or afford the funds necessary to buy housing, because of higher interest rates on mortgage loans, and higher price tags on the new housing built with the higher interest charges.

In a profit-based system of housing production, whether new housing gets built, whether older housing gets repaired or rehabilitated, and whether families can afford to buy homes depends largely on the overall condition of the economy, as well as federal fiscal and monetary policies. In times of recession or depression, or rising interest rates, housing production tends to fall dramatically.

Cost of Credit. A second problem in a capitalist housing system is the fact that a large percentage of the cost of buying a home is the cost of credit, thereby reducing the money available for actual construction of housing units. For example, if a home costs $45,000, and if $40,000 of the purchase price is financed over 25 years at an 11 percent interest rate, then during the course of the loan, the purchaser will pay out a total of $117,615, or almost three times the purchase price of the home.

Yet according to Charles Abrams's detailed study of housing, an interest rate of no more than 2 percent is necessary to meet the normal servicing costs and risks of a mortgage loan.[9] (Indeed, Federal Housing Administration [FHA] interest rates did not exceed 4.5 percent from July 1939 to December 1956.[10]) That is, if money loaned for home purchases did not have to earn a profit or a return competitive with other investments, an interest rate of about 2 percent on mortgage loans would cover the management costs of handling the loans and the risks of default on the loans. At such an interest rate a buyer would pay only $50,862 over the life of a $40,000 25-year loan. Moreover, because a home mortgage loan is secured by a deed of trust on the property, a lender faces little risk of loss in the event of default on the loan; it can simply foreclose on the property and thereby be paid off on the loan. Only in times of decreasing home values will a lender risk failure to recoup full payment on the loan in the event of default. Yet even this risk has been eliminated on FHA- and VA-insured loans, as well as privately insured loans, for the lender can look to insurance to pay any losses it might sustain.

Not only is much of a homeowner's cost of purchase tied up in interest payments but the interest expended on housing is increased by the fact that most homes are resold several times. Each time the property is resold, it is refinanced. Most of the house payments made in the early years of a loan go to interest rather than to principal. With homeowners moving on the average of every five years, many homeowners scarcely build up any equity in their homes before they move and have to start all over with another home. Financial institutions are the ones that profit from this repeated turnover of mortgage loans. They earn money on loan fees, closing costs, and points, as well as on the higher amount of interest paid each month on a newer loan as opposed to an older loan.

Thus, high interest rates and frequent loan refinancings lead to a much smaller percentage of total housing expenditures paying for the bricks and mortar of housing construction than would be the case if interest charges were based merely on the cost of lending. The original cost of construction of virtually all homes is paid for many times over as the home is sold and resold, each time with a new mortgage.

Filtering. Finally, the filtering of housing from richer to poorer that is supposed to occur under capitalism often does not proceed as smoothly as predicted by theory. For one thing, the housing market is highly segmented between different classes and races, as well as by location. Second, people do not immediately move to the next car on the housing train simply because a car near the front of the train in their area has been vacated. While filtering does certainly happen, it is an insufficient way to allocate housing to lower-income persons, and, since the late 1970s, to moderate-income persons as well. Filtering fails to provide better housing for low- and moderate-income households in three additional circumstances: (1) When the number of housing units at a particular income level on the housing continuum is being reduced at a faster rate than housing at the next higher level is being freed up, then persons at the lower income level face a housing shortage. (2) When the number of lower-income households is growing faster than the number of new housing units being built for upper-income households, then there are insufficient numbers of housing units filtering downward. (3) When gentrification displaces persons in lower- or moderate-priced housing, their homes become freed up for occupancy by middle- and upper-class households. Gentrification is the reverse of filtering, or perhaps more accurately, it is filtering with a vengeance, as formerly poor and working class housing is filtered *up* to the middle and upper classes. (See Figure 7.)

Figure 7
Breakdowns in Filtering

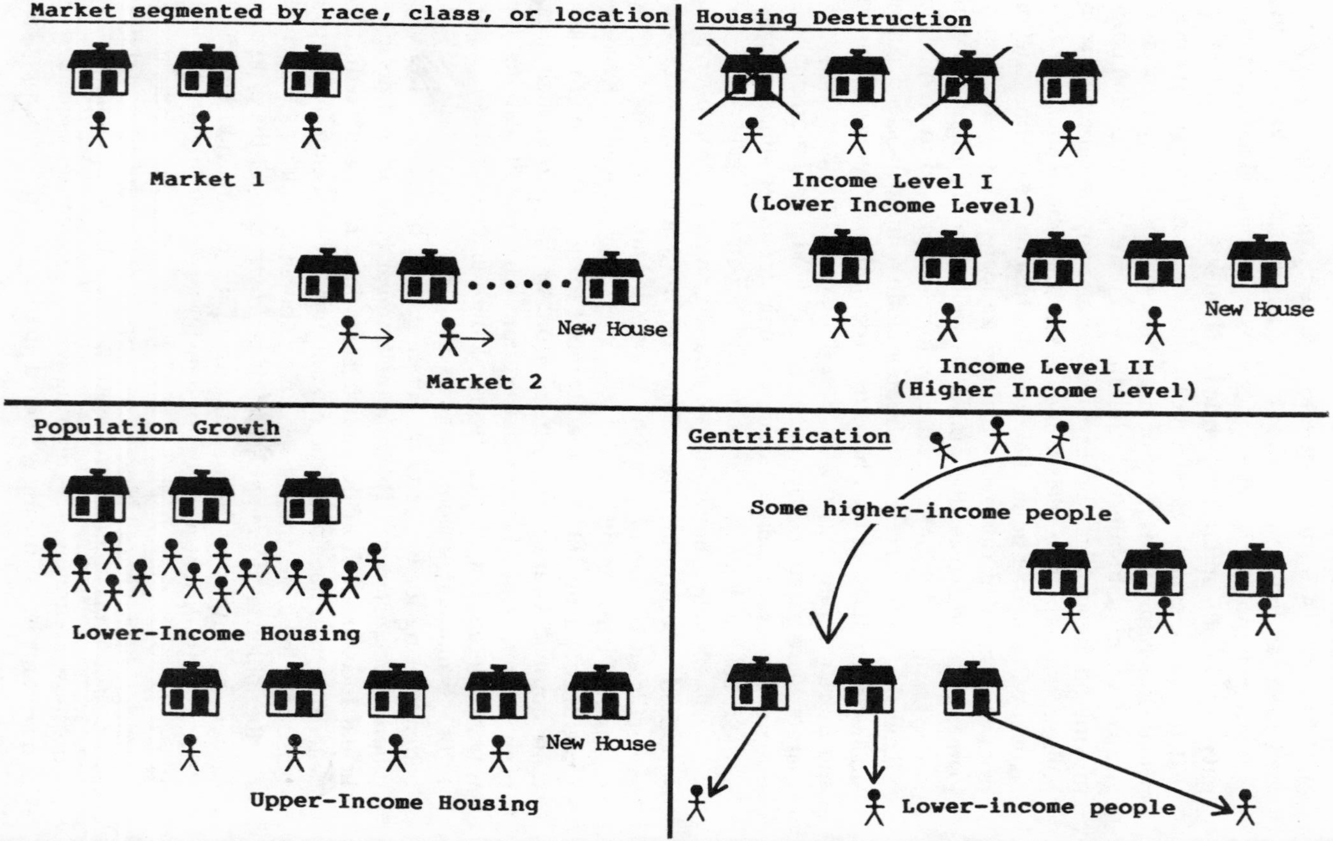

Market segmented by race, class, or location

Market 1

New House

Market 2

Housing Destruction

Income Level I
(Lower Income Level)

New House

Income Level II
(Higher Income Level)

Population Growth

Lower-Income Housing

New House

Upper-Income Housing

Gentrification

Some higher-income people

Lower-income people

Alternative Methods of Production

In societies where the state either builds the housing directly itself, or contracts with private contractors to build the housing for the state, there should not, in theory, be the ebbs and flows of housing production that are found in the United States, since the state can plan the number of units to be built each year. The degree of central versus decentralized planning can, of course, vary. (See Chapter 5 for further discussion of planning.)

In practice, however, few countries that have had one degree or another of socialized production of housing have successfully eliminated their housing shortages. The reason for this lack of success seems to hinge on a lack of commitment to ending the housing shortage. For example, in the Soviet Union and Eastern European countries, the governments have often seen housing as an unproductive consumer item, and therefore have concentrated their attention on industrial development at the expense of consumer production.[11] While Cuba has given attention to housing issues from the very beginning of the revolutionary period, it is simply too underdeveloped to have solved its housing problem. In Britain, since World War II, the production of council housing has ebbed and flowed with the shifts in political power between the Conservatives and the Labour Party, and now the Conservatives are moving to privatize council housing.

In devising a housing production system that will be successful in ending the housing crisis in the United States, then, an essential requirement is a long-term commitment to ending the housing crisis. There must be a long-term commitment to producing an adequate supply of affordable, decent, safe, sanitary, and handicapped-accessible housing, particularly since it takes a number of years of construction to add significantly to the total housing stock. This long-term commitment has never existed in the United States. While the 1949 Housing Act called for eliminating the lack of decent, safe, and sanitary housing, that legislation has never received the long-term financial and political support necessary to build affordable and adequate housing for all persons in the United States. Indeed, of the countries discussed in this book, only Sweden, which maintained a commitment over forty years to eliminate the housing shortage, and Norway, which has had a consistent system for promoting housing production over several decades, can be termed successful in ending their housing shortages.

Once the commitment to ending the housing shortage is made, the next question is how the housing actually will be built. Will it be built by for-profit private contractors, who receive subsidies from the government to induce them to build more housing? Will it be built by nonprofit and cooperative builders? Will the government itself build the housing as the general contractor, hiring private subcontractors to supply the components of housing? Will there be any controls over the prices charged by contractors or subcontractors under any of these methods of production? Will the government, on the other hand, itself provide the supplies and labor for the production of housing?

Government Subsidies to For-profit Contractors. A system of subsidizing private builders can result in the production of more housing for lower-income consumers than would otherwise be built. Such subsidies can also reduce the price to the consumer of the housing that is ultimately sold or rented, where restrictions are placed on the prices or rent charged by developers. Such a system does not, however, eliminate profit considerations from housing. Rather, it simply increases the profit that would otherwise be realized in lower-priced housing construction, in order to encourage investors to put their money into such housing production rather than into other investments.

Production by Nonprofit/Cooperative Builders. Production by nonprofit and cooperative builders eliminates the profit motive at the builders' end of the production of housing, but it does not end the need of such nonprofit and cooperative organizations to buy supplies and borrow funds. If these supplies are bought and funds are borrowed from private sources, then the suppliers and banks will be making profits from the construction of housing. While control over materials prices and credit charges would be necessary to ensure that the construction of the housing is truly "nonprofit," this would lead to a large and unwieldy bureaucratic system of price control. Excessive credit charges could be dealt with via establishment of a housing bank. (See Chapter 4.) To make sure that "profits" are not, in fact, being made by way of excessively high salaries paid to the management of the nonprofit organization, it might also be necessary to have some sort of government scrutiny of the nonprofit developers.

Production by the Federal Government. When the government builds housing with the help of private subcontractors, the government is still hostage to the prices charged by the subcontractors, who, in an otherwise capitalist system, will charge whatever the market will bear to maximize their profits. If the government establishes a system of price controls, or a requirement that the contractors or subcontractors be nonprofit, this might give the government control over the cost of building housing. A result of such price controls, however, may be low bids submitted by contractors and subcontractors who do shoddy work. If, on the other hand, the government itself does all the building, and uses state-owned suppliers, then there is an enormous coordination effort needed to ensure that supplies are available when needed. These problems have been chronic in the Soviet Union. It may be, however, that the problems of lack of supplies can be resolved with the developments in computer technology (since computers can help ease the burden of coordinating information). But without any competition from nongovernmental builders, there will likely be less consumer choice, as the government is not forced by competition to vary its product to meet the wishes of consumers.

Local Government Production. The problems involved when the national government takes charge of housing production might be surmounted with a system of local control over housing production. This could include local residents as active participants in the design and location of housing and local government or nonprofit companies as the actual builders of housing. Such an arrangement would ensure that differences in local tastes and needs would be reflected in the type and amount of housing produced. The local government, however, would still be hostage to national economic trends; if the local area is depressed economically, it will not have sufficient funds to build adequate amounts of housing for its populace. National involvement is needed, to ensure more equal distribution of funds across the nation for housing production.

ALLOCATION OF HOUSING

Allocation under Capitalism

Under a capitalist system, housing is allocated by money. Those who can buy housing are those who can afford to pay the rent or can get loans to pay the purchase price. Those who rent have a right to remain in the housing only so long as they can afford to pay the price demanded and only during the term of their lease.

Financial institutions that lend money for mortgage loans or home improvement loans will lend their money to borrowers who appear to be the safest financial risks. A lending institution will look not only at the income of the potential borrower but also at the price of the property for which the borrower wants to obtain money. The price of the house in question is determined not merely by the actual physical condition of the house but, more importantly, by the neighborhood in which it is located. The perceptions, which can be distorted by racism, of the financial institution about the stability of the neighborhood also influence lending decisions. Thus, the decision to lend will not be based primarily on need, or on an effort to preserve the housing stock that already exists, but on perceived profit considerations. A larger loan for a higher-priced house will generate higher profits for the lender.

Filtering is the primary mechanism of allocation of housing to lower-income families. Yet, because of the inadequacy of filtering as a mechanism of allocation, allocation does not always proceed according to the train analogy. Instead of the housing stock in a metropolitan area being like a train, with the cars at the end of the train being removed as new ones are added at the head of the train and everyone moving into a higher-class car, a different picture can develop in certain urban areas: the last cars are uncoupled and left to rot on the tracks, with the people still in the cars, while persons in the next to last cars are pushed off the train to provide *lebensraum* for people in the middle- and upper-class cars. The promise of capitalism that it will provide adequate housing for all becomes a mirage.

In the United States, there have been modifications of the purely capitalist system of allocation, although the capitalist one still predominates. Public housing and certain subsidized housing provide homes for some households whose incomes are below certain standards set by law. Allocation in public housing is by waiting list. Section 8 subsidized housing is allocated partly by a waiting list: the certificates for Section 8 housing are allocated by a waiting list, but once a person has the certificate, he or she must find a landlord willing and approved to rent to the family under the Section 8 program. If no such landlords exist, then the Section 8 certificate holder is not allocated any housing under the Section 8 program.

Further modification of a purely capitalist mode of allocation derives from racism. A minority household and a white household with equal incomes will not be equally considered in the allocation of housing, if the seller or landlord engages in discrimination. Discrimination also skews a purely capitalist mode of allocation with regard to receipt of public benefits, if lenders or landlords refuse to consider welfare dollars received from the government the same as dollars received from an employer.

Allocation under Administrative Systems

In contrast to a capitalist system of housing allocation is an administrative system of housing allocation. Such a system can distribute housing using criteria other than money. If administered according to uniform criteria, an administrative system theoretically can assure that all persons have decent, safe, and accessible housing, *assuming* that there is a sufficient supply of housing available to allocate. This assumption, however, is generally fallacious in today's industrial countries, and therefore administrative housing systems have developed their own inequalities.

In socialist countries where housing allocation is based on a principle of need rather than on household income, so long as there is scarcity of housing, there will be inequality in the distribution of housing. The reason for this is that whenever there is scarcity of housing, the society then must decide what criteria other than need will be used to allocate scarce housing to equally needy people. While a waiting list can be used for this purpose, it is not generally an adequate resolution of the problem when the waiting list is years long. As a result, other criteria, such as social merit, determine which persons will first be allocated the scarce housing.[12]

Consequently, administrative systems of allocation in socialist countries have developed unexpected degrees of inequality, although the extent of inequality has not been nearly so great as in the United States. This inequality derives from the tendency of the administrators of such systems to reward those in society who are deemed more worthwhile, by giving them priority in the allocation of housing. Even if there is an adequate supply of housing, administrators are likely to allocate the better quality housing to those who are preferred. Yet those who are deemed most meritorious by society, or those who are in the most essential jobs, tend to have the highest wages. As a result, those who are already somewhat better off financially in the society, and who could therefore better afford to pay more for their housing, receive greater subsidies than the less well-off. Thus, analyses of state housing in Eastern Europe have demonstrated that the better-quality state housing tends to be occupied by the middle class (clerical workers, intellectuals, professionals, bureaucrats, and skilled workers), rather than by the working class. In addition, because of the shortage of housing, there is inequality between those who are able to get a housing allocation from the state (generally the better-off) and those who are not able to get an allocation, and between those who are older urban residents (who already have housing) and those who are new migrants to urban areas.[13]

Employment and Housing

One of the social criteria that often has been used in Eastern European countries to allocate housing is employment. Certain housing has been tied to jobs, meaning that a person is eligible for the housing only if he or she works for the industry that built the housing. This system has also been used by employers in "company towns" in the United States. This rewards those who have jobs and encourages people to work. Indeed, if the consequence of not having a job is certain loss of one's housing, this is a powerful incentive to conform to the demands of the workplace and not to rebel, for fear of losing one's job. Tying housing to jobs can be used to reduce worker mobility for those who already have jobs and housing; it can also be used as a strong inducement, when housing is scarce, to lure workers to jobs in less desirable areas (e.g., Siberia).

Thus, a system that ties housing to jobs can lead to a harsher situation for unemployed persons than a capitalist system that separates employment from housing. Loss of employment in such a capitalist system, for example, can result in foreclosure when the homebuyer becomes unable to meet the mortgage, or in eviction when the tenant becomes unable to pay the rent. The loss of housing when a person becomes unemployed is not, however, a foregone result, because the worker may be able to use savings or certain benefits (e.g., unemployment benefits) to keep up with the mortgage or rent payments.[14]

If, however, a housing system linking housing to employment allows a worker to remain in housing belonging to the employer after he or she leaves the job, then this can lead to workers taking jobs just to get better housing, with no intention of remaining in their jobs. This problem can be reduced through requirements that the worker remain on the job for a certain period of time before the worker acquires any "right" to the housing. Yet such requirements can be abused if the employer (whether private or public) routinely discharges workers just before their right to the housing accrues.

Security of Tenure

The discussion of employment and housing relates to another issue in the allocation of housing—security of tenure. In most urban societies, there is some amount of security of tenure, although this security varies widely. Its extent can range from absolute security to security as long as the occupant is not destructive of property or disruptive to neighbors, to security for a term of years, to security merely from month to month (which scarcely qualifies as "security"). Under capitalism there is security of tenure for those homebuyers who consistently make their mortgage payment on time and pay their taxes (except where eminent domain is used to take homes away from people); for tenants, security exists for the length of their lease if they regularly make the rent payments. Anything that interferes with the ability of a homebuyer or a tenant to pay the full monthly payment on the dwelling unit threatens the tenure of the household. While Cuba initially had a system of virtually absolute security of tenure, this system had to be modified to take into account divorce, and the problem of visitors outstaying their welcome.[15] The Soviet Union has a system that approximates security of tenure as long as the tenant is not destructive or disruptive.

DISCRIMINATION

There are several different types of discrimination presently existing in the United States: race and ethnic discrimination, class discrimination, handicap discrimination, and discrimination based on marital status. Each poses somewhat different issues.

Racial and Ethnic Discrimination

The most visible discrimination is racial and ethnic discrimination, which has resulted in the extensive segregation found in most urban areas, and which was discussed in Chapter 1. Since racial and ethnic minorities are easily identifiable, the modes of discrimination can be myriad. For example, minority renters and homebuyers who are steered away from certain neighborhoods by rental agents and realtors may not even realize they are being steered. Neighborhoods intent on keeping out racial or ethnic minorities can, in subtle and not-so-subtle ways, make life sufficiently unpleasant for minority occupants that they move out. A person who has to find a new place to live fairly quickly (for example, because of a new job, or because of eviction) often will not have the time and energy needed to determine if discrimination is occurring. Finally, given the fact that most people consider their home a refuge from the rest of the world, most minorities will not willingly place themselves in an environment where their home will have to be a fortress rather than a refuge.

While policies certainly can be developed to counteract housing discrimination, these will have to be coupled with efforts in other areas (such as education) designed to combat existing prejudice. For example, while laws can be passed to attack discrimination, the enforcement of those laws will depend in large part on the prevailing societal attitudes toward the elimination of racial prejudice. If there is not a commitment to end prejudice and racial discrimination, the laws will remain idle on the books.

A controversial issue that has arisen even among those committed to eliminating segregation is that of integration management. This consists of methods set up to assure that an integrated community does not become all-minority. Usually, this is done by setting quotas on the number of minorities in the community or by steering minorities away from the community if they threaten to become too numerous. Those who support integration management programs argue that, without such "benign" quotas, integrated communities will become predominantly minority in short order, and whites will leave when the "tipping point" is reached. The tipping point is considered the point at which the percentage of minorities in the community is sufficiently high that whites begin to leave or refuse to move in, because they do not wish to be in a predominantly minority community. Supporters of integration management programs generally argue that whites must remain in the majority in a community and must be guaranteed that they will remain in the majority, or else they will leave.[16] To the minority person who is excluded from occupancy based on his or her race, such "benign" quotas have precisely the same effect as quotas motivated by prejudice: they prevent the minority person from residing in the community based on that person's color. Those who oppose integration management argue that the policies developed to fight housing discrimination must be ones designed to increase minority choice, rather than ones designed to impose integration by discriminating against minorities. An additional consideration is the fact that some minorities prefer living in a predominantly minority community, not because of the hostility they might face in other communities, but as a way of increasing minority political power and representation in legislative bodies. Chapter 6 discusses this issue in more detail.

Class Discrimination

Class discrimination, while certainly overlapping with racial and ethnic discrimination, presents somewhat different issues. As long as houses and apartments have different price ranges, there inevitably will be some segregation by economic status. This can, of course, be reduced by laws that require housing developers (whether private or public) to include a range of housing prices in their developments (whether subdivisions or apartment buildings). But, without extensive construction of lower-priced housing and apartments in existing upper-class areas, class segregation is likely to continue. Likewise, full employment, enforcement of employment discrimination laws, and equal educational opportunities are essential to ensure that those born into poor, working-class, and minority families are able to pay for higher-priced housing. Laws that prohibit discrimination against women and children also can aid in reducing class discrimination. But without adequate child support laws and enforcement of such laws, single women with children will be relegated to sectors of lower-quality and lower-priced housing.

Handicap Discrimination

Discrimination against the handicapped is manifested not so much by overt refusals to sell or rent to the handicapped (except for those who are mentally handicapped or have illnesses such as AIDS) but by the simple fact of unavailability of units that are accessible to the handicapped. While the 1988 amendments to the Fair Housing Act prohibit discrimination based on handicap and require new construction to be handicapped-accessible, the vast majority of the housing stock is existing housing that is not accessible. The question becomes: under what circumstances will buildings be required to be converted to handicapped-accessibility, and who will bear the cost of such conversion? This issue is discussed in Chapter 6.

Marital Status Discrimination

Nonmarried cohabitants are most likely to experience discrimination in those communities that have ordinances prohibiting persons unrelated by blood or marriage from living together. In addition, lesbian and gay renters face the risk of eviction whenever their sexual orientation is discovered, unless the jurisdiction has security of tenure laws. While laws prohibiting discrimination based on marital status or sexual orientation would alleviate discrimination against gays and lesbians, the history of continuing discrimination against racial minorities and women, despite the passage of civil rights laws a generation ago, illustrates the inadequacy of antidiscrimination laws as the only solution to the problem.

DISPLACEMENT

Displacement, as discussed in Chapter 1, results from a variety of causes: inability to pay the rent or mortgage, shrinking supply of lower-priced units, and public and private revitalization. These different causes of displacement raise somewhat different issues in devising policies to combat displacement.

Measures that make housing affordable will, of course, reduce displacement caused by failure to pay rent or mortgage payments, provided that there is a sufficient supply of housing. Thus, measures that increase the supply of lower-priced housing, as well as those that decrease the price of housing, are important parts of an effective anti-displacement policy. Full employment policies and welfare programs can also reduce displacement caused by inability to pay rent or mortgage payments, provided that rents and housing prices do not simply increase in tandem with increases in household income.

Displacement caused by the shrinking supply of lower-priced housing can be combatted by measures to increase the preservation and production of lower-priced housing, the subject of Chapter 5. In the rental market, landlord notice and property deterioration ("constructive eviction") also cause displacement. Such displacement can be dealt with through laws requiring security of tenure and property maintenance (see Chapter 7).

Displacement caused by public and private redevelopment is likely to be the most difficult problem, as such redevelopment often appears to be in the general public interest, although causing harm to those facing displacement. In an ideal world no one would be displaced. In the real world, which already has existing patterns of development, some of which impede community betterment, the local government sometimes will have to use its eminent domain power to ensure rational land use. For example, if a city decides to build a rapid transit system to decrease use of automobiles, this may well require some dislocation to construct the necessary rights of way, if existing roadways are not adequate for development of an extensive public transit system.

In debates over proposed government action that may cause displacement, there often will be disputes as to whether a particular plan will benefit the public, or merely a small powerful sector of the public. Although increased public participation and decision making in urban development might decrease dislocation, those involved in the planning process might simply impose dislocation on disfavored and less powerful segments of the public.

By requiring more adequate compensation and relocation for those displaced, relocation laws can decrease unnecessary displacement by requiring those causing displacement to bear the true costs of dislocation. Moreover, by severely limiting the circumstances under which redevelopment projects will be approved, and building and demolition permits will be granted, the local government can reduce substantially the amount of displacement caused by redevelopment and incumbent upgrading. Proposals to counteract this type of displacement are made in Chapter 7.

There is no "perfect" system of housing pricing, production, and allocation, nor any "perfect" system to eliminate discrimination and displacement. Any system will have its limitations and its problems. The task, then, is to propose a housing system that will result in a more just housing system in the United States and that will have as few built-in problems as possible. The remainder of the book proposes a comprehensive framework to solving the housing problem and makes specific proposals in the realms of pricing, production, allocation, discrimination, and displacement. Chapter 3 provides a brief overview of the framework, and subsequent chapters provide the details.

Chapter 3

A Housing Platform for the United States: An Overview

It is not an easy task to develop proposals for a more just and equitable housing system in the United States. The preceding chapter has pointed out the problems involved in the different types of housing systems. Therefore, the proposals in this book are an amalgamation of the best of the various policies that have been adopted or proposed in other countries or in this one. Debate and discussion generated by these proposals undoubtedly will cause modifications in the platform.

Before going into the specifics of the platform, some general points should be mentioned. First of all, I do not favor the elimination of homeownership, not only because such a policy would give too much power to the governmental entities who would be leasing property to renters, but also because this society strongly values homeownership as a goal. Instead, I favor a mixed system of housing options, including homeownership, renting (public and private), and cooperatives. Private builders and landlords should be allowed to coexist with publicly owned housing, as private builders and owners will serve as a check on publicly owned housing, ensuring that such housing is meeting the needs of the people. If it is not, a privately funded entity may be able to produce better housing that meets these needs.

Second, regardless of the type of housing system adopted, there will need to be subsidies of some sort for the poorest, particularly so long as unemployment idles millions of potential workers. Even if the unemployment problem were solved, subsidies will still be required for those who earn too little to afford the price of their dwelling unit, and for those who are unable to work. In order to avoid stigmatizing those who are receiving subsidies, housing should not be segregated for the poor.

Finally, in order for the housing crisis in the United States to be solved, there must be a long-term sustained commitment to eliminating the lack of adequate and affordable housing. This probably will require at least a generation. Given the vagaries of politics in the United States, with housing policies changing every four to eight years depending on presidential and congressional elections, this may be the most difficult condition to meet. Even if the nation as a whole will not make a long-term commitment, it may be possible to design long-term goals and the policies to achieve some of those goals on a state-by-state or city-by-city basis. At whatever level the plans are made, however, the solution to the problem will come not in a limited short-term program but only in a long-term comprehensive program that takes into account the various aspects of the housing problem.

It is the goal of this book to suggest a comprehensive approach to the housing problem. One component of the proposed housing program cuts across all the areas for which proposals are made in the following chapters: the proposal that there be a Social Housing Sector in the United States. Therefore, the first part of this chapter explains the proposal for social housing in detail, while the remainder of the chapter merely summarizes proposals that are discussed more thoroughly in subsequent chapters. The proposals made in the book are designed to comport with the requirements of the United States Constitution; Chapter 8 discusses these constitutional considerations.

SOCIAL HOUSING SECTOR

Types of Social Housing

Under the present housing system that we have in the United States, the construction costs of most houses and apartment buildings are paid for many times over during the life of the structure, as discussed in Chapter 2. If the constant cycle of mortgaging and remortgaging property at ever-higher prices could be broken, then, as the currently existing mortgage debt in the United States is paid off, the financial burden of housing costs would be dramatically reduced. A way to accomplish this is through the development of a Social Housing Sector, that is, a sector consisting of housing that will never be sold for profit.[1] Thus, once the mortgage is paid off on a piece of property in the Social Housing Sector, housing costs for that property should drop dramatically, with monthly housing expenses being only those needed for repairs, maintenance, management, and utilities.

Social housing, then, would be any housing that:

1. would never be resold into the private housing market *and*
2. is owned by the local government, a public housing authority, a limited equity cooperative, a mutual housing association, a community land trust, or a nonprofit organization.

Occupants of social housing would have security of tenure, except that eviction would be authorized for malicious destruction of property, refusal to pay rent if the person is able to pay it, or repeated disturbance of or assault on others. Occupants also would have the right to improve their dwelling units. The different forms that social housing could take are described below.

Public Housing/Locally Owned Housing. These forms of socially owned housing could be much the same as the current public housing program, though with more tenant control than exists in many projects. Public housing, however, need not be limited to low-income persons, as is the current practice in the United States. For one thing, such a policy almost guarantees recurring financial crises in public housing, for poor people simply cannot pay enough rent to cover the costs of housing. Thus, to make public housing financially viable, it is essential that it be available to higher-income tenants who can pay unsubsidized rents. An initial step that could be taken is to allow persons who are in public housing to remain in public housing even if their incomes increase. The only thing that should change is the amount of rent that they pay; as they become able to pay unsubsidized rents, they should be required to do so. As for making public housing available to new applicants who are not poor, this can only be done if the supply of public housing is increased. At the present time, the number of poor people on the waiting list is so great that it would be unfair to give priority to persons who have not been on the waiting list just because those persons have greater income. Thus, opening up public housing to higher-income persons would have to be a gradual process. However, as public housing becomes more economically mixed, this is likely not only to make public housing more solvent financially but to destigmatize public housing, particularly if it were designed to be attractive and comfortable.

Community Land Trusts and Limited Equity Cooperatives. Community land trusts (CLTs) are organizations that acquire land and hold the land in perpetuity, with residents on the land having long-term or lifetime inheritable leases. The trust is operated on a not-for-profit basis, with board members elected from the local community and residents of the land trust. Those living on land owned by the community land trust pay a lease fee, which is based on a land use fee, plus the costs of real estate taxes and assessments, insurance, and debt service, if any, on the land. Those leasing land in a land trust cannot own the land, but they can own the improvements built on the land. If a resident of the land trust wishes to sell his or her improvements, the land trust has the first right to purchase the improvements, or the right to approve the sale of the improvements to a low- or moderate-income household, with the price being based on the amount that the seller paid down on the property, with adjustments made for inflation, improvements, depreciation, and damage.[2]

A limited equity cooperative (LEC) is a cooperative in which each member owns a share of the total value of the cooperative's property; the sale price of an owner's share is limited according to a formula, to prevent inflation in the value of shares from pricing low- and moderate-income households out of an opportunity to buy into the cooperative. Typically, the resale value of a share is limited to the owner's cash investment in the cooperative, plus a small return on investment.[3] While the rights of members of LECs vary with each LEC, generally members have the right to live in their housing unit in perpetuity and to pass their housing unit on to their heirs. They agree, however, that their equity appreciation in their home will be limited. The formulas for limiting equity appreciation generally provide that the member will, upon sale of the housing unit, get only an amount equal to the initial investment of the member in the cooperative and the improvements made by the member to the unit, often adjusted in some fashion for inflation as well as depreciation. The LEC has the first option to buy the property at the price established by the formula and can then resell the property to a subsequent member of the cooperative.

The United States in recent years has seen the development of limited equity cooperatives with underlying land trusts as a method of production and rehabilitation that assures lower housing costs for members of the cooperative. Most LECs have acquired existing vacant or deteriorated housing and rehabilitated it for members of the cooperative, though some have also produced new housing. A separate community land trust is established as the entity that actually owns the land under the properties that are owned by the limited equity cooperative, to reduce the chance of all the members of an LEC deciding to convert the LEC to privately owned market-rate housing.[4] The LEC rehabilitates the property on the land that is leased from the CLT, with members of the cooperative given ownership shares in the cooperative.

Only those CLTs and LECs that require the property to remain in the Social Housing Sector forever should be treated as part of the Social Housing Sector. Since a land trust or cooperative might eventually dissolve, there should also be a provision that, if dissolution occurs, the land or property owned by the trust or cooperative must be transferred to another portion of the Social Housing Sector, to ensure that the property does not revert back to private for-profit ownership. Moreover, to be deemed social housing, a CLT or LEC should prohibit discrimination based on race, color, sex, age, national origin, religion, handicap (including health-related condition), marital status or sexual orientation.

While CLTs and LECs have the advantage of decentralizing control over social housing so that it is not just public housing authorities that control social housing, they do require a high level of involvement, skill, and commitment by board members and residents to make them work successfully. Therefore, a significant factor in the development of such forms of social housing will be state and federal grants to provide technical assistance and training for members of CLTs and LECs. Otherwise, such forms of social housing are likely to remain a very small fraction of the housing economy.

Nonprofit Housing Corporations. A third type of social housing would be housing controlled by nonprofit housing corporations. Nonprofit corporations could help to increase the supply of social housing and provide for another form of decentralized control of such housing, in addition to land trusts and cooperatives. While a limited equity cooperative or a land trust could be organized in the form of a nonprofit corporation, there also could be nonprofit housing corporations that are not land trusts or cooperatives but that should be entitled to be regarded as part of the Social Housing Sector if they conform to five principles. (1) The property owned by the corporation would never be resold into the private for-profit sector. (2) It would not discriminate on the basis of race, sex, national origin, age, religion, handicap, household composition, or sexual orientation. (3) It would use a cost-rental system of setting rent rates, modified by taking amenities into account in setting rent levels (see Chapter 4). (4) Its tenants would have security of tenure (see Chapter 7). (5) A certain percentage of its apartments would be available to low- and moderate-income persons. The most likely sources of nonprofit housing corporations would be religious organizations, community groups, and employment-related organizations (unions, employers, or employees).

Development of the Social Housing Sector

Any of the forms of social housing could be pursued at the local level, even if the federal or state government did not adopt a social housing program. Having state or federal backing for such social housing programs would, however, be a substantial aid to their success. Therefore, in order to encourage the development of a Social Housing Sector, the government should provide funds for the training of people for the Social

Housing Sector. This training should consist of education in housing management and building maintenance, as well as the organizational and financial structures for establishing, organizing, and running CLTs and LECs. Property acquired by the government by foreclosure on government-insured mortgages, for failure to pay back taxes, for failure to maintain rental housing at minimum code standards, and for violation of antidiscrimination laws (see Chapters 5 and 6) should be sold to entities in the Social Housing Sector. In addition, those entities that are in the Social Housing Sector or that propose to build in the Social Housing Sector should be entitled to special low-interest loans from the Housing Bank (described in Chapter 4).

THE HOUSING PLATFORM: A SUMMARY

The remainder of the book discusses in detail four aspects of the housing crisis—financing and affordability, production and allocation, discrimination, and displacement—and presents proposals in each of those areas. There are no separate proposals on the homeless, because policies to build housing and to provide subsidies to those unable to pay the full price of housing should eliminate the problem of involuntary homelessness. The proposals in the different chapters overlap with each other. For example, policies given in Chapter 4 to make rents affordable to lower-income households should also reduce displacement, which is discussed in Chapter 7. Moreover, while the housing platform would be most successful if adopted in total, certainly cities, states, or the federal government could decide to adopt only parts of the platform.

In brief, the housing platform calls for the establishment of a nonprofit Housing Bank, which would provide low-interest, low-down-payment loans to homebuyers and low-interest loans to builders, with interest rates lower for buyers and builders in the Social Housing Sector than for those in the private sector. Resale price controls, antispeculation laws, and rent control should be adopted to help stabilize housing prices. Since there are some households, however, that will be unable to pay the full price of housing, subsidies will be necessary for low-income households. All these matters are discussed in Chapter 4.

While the Housing Bank will decrease the finance costs associated with housing, and resale price controls, rent control, and anti-speculation laws will reduce the escalation of housing prices, this will not be sufficient to ensure the preservation and production of housing affordable by lower-income households. Therefore, Chapter 5 proposes measures to ensure the preservation of the existing stock of lower-priced housing, as well as measures to increase the production of affordable housing. Currently existing public and subsidized housing should be preserved, and property acquired by FHA and VA through mortgage foreclosures should be transferred into the Social Housing Sector to take it out of the private for-profit housing system. Those absentee landlords who fail to maintain their properties or who fail to pay their property taxes should have their property taken from them, and its ownership transferred into the social sector. Systems should be developed to plan for the production of adequate amounts of new lower-cost housing; inclusionary zoning programs, as well as housing construction by the cities themselves, should be used to ensure its production. Building requirements not necessary for health and safety should be eliminated, as should exclusionary zoning devices that serve to keep lower-priced housing entirely out of some suburbs.

To ensure that minorities benefit from the inclusionary zoning programs and production of lower-priced housing, Chapter 6 proposes vigorous enforcement of existing civil rights legislation, as well as strengthening of such legislation to increase the penalties for discrimination. Such penalties could include forfeiture of the real estate involved in the discrimination and suspension of real estate licenses or the right to sell homeowners insurance. Moreover, communities need to take steps to provide public information on the availability of housing, so that minorities are not denied access to information by private listing agencies. Information as to the extent and location of home mortgage loans made by lending institutions, and as to credit practices of financial institutions, should be available to communities with sufficient detail that they can effectively take action when discriminatory lending practices become apparent. The newly enacted law against handicap discrimination should be amended to provide assistance to handicapped persons for modifications of existing housing units. The Fair Housing Act should also be amended to prohibit discrimination based on marital status and sexual orientation. Chapter 6 also proposes changes in zoning laws to end discrimination against unmarried cohabitants.

Many of the measures proposed in Chapters 4, 5, and 6 will aid in the elimination of displacement, which is the primary concern of Chapter 7. Thus, rent control, subsidies to lower-income households, low-interest loans to lower-income homeowners for home repairs, preservation of the existing stock of lower-priced housing, and creation of a Social Housing Sector that preserves housing as a resource for low- and moderate-income households, will all aid the fight against displacement. In addition, Chapter 7 proposes security of tenure laws, which would require that eviction be only for cause or for certain other limited situations. Various proposals are made to strengthen current relocation assistance laws, including an extension of such laws to landlords who displace tenants in violation of law. Antidisplacement zoning laws, restrictions

Table 1
Housing Platform

Proposal (Chapter)	Issues Addressed by Proposal			
	Afford.	Produc. Preserv.	Discrim.	Displmt.
Antidisplacement zoning (7)		x		x
Antiredlining measures (6)			x	x
Antispeculation laws (4)	x			
Demolition controls (5)		x		x
Elimination of marital status discrimination (6)			x	
Elimination of private eminent powers (7)	x	x		x
Enforcement of anti-discrimination laws (6)			x	
Handicap accessibility (6)			x	
Housing Bank (4)	x	x		
Incentives for employers (4)	x			
Inclusionary zoning (6)	x	x	x	
Increased penalties for discrimination (6)			x	
Low down-payments (4)	x			
Low-interest loans to poor homeowners (5)	x	x		
Municipal production (5)	x	x		
Municipal liability for faulty construction (5)		x		
Planning (5)	x	x		
Preservation of FHA- and VA-foreclosed property (5)	x	x		x
Preservation of public and subsidized housing (5)	x	x		x
Public information on housing availability (6)			x	
Racial impact studies (6)			x	x
Reduction in development costs (5)	x	x		
Regulation of building permits (5)	x	x		
Rent control (4)	x	x		x
Resale price controls (4)	x	x		
Restrictions on condominium conversions (7)	x	x		x
Security of tenure (7)		x		x
Social Housing Sector (3)	x	x	x	x
Strengthen property maintenance laws (7)		x		x
Strengthen relocation assistance laws (7)		x	x	x
Subsidies (4)	x			x
Support for integrated areas (6)			x	
Taking deteriorated and tax-delinquent property (5)		x		x

on condominium conversions, and an end to the grant of eminent domain powers to private entities are further components of the anti-displacement proposals made in Chapter 7.

Table 1 lists the components of the housing platform. These components of the housing platform are developed in more detail in the remainder of the book. Chapter 8 gives attention to the legal issues that have arisen or that may arise in the four major areas, as well as to financing mechanisms. Each chapter summarizes the history of urban housing policies (pertaining to the topic of the chapter) that have been followed in the United States. Alternatives to the dominant policies are analyzed in the sections on financing, affordability, production, preservation, and allocation. All chapters, including those on discrimination and displacement, then present the author's proposals.

Chapter 4 _____

Financing and Affordability

A necessary precondition for ensuring the construction or rehabilitation of an adequate supply of decent affordable housing for all income groups is a consistent supply of credit at a guaranteed low rate of interest. The type of fluctuating interest rates that the United States has experienced over the past two decades does not permit rational planning. When the financial feasibility of a project depends on the vagaries of the overall economy, there will not be a consistent rate of housing production. High interest rates make some projects simply impossible to do, and for other projects, make housing excessively expensive for both homebuyers and renters. For homebuyers, high interest rates translates into higher prices for homes and higher monthly payments; for renters, high interest rates translates into high rental charges. As discussed in this chapter, most federal housing policies, whether carried out through the tax code or through subsidy programs, have not attempted to reduce the total cost of housing finance. Instead, the programs have, at best, merely helped consumers pay the price charged. The underlying interest rates have not been challenged.

The issue of financing and affordability breaks down into three questions: How should new construction and rehabilitation be financed? What controls, if any, should there be on prices and rents? Should homebuyers' and tenants' expenditures be subsidized, and, if so, how? To the extent that the cost of new construction and rehabilitation can be lowered through financing mechanisms that reduce cost, this should result in lower prices to both homebuyers and tenants. This is the subject of the first part of the chapter. But merely lowering finance costs will not prevent prices of existing real estate from appreciating nor rents from rising. The questions of housing price controls therefore are the subject of the middle portion of the chapter. Since some people will be unable to pay the full price of housing even if housing prices and rents stabilized, the question of subsidies is the subject of the last part of the chapter. While not discussed in this book, full employment programs are a final essential component of a housing policy, for people must be employed at livable wages to be able to pay the price of housing.

FINANCE COSTS

Past Policies in the United States

Prior to the Depression, the federal, state, and local governments generally were not involved in financing housing, and the only restrictions on finance charges were state usury laws. Home mortgages before the Depression generally were short-term balloon notes that had to be refinanced every few years.

As a result of the collapse of the housing finance system owing to the Depression, the federal government restructured the financial system, providing indirect support for the financing of housing. Congress created a variety of federal agencies whose purpose was to shore up the staggering financial institutions, with the hope that, with increased financial stability, the economy would take off again.[1] Four of the institutions established to stabilize the financial system still exist today in forms similar to that designed during the Depression: the Home Loan Bank Board (HLBB), the Federal Housing Administration (FHA), the Federal National Mortgage Association (FNMA), and the federal deposit insurance system.

The first of these, the HLBB, was established in 1932 and had twelve regional banks. Each of the regional banks could lend money to savings and loan associations that belonged to the system, with the money to be used by the savings and loan institutions to make mortgage loans. The intent of the act establishing the HLBB was to preserve the assets of savings and loan associations by lending money to them. This, in turn, would save the small depositors by preventing collapse of the savings and loan associations and would stimulate the availability of credit for mortgage loans.

The second agency, the FHA, established in 1934, was designed to encourage lenders to lend money and contractors to build housing. To achieve this goal, homeownership was promoted so as to provide a market to purchase the houses that were built. The mortgage loan, which prior to the Depression had been a high-down-payment short-term loan, was changed to a low-down-payment long-term loan. FHA insured the loan, so long as the lending institution made the loan in the amount of at least 90 percent of the value of the property for a 20- to 30-year period. The low down payment and FHA insurance made home mortgages available to a much larger percentage of the white population than had been the case before the Depression. (Racism in the administration of the FHA program limited its availability to minorities—see Chapter 6.) If the borrower defaulted on an FHA-insured mortgage loan, the federal government paid off the balance owed to the financial institution. Although it was the financial institutions that were protected by the insurance, it was the homebuyers, not the financial institutions, who had to pay an insurance premium to FHA. Thus, FHA was (and still is) similar to a private insurance business, but with the federal government, instead of a private company, bearing the risk of default, and with the homebuyer, and not the insured lenders, paying the insurance premiums. In 1944, the mortgage insurance program was supplemented by establishment of a Veterans Administration mortgage guarantee program.

The creation of the FNMA, also known as "Fannie Mae," in 1938, provided further support for mortgage lending, by creating a market for the sale of federally insured mortgages. One of the purposes of the FNMA was to help smooth out the housing cycles, by FNMA buying more mortgages when credit was tight, and fewer mortgages when credit was easy to obtain.[2] Mortgage lenders were assured a market on which they could sell their mortgage loans and therefore could obtain funds when they needed cash in order to be able to make additional mortgage loans.

The final innovation was federal deposit insurance, established in 1933 and 1934 to ensure that financial institutions would have money to lend and to restore confidence in the financial system. Congress sought to accomplish this by insuring accounts in federally chartered banks (through the Federal Deposit Insurance Corporation) and in federal savings and loan associations and local thrift institutions (through the Federal Savings and Loan Insurance Corporation) to encourage people to put and keep their money in savings accounts.[3]

In addition to these four institutions developed during the Depression years, which were designed to maintain the flow of mortgage funds, since the Depression the government has subsidized the finance costs for housing for lower income households in a variety of programs. Most of these programs now have either been eliminated entirely, or severely cut back. These programs included public housing (where the federal government paid directly the debt service on bonds floated to construct public housing), programs that subsidized the mortgage interest rate on the construction loans or mortgage loans for housing for low-income households (Sections 221(d)(3), 235, and 236 programs), and programs that provided federal low-interest loans for the construction or rehabilitation of housing (Section 312 loan program and, until 1974, the Section 202 program). All of these programs, except the low-interest direct loan programs (Sections 202 and 312), accepted the prevailing market interest rates, seeking merely to pay or subsidize those interest rates. Moreover, these finance subsidy production programs have resulted in the production of only about 2.5 million units, compared to a total of 56 million housing starts in the period from 1950 to 1985 alone.[4]

Alternative Financing Models

Both Norway and Sweden have extensive state-supported housing finance systems that are based on special housing banks and/or government loans and subsidies. These finance systems, together with extensive housing allowance programs (see "Subsidies"), have been the primary reasons that both countries have made affordable decent housing a reality for virtually all of their citizens.

Norway has state housing banks that provide loans for cooperatives, private housing contractors, and owner-occupiers. By 1976, the housing banks were providing 75 percent of the credit for new housing development. There are no income restrictions limiting the persons eligible for loans from the banks; rather, the only restrictions pertain to the cost and size of the dwelling unit that can be constructed with proceeds from a state housing bank loan. Borrowers can choose to repay the loans in one of two ways: by entering into a leveling loan or a nominal loan. Under the leveling loan system, payments are based on 20 percent of the average annual male blue-collar earnings, with the principal carrying a 6.5 percent interest charge (which can be varied by the government). Nominal loans are paid as a percentage of the principal balance of the loan and carry a 6.5 percent interest rate; repayments of the principal are set at 1 percent per year for the first ten years, and 2 percent for the next five years. The government can change the rate of the nominal loans and must amortize the nominal loans as quickly as the leveling loans. As of the beginning of the 1980s, 85 percent of borrowers chose the leveling loans. The housing finance system is capitalized by the government selling government bonds to savings banks.[5]

Sweden has aided the financial costs of housing for both housing developers and housing buyers, through specially chartered banks whose funds are guaranteed by the government. These banks provide first- and second-mortgage 40-year loans for construction at below-market interest rates for the first 70 percent of land and development costs. The state provides low-interest third-mortgage loans for a portion of the balance of the construction costs, depending on whether the builder is a publicly owned corporation, a cooperative, an owner-occupier, or a private landlord. Public builders can obtain third-mortgage loans for the full 30 percent remaining of the land and development costs, cooperative builders can borrow 29 percent, owner-occupiers 25 percent, and private landlords 22 percent. The central government rations the number of loans available in each category from year to year. In addition, the central government subsidizes the interest payments of individuals on mortgage loans, with the subsidy being greater for those who are acquiring property for cooperatives or rental units than for those purchasing owner-occupied homes.[6]

The National Pension Fund supports housing indirectly through its purchase of bonds issued by mortgage banks, housing credit societies, and mortgage companies, thereby increasing the flow of money into housing credit. By the 1970s, over 40 percent of the pension fund was invested in housing.[7]

Proposal: Housing Bank

To provide sufficient low-cost credit for housing construction and mortgage loans, a Housing Bank should be established on a nonprofit basis.[8] The sole mission of the Housing Bank should be to provide residential construction and mortgage loans at low interest rates, with the interest rates for housing in the Social Housing Sector set at an amount that will just cover administrative costs and reserves for defaults on loans. Interest rates for housing in the private sector should be marked up slightly, with the interest rate increasing with the price per square foot of housing. As in Norway, there should be a cap on the size and price of housing eligible for loans from the Housing Bank. Furthermore, borrowers should not be permitted to obtain Housing Bank loans for second homes. Thus, interest rates should range from 2 percent to 6 percent, with the lowest rates being for Social Sector housing and the highest rate for the most expensive private sector housing for which Housing Bank loans are permitted. Since the risk on construction loans is greater than the risk on mortgage loans, the interest rate for construction loans should be slightly higher than for mortgage loans. There should not, however, be any difference in rate based merely on the location of the property; no "redlining" should be permitted.

A reduction in the cost of credit would result in a substantial reduction in the price of housing, for the cost of credit has been one of the prime causes of the increase in housing prices since 1970.[9] For example, if a purchaser borrows $40,000 on a 25-year loan at 12 percent interest, his or her monthly payments are $421.29, and the total amount paid over the course of the loan is $126,387. The same loan at 6 percent interest results in a monthly payment of $257.52, or $77,316 over the life of the loan, while at 2 percent interest, the monthly payment is only $169.54 and the total payment over the life of the loan is $50,862. Thus, over the life of the loan, a homebuyer in the private sector would save $49,071 by being able to pay a 6 percent interest rate rather than a 12 percent interest rate. For those building or buying housing for the Social Sector and paying a 2 percent interest rate, the savings would be $75,525.

It is preferable to establish a Housing Bank, which provides low-interest loans to builders and buyers, than to subsidize market interest rates, for four reasons. First, in an interest rate subsidy system, the financial institution making the loan recovers the same amount of money from the loan as it does when the interest rates are not subsidized; the only difference is that the purchaser is paying only part of the interest charge, while the government (i.e., the taxpayer) is paying the rest. Thus, an interest-subsidy system does nothing to reduce the total amount of money paid in excessive interest charges to lenders (i.e., interest that exceeds the amount necessary to pay for administrative costs and bad debt risk). Second, a low-interest loan program is self-financing, once the initial capitalization is made. As the loans are repaid, the bank recovers the funds that it loaned out. In a private market subsidy system, the state never gets repaid the money it has paid out to private financial institutions. Third, and related to the second reason, a market interest-rate subsidy is a continuing expense throughout the period of the loan. Thus, a market subsidy program is a very expensive way to finance housing. Fourth, by having a Housing Bank, developers can go to one single source for financing for projects, rather than having to package financing from a half-dozen sources, as is often the case today with nonprofit developers.

There are two problems likely to arise with a Housing Bank. First, there may be more demand for credit than the bank is able to provide, particularly in the early years of the program, because of pent-up demand for affordable housing. Therefore, there will have to be a system of rationing the available credit, to ensure that credit is not distributed solely to those least in need of credit (i.e., better-off families, or builders constructing higher-priced housing). Credit should be allocated to localities in the state (or to each state in the country), based on the housing production plans of that locality and the anticipated credit needs for that production. (See Chapter 5 regarding planning.) If there are insufficient funds for all requested loans in a locality, then first priority should be given to those entities that are rehabilitating, constructing, or buying housing for the Social Housing Sector, particularly community land trusts, limited equity cooperatives, and nonprofit housing corporations, as well as persons displaced by government-supported activity (see Chapter 7). Second priority should be given to low- or moderate-income households wishing to purchase housing, and third priority to those credit-worthy households unable to obtain loans from the private sector.

Second, a Housing Bank is likely to face the "incipient yuppie" problem in situations where it has insufficient funds to lend money to all applicants. Recent state programs that have subsidized the costs of homeownership through mortgage bond revenue programs have given an extremely high percentage of the subsidized loans to whites, often young professionals who are at the beginning of their careers (or who still are in graduate school) and who therefore meet the definition of low- or moderate-income.[10] To avoid "incipient yuppies" from getting the bulk of limited credit from the bank, those who are in professions requiring advanced degrees or who are in graduate programs should not be considered low- or moderate-income, regardless of their actual income. Furthermore, in determining whether or not a household qualifies as low- or moderate-income, the income of all the members of the household over the preceding five years should be averaged, and this average used to determine the person's eligibility. This will prevent a household from becoming eligible for the program simply by having one year of lower income. It also will prevent a household composed of two or more working adults that are unrelated by legal marriage from qualifying simply by having only one member of the household apply for the loan.

Proposal: Low-Down-Payment Requirements

Higher down-payment requirements have been one of the factors causing homeownership rates to decline.[11] Therefore, to enable low- and moderate-income households to be able to buy housing, should they so desire, the Housing Bank should not require any down payment for the lowest-income borrowers, and it should gradually increase the down-payment requirement for higher-income borrowers, to a maximum of 5 or 10 percent down payment. Persons making no down payment or a low down- payment should be given pre- and post-purchase counseling, to minimize the risk of default. A no- or low-down-payment requirement will ensure that those who have the income to make regular monthly payments are not precluded from buying simply because of down-payment requirements that make it impossible for the family to obtain a loan.

Proposal: Employee Housing

Employers should be encouraged to provide funds for housing for their workers through the tax code. Employers willing to make low-interest loans to their workers for the purpose of purchasing housing in the Social Sector should be taxed only on the interest income that they actually receive from the loan payments; there should not be any imputed payroll tax on the interest foregone (that is, on the interest not charged because the loan is a below-market-rate loan). Similarly, employees should not have to declare the interest saved (through the lower interest rate) as imputed income.

SALE PRICES OF HOUSING

In addition to the cost of credit, rising land prices have been another prime cause of increasing housing prices since 1970.[12] In the United States, there generally has not been any regulation of land prices or construction costs. Owners of residential property, whether homeowners or owners of rental property, get the benefit of any increase in the price of the property, even if they have not made any improvements to the property. Moreover, real estate speculators can buy land in anticipation of future development and then hold the land vacant until its price rises sufficiently to satisfy the speculator's profit needs, only then paying taxes on the gain (until 1986 capital gains were taxed at a lower rate than earned income, and proposals are being made to reinstate a lower tax rate on capital gains).

Yet the market price of urban land and improvements reflects the investment of the entire community, for a piece of land that is close to certain urban amenities will have a higher price than land that is isolated. Thus, the price of a piece of property reflects the surrounding community—the streets, sewers, schools, employment opportunities, transportation—as well as the size and quality of the physical structures on the property. The price of property often rises as a result of extraneous factors with which the owner has had nothing to do, such as community development, construction of a factory, or increased demand. As a result, owners can find the prices of their houses increasing although they themselves do nothing to improve them.[13]

Without some sort of control over land and housing prices, it will be difficult to stop the type of market forces that can cause prices to soar. A substantial part of Housing Bank loans might end up being used to pay for the appreciation in the price of property that is due to speculation or increases caused by surrounding developments. Accordingly, the community should control the price of property, since it is the community as a whole that is a large source of its value.

Since the revolution, Cuba has promoted homeownership, but, at the same time, has taken steps to control prices. Thus, because it is a country that emphasizes homeownership as a goal, Cuba provides an interesting Example. Immediately after the revolution, Cuba adopted vacant lot laws, which required landowners of vacant lots either to start construction on the lots within six months, or else to sell the lot to someone willing to do so. The sale price of vacant land was set at a maximum of 4

pesos per square meter. An additional step taken to reduce price inflation was limiting property ownership to one's own residence, plus a vacation home. This was designed to reduce speculation. Homeowners
could continue to buy and sell property, but only at government-set
prices, with the state having the first right to purchase. In 1984, the Urban Reform Law was adopted, which gave tenants in government-owned
housing the option to purchase the property, with the price being based
on type of construction, floor area, location, depreciation, and yard
space.[14]

Proposal: Resale Price Controls

In order to prevent substantial housing price increases that are not
related to improvements by the owner, both land and housing prices
should be controlled. While Cuba's experience provides a model, its
land-price controls are too rigid, as they fail to take into account the
varying quality of land. The proposal presented here would use price
to reflect difference in value but would prevent the seller of property
from making windfall profits simply because the land or property has
increased in value due to community developments.

Land prices should be set by county assessors, who would establish
the value of urban land in a manner similar to the way in which they
set the value of agricultural land. That is, agricultural land is differentially
assessed for tax purposes according to the quality of the land, because
it would be unfair to tax a farmer with ten acres of poor land at the same
rate as a farmer with ten acres of top quality land. Similarly, assessors
could set a certain number of dollars per square foot as the value of land
in each neighborhood in the community, with the number of dollars
varying, based on the surrounding developments. These values would
be adjusted periodically, as changes in the community make one area
or another more or less desirable.

Whenever the property in an area were sold, the seller could not
receive more than the assessed value per square foot of land that had
been in effect at the time that the seller purchased the land. If the
assessed value per square foot had increased during the time that the
owner held the property, then the buyer would pay to the Housing Bank
any increase in the assessed value.

Such a system not only would stabilize land prices, by preventing any
profit from being made from the speculative buying and selling of land,
but also would ensure that buyers are not able to acquire valuable land
at bargain prices. Because improvements by a community may increase
the value of land, the buyer of urban land would have to pay for the
increased land value as the assessed value of the land increased. However, instead of the seller of the land making a profit from the increase
in value of the land (which the seller had nothing to do with), the buyer

would pay the increase in value to the Housing Bank. The money received by the Housing Bank could, in turn, be used to support further housing loans in the community. (It is preferable to give the money to the Housing Bank, rather than to local government, because, as pointed out by Alan Mallach, local government often lacks the capacity to undertake housing construction projects itself).[15]

Sellers would be likely to try to get around land price controls by claiming that the sale price of the property is based on the housing constructed on the land, rather than on the land. That is, sellers would argue that property improvements on the land, rather than land price increases, had pushed the price upward. To avoid this problem, there should also be resale price controls on urban housing, which would restrict the increase in price from initial purchase to resale of the property. Such restrictions would limit the increase in price to the cost of improvements (less depreciation), plus a fraction of the amount of inflation since the date the property was purchased (measured by the local Consumer Price Index). The increase in price should not be allowed to increase at the rate of inflation for two reasons. First of all, only operating costs (and not fixed mortgage costs) rise with inflation.[16] Second, if resale price is allowed to rise at the same rate as inflation, this may result in home prices rising quickly out of reach, if the inflation rate is high. (An alternative approach would be to set the resale price at a level that a household earning a certain percentage of the median income in the area could afford, or at the market price, whichever is less.[17])

An example shows how such a system would work. Assume that a family bought a house for $40,000 in 1990. The land at the time was assessed as worth $4,000, meaning that the improvements had a price of $36,000. After five years the family wants to sell the house. In 1994, the family had put in a new kitchen, at a cost of $3,000. (Assume that the kitchen improvement has not depreciated.) The CPI has increased in the metropolitan area during the period by 25 percent. The land has increased in value to $6,000 due to surrounding improvements and increased demand for the neighborhood. Assuming that the resale price controls limited price increases due to inflation to 40 percent of the increase in the CPI,[18] then the buyer would pay $48,600 for the house, calculated as follows:

Original price of house and land	$40,000
New kitchen	3,000
Increased value of land ($6,000–$4,000)	2,000
40% of increase in CPI ($36,000 x 25% x 40%)	3,600
Total	$48,600

The seller would receive $46,600, as the $2,000 increase in the value of the land would be paid to the Housing Bank.

Under such a system, house prices should begin to stabilize, particularly when coupled with low-cost credit from the Housing Bank. If the system were instituted nationwide, then, even though a seller would not make the amount of capital gain that might be made under the present system, the prices of houses in other communities also would have stabilized. Therefore, a large capital gain on the former home would not be necessary in order to have funds to purchase another home, particularly if the Housing Banks are providing low-down-payment loans.

If resale price controls were not adopted nationally, this would, of course, make it more difficult to adopt resale controls at a local or state level. Property owners may want to capture the full increase in market price of their property so that they can use the equity to buy a house in another community should they need to move out of town. That is, if resale price controls were in effect in a single municipality, a homeowner there that needed to move elsewhere would be limited in the amount of gain from the home that he or she would have to use in acquiring another house. This would put that property owner at a financial disadvantage in those communities where resale price controls were not in effect, and where, accordingly, housing prices are higher.

On the other hand, experience with resale controls in inclusionary zoning programs (see Chapter 6) indicates that homeowners in such programs generally do not object to resale price controls.[19] Moreover, to the extent that resale price controls, together with the other proposals made in this book, succeed in reducing the cost of homeownership to purchasers, purchasers can use their savings toward the purchase of another home, should they move to a jurisdiction that does not have resale price controls.

In addition, even without full-blown resale price controls, a state or municipality could still adopt at least limited controls. For example, land prices could still be controlled. This would reduce one of the sources of price inflation in the housing market but would still enable homeowners to capture the gain in the market price of the structure on the land. From the selling price of the house would be deducted the gain in price of the land under the house, with this amount paid to the Housing Bank instead of the seller. A municipality might also decide to impose resale price controls only on multifamily structures that are not owner-occupied, so that absentee landlords would not have an incentive to speculate in the purchase and sale of real estate in the community. This would, however, give owner-occupiers the ability to capture the gain in price of the structure, in the event that he or she wished to move.

It is a reality, however, that under the present economic system, some people buy houses at least in part so that they will have property that is increasing in price. This provides them with a sense of security that they will be able to provide for themselves in old age, through the increase in the price of their assets. While this sense of security often turns out to be false (because the homeowner defaults on the mortgage loan and is foreclosed upon before reaching old age, or because health care costs outstrip assets), it is a very real concern for most Americans. Thus, many people are likely to be opposed to a system of resale controls, because they will view it as a restriction on their ability to build security. The only way that such a system could be viable is with a greatly expanded social welfare system, including such items as national health care and adequate Social Security. With a viable social welfare system, people would not have the need that they do now to accumulate a lot of assets to protect themselves for times of crisis.

Proposal: Antispeculation Laws

As an alternative to resale price controls, a municipality or state could pass antispeculation laws, designed to prevent the speculative buying and selling of rental housing. Such laws could allow landlords that hold their housing for a certain period of time to keep their gain but tax stiffly those who hold property for only a short period. Social Sector entities could be given the first right to purchase property put up for sale that has been held for less than a certain minimum period of time. For example, Sweden has imposed a capital gains tax of 75 percent on short-term gains (less a small deductible), and municipalities there have the first right of refusal to purchase urban land that is put up for sale.[20] Vermont has a sliding capital gains tax on the sale or exchange of land of under ten acres that is not used as the principal dwelling unit of the purchaser. Under the law, the amount of the tax depends on how long the property is held by the transferor and on the percent of gain in value from the basis (tax cost) of the property. Thus, a transferor holding land for less than one year and making a gain of 200 percent pays a 60 percent capital gain tax, while a transferor holding land for between five and six years and realizing a gain of 0 to 99 percent pays a tax of 5 percent on the gain.[21]

RENT IN PRIVATELY OWNED BUILDINGS

The Housing Bank, resale price controls, and/or antispeculation laws should, over time, result in lower housing prices. To ensure, however, that owners of private apartment buildings constructed with low-interest loans from the Housing Bank do not make excessive profits by charging as high rents as would be charged in a purely private free-market economy, there should be rent control on such buildings. In addition, rent control may be necessary for other buildings as well, when the community is experiencing high rent increases.

Alternative Methods of Rent Control

A variety of different methods of rent control have been used, both in other countries and in the United States. These include strict limits on rents charged (Soviet Union), rent-splitting (Sweden), rent-pooling (Sweden), collective bargaining (Sweden), rent based on income (Cuba), and moderate rent control (most cities in the United States where rent control is in effect).

Soviet Union. In the Soviet Union, rent is set at a very low base per square meter, with adjustments to the rent based on the distance of the apartment from the center of town, the amenities provided, the overall condition of the apartment, the tenant's income, and the type of job held by the tenant. Pensioners, holders of medals, and members of the armed forces receive a reduction in rent, while those working outside the government pay more, as do those who do not have a job. Tenants pay only for current repairs to their living area and to common areas, as well as a pro rata amount for utilities, while management is responsible for capital repairs and garbage disposal. Rent rates have not been increased since 1926 and average only 3 percent of income. Because rents are so low, they cover only about 40 percent of the operating and repair costs of the apartment buildings.[22]

Sweden. Sweden has used, at varying times, three different methods to control rent: rent-splitting, rent-pooling, and collective bargaining. From 1942 to 1968, Swedish rent control was based on the concept of rent-splitting, which guaranteed profit to private landlords but ensured that "excessive" profits would not be made. Under this system, rents in newly constructed apartment buildings were allowed to be sufficient to cover capital and maintenance costs. In older apartment buildings, by contrast, the government restricted the amount by which rents were allowed to rise, generally limiting rent increases in those buildings to increases in the costs of maintenance, plus a percentage of the per square foot construction cost increase in new buildings. The reason for the difference in treatment of older buildings compared to new buildings was the fact that in an unregulated market, rents in older buildings will tend to rise as new apartments with higher rents are constructed. That is, the rent will generally rise in an area, even if the landlords' costs in the older building have not increased. The rent-splitting system was designed to dampen the superprofits that could be made on the rental of older buildings, where costs were less than for newer buildings (since mortgage costs were fixed through long-term mortgage loans). At the same time, this system was intended to allow "normal" profits.[23]

While private landlords were subjected to rent-splitting from 1942 to 1968, public housing corporations in Sweden were required to base their rents on a cost-rental (also called "rent pooling") system. Under this system, all the housing owned by a public housing corporation had the same rent for equivalent dwelling units, even if they were located in different buildings that had been constructed at different costs in different years. Thus, a public housing corporation would add up all the costs of construction and maintenance on the various buildings that it owned and then set rents the same in all equivalent dwelling units (new or old) at a level sufficient to pay the mortgage and maintenance charges on all the buildings. In order for a cost-rental system to result in generally lower rents, there must be a large number of buildings, constructed over a number of years and owned by one entity, so that the tenants in the lower-cost older buildings can subsidize the rents of tenants in the higher-cost newer buildings. In Sweden, it took two decades of construction by public housing corporations before their rents could begin to undercut significantly the rents charged by private landlords. By 1968, there were sufficient numbers of buildings in the cost-rental system to be competitive with private landlords.[24]

In 1968 a system of collective bargaining was instituted in Sweden, under which the rent levels in the public sector for both newer and older buildings are set by negotiations between the National Federation of Cost-rental Housing Corporations and the National Tenants' Union. Rents in privately owned apartments buildings are set by county rent tribunals, which follow the level of rents that have been negotiated in the public sector. Negotiated rents are based on the rent-pooling principle, as well as on the principle that dwelling units of equal quality should have equal rents, regardless of location or the cost of building the unit.[25]

Cuba. As mentioned previously, Cuba has emphasized homeownership in its housing policies. Accordingly, tenants are entitled to buy their apartments (the government prohibited private ownership of investment property after the revolution and bought from landlords all property that tenants did not buy), with the price being amortized through the monthly rent payments. Rent is set at 10 percent of family income. If a tenant falls behind in rent, the arrearage, plus a penalty, is deducted from the tenant's paycheck.[26]

United States. About 10 percent of the private rental units in the United States are subject to one or another form of rent control. Most rent control laws attempt to stabilize rents, while providing for a "fair" profit for landlords. The majority (60 percent) of jurisdictions with rent-control laws allow landlords to maintain the level of net operating income that was in effect prior to rent control. The basic formula is:

Gross building rent = base period rent + (current operating expenses
    − base period operating expenses).

That is, owners may obtain rent increases to cover increases in operating expenses, but the cost of debt service is not included in the rent determination. Under this method of rent control, appreciation (or depreciation) in price of the property is not included in the calculation of permissible rents. Under almost all ordinances, landlords can petition for additional rent increases to cover the cost of capital improvements, which are amortized over a period of time.[27] Some rent control laws allow controls to be lifted whenever the unit is vacated, in which case rent control is not very effective in holding down rents, while others do not allow vacancy decontrol.[28]

The issue of inflation is a critical but often lightly analyzed aspect of the maintenance-of-net-operating-income system of rent control. Some of the jurisdictions with this type of rent control do not allow for any adjustment for inflation; others allow the operating income base to increase at the same rate as inflation; others allow net operating income to increase at a fraction of the inflation rate. Historically, over the past 70 years, rents have increased at about two-thirds the inflation rate.[29] This undoubtedly is related to the fact that between one-third and one-half of landlords' costs are unaffected by inflation (for example, monthly mortgage payments).[30] Thus, allowing the net operating income base to increase at the rate of inflation allows landlords in those jurisdictions to increase their rents at a rate higher than the historical average. In general, those jurisdictions with strong rent control allow for rent increases at less than the rate of increase in the CPI.[31]

There are other, less commonly used, standards for rent control in the United States: return on value (15 percent of jurisdictions), return on investment (7 percent), maintenance of cash flow (5 percent), percentage of net operating income (3 percent), return on gross rent (2 percent), and a combination of the above (8 percent).[32]

Analysis of Alternative Methods of Rent Control

The system of rent control used in the Soviet Union can work only when the government owns the housing. By its very terms, rent is not sufficient to pay expenses, and massive subsidies are necessary. The preference in terms of rent level given to those who work for the state, or who occupy positions in certain preferred sectors of the economy, is unacceptable in a society that values individual choice and privacy. Even though the Soviet Union has reduced rent to an almost *de minimis* level, its policy that one who is unemployed pays *more* for rent than one who is employed is simply perverse.

Cuba has rents that are much lower than those prevailing in the United States, 10 percent of income, compared to a median rent burden in the United States of about 30 percent. Cuba's policy of allowing tenants to buy their apartments, however, runs the danger of losing publicly owned housing to the private sector. This danger is ameliorated, on the other hand, by Cuba's resale price controls, which tend to prevent home-buyers from making profits on the resale of their house or apartment.

Sweden's system of rent-splitting did succeed in eliminating most superprofits, but rents did, nonetheless, rise. This was due to the main-tenance costs on older buildings and to the fact that landlords could raise rent on older buildings by a percentage of the increase in construc-tion costs on new buildings. Thus, an inflation factor was built into the system.

The advantage of the Swedish rent-pooling system is that it reduces the amount of rent that tenants in newer buildings have to pay, de-creasing the very high rents needed to cover the costs of building the newer buildings. There are, however, several difficulties with the sys-tem: the time required before it produces results, the potential for fi-nancial problems, pressures from older tenants not to build new buildings, and problems of inequity.

A cost-renting system requires at least one or two generations of house building before there are enough buildings in the system in various stages of paying off their finance costs to make rent pooling result in lower rents than the market. In the early years of the system, all the buildings are of a similar age, so that their costs are likely to be similar. Since there are no old buildings in the system at the beginning of the rent pooling system, there is no subsidy available from rents from older buildings to help keep down the rents in the newer buildings.

A cost-renting system also can quickly run into major financial diffi-culty if interest rates skyrocket. Then the cost of new construction jumps, unless there are controls over the interest rates charged on construction loans. This problem, however, can be resolved by the Housing Bank proposed earlier in this chapter.

A third problem with a cost-rental system is the fact that existing tenants will tend to face increased rents whenever a new building is constructed (because the new building is likely to cost more to construct than those already in the system). This will result in pressure from the existing tenants on the management not to buy or construct additional buildings. In addition, poorer tenants may find themselves saddled with a rent increase to pay for the costs of a newer building. This problem can be solved, however, by a system of housing allowances that cushions existing tenants from rent increases caused by new construction.

A final, but significant, problem with cost renting is the fact that tenants in older units subsidize those in more modern units. This prob-lem could be reduced by taking the amenities provided into account when setting rents for tenants in the cost-rental system. As the mort-gages on the buildings are paid off, rents for everyone in the system should tend to fall, reducing dissatisfaction over rent by tenants in older buildings.

The Swedish system of negotiated rents is, at the present time, unlikely to be feasible in the United States. Most tenants do not belong to a tenants' union, and the public sector of housing is too small to provide a basis for establishing rent standards for the rest of the private rental sector.

Proposal: Rent Control

Rent control should be imposed on all apartment buildings constructed with Housing Bank loans, and in those jurisdictions where rents are increasing substantially. Rent should be based on the amount of rent that was charged on a specified date (the base period), plus an amount sufficient to pay for the actual increase in operating expenses since the base period. The base period should be set on a date sufficiently preceding the introduction of a rent control bill so that landowners do not increase their rents in anticipation of passage of the ordinance. (While courts have generally upheld relatively short rollbacks of six months to one year, rollbacks for a longer period of time are likely to run into a constitutional challenge that such rollbacks impair existing contracts, in violation of Article I, Section 10 of the United States Constitution.[33]) Since landowners will be allowed to raise rents to meet any increase in operating costs that are the result of inflation, they should not be allowed a separate inflationary increase in their net operating income.

This system of rent control would not eliminate private profits in the private rental system, but it should eliminate super profits. It does not allow owners to raise rents simply because property prices in an area have risen. Rent increases would be allowed only when an owner could show that his or her operating expenses had increased. In order to evaluate adequately owners' requests for rent increases, the rent board would have to have complete access to the owner's financial records for the building for the period during which the owner claimed that he or she did repairs to the building. Moreover, the municipality would have to allocate sufficient funds so that the rent board could hire sufficient personnel to review owner records, to ensure effective enforcement.

However, there should be some adjustments to the above rent control model. First of all, an owner should not be able to pass through to tenants 100 percent of the increase in utility charges, unless the owner has installed insulation and weatherproofing sufficient to meet the minimum standards set by the rent control board. Otherwise, if an owner can pass all utility cost increases directly on to tenants, he or she will have absolutely no incentive to weatherproof the building to help reduce utility costs. Second, in order not to penalize owners who held their rents below market rates while others raised rents (for example, a small landlord who has owned only one or two buildings for years), the rent control ordinance should exempt such owners from rent control, so long as their rents continue to remain below the average base period rent for their size apartment and neighborhood.

A difficult problem of administering rent controls arises with capital improvements to the property. If owners are permitted to recoup the entire expense of remodeling or upgrading the property through rent increases, then they will have no incentive to maintain their properties in a rent range that is affordable to low- or moderate-income persons. At the same time, when an apartment building does need major repairs, the owner should be able to recoup the expense necessary to maintain the property in its prior condition. The solution is to permit only the following capital improvements to be included in rent: either those that are necessary to maintain the building at minimum housing code standards, or those needed to maintain the building at its previous standard, whichever standard is higher. Those capital improvements that are designed to improve the building beyond the condition of the building in the base period (provided that the building met minimum code in the base period) would not be allowed to be included in the rent.

A corollary problem is the period of time over which the owner would be permitted to recoup the capital expenditure from the tenants. The rent control board would have to establish standards for a reasonable period of amortization based on the cost of the capital improvement, so that the tenants do not have to bear the expense of the improvement over too short a period of time.

There must be several other components of an effective rent control system. No vacancy decontrol should be allowed, to ensure that rents do not jump upward when a tenant vacates. To prevent landlords from extorting illegal side payments or "key money" from tenants by threatening to evict tenants who do not agree to such payments, there should be no evictions except for cause (see "Security of Tenure," Chapter 7); landlords who are found to have engaged in such practices should have their property taken by eminent domain. There must also be strict code enforcement, coupled with eminent domain powers against landlords who fail to comply with the housing code, to ensure that landlords do not seek to increase their profits by allowing their buildings to fall into disrepair. (See "Strengthen Property Maintenance Laws," Chapter 7, and "Proposal: Take Absentee-Owned Deteriorated and Tax-Delinquent Property," Chapter 5.) Since code enforcement, as well as eminent domain proceedings, may take a substantial period of time, the rent control board should have the authority to reduce rents in buildings that are not adequately maintained. Since some landlords may try to avoid rent control through demolition or conversions to condominiums, strict demolition controls should be established (see "Proposal: Demolition Controls," Chapter 5), as well as restrictions on condominium conversions (see "Restrictions on Condominium Conversions," Chapter 7).

The type of rent control proposed above should put strong reins on landlords who buy and sell apartment property on a speculative basis to maximize their profits, while providing an adequate income to small landlords. Rent rates should stabilize, and displacement caused by rent increases should be reduced significantly.

Proposal: Cost-Rental System in the Social Housing Sector

For those buildings held by public housing authorities, or other entities in the Social Housing Sector, base rents should be calculated on a cost-rental system. The rents arrived at by averaging the operating costs of all the buildings in the system would need to be modified to take into account different amenities provided in the units. Moreover, subsidies will be necessary for those households unable to afford the rent.

SUBSIDIES

Past Policies

The principal subsidies used in the United States to reduce the cost of housing are the indirect subsidies provided through the tax system to certain homebuyers: the mortgage interest and real estate tax deductions. These two subsidies doubled between 1980 and 1987 and now exceed $50 billion per year.[34] As a result of these subsidies, far fewer federal taxes were paid than would otherwise be paid without these deductions. In 1984, 26.3 million taxpayers paid an average of $889 less in taxes as a result of claiming the mortgage interest deduction. Yet fewer than half of all taxpayers took the mortgage interest deduction, either because they could not itemize their deductions, or because they had no mortgage interest to deduct.[35] The mortgage interest and real estate tax subsidy benefits primarily higher-income homebuyers, for lower-income homebuyers often do not have enough other deductions to be eligible to itemize their deductions. Moreover, the more expensive the home, the greater the deduction. Thus, those wealthy enough to buy larger houses benefit doubly by the deduction: both by their ability to take the deduction and by the greater amount of the deduction they can take as the price of the house increases. In 1987, two-thirds of the deduction was taken by taxpayers who earned over $50,000.[36]

In addition to the mortgage interest and real estate tax deductions allowed by the federal tax code, other tax code provisions have been used to subsidize owners of real estate indirectly. Provisions included accelerated depreciation, favorable treatment for capital gains, offset of losses in real estate against other income, and tax exemption on the interest earned on municipal mortgage revenue bonds. While these tax subsidies were reduced or phased out by the 1986 Tax Reform Act, there is pressure to restore the favorable treatment of capital gains.

In addition to indirect subsidies through the tax code, the federal government has also sought to reduce the cost of housing through various direct subsidy programs. Some of these programs subsidized the interest rates on mortgage loans (Sections 221(d)(3), 235, and 236 programs), and some subsidized tenant rental costs (primarily the Section 8 program; the operating subsidy programs associated with public housing after tenant rents were limited to 25 percent—later 30 percent—of household income; and the new housing voucher program). These direct subsidies have been far smaller than those to homebuyers through the mortgage interest and tax deductions. From the late 1930s through 1986, *total* federal spending for these direct subsidies, as well as for the public housing program, was $86 billion; in 1987 and 1988 *alone*, the homeowner mortgage interest and tax deductions were $107 billion.[37] Virtually all of the direct subsidy programs (except public housing) accepted the prevailing interest rates or rental charges as the norm, seeking to reduce the price paid by homebuyers or tenants by subsidizing the interest or rental expense.

Critique of Housing Subsidy Systems

The housing subsidy systems that have been developed in the United States generally serve to aid middle- and upper-income homebuyers and to guarantee lender profits (by guaranteeing lenders interest rate payments) or landlord profits (by guaranteeing landlords market rents). While housing subsidies certainly are necessary for those whose income is so low that they cannot, under any system, pay the full cost of housing, subsidies should be targeted to persons with lower income, not to those who are most able to pay housing costs.

In Norway, housing allowances, which supplement the finance system, are targeted to those with below average incomes. The lowest-income households do not pay more than 15 percent of their income for rent, while those with higher (but still below-average) incomes are expected to pay no more than 20 percent of their income for rent.[38] Sweden likewise has an extensive system of housing allowances, which are available to about 40 percent of the population, and which assure that no one pays more than 20 percent of their income for housing.[39] Both Norway's and Sweden's housing allowance systems exist in the context of government programs that reduce total housing finance costs. While housing allowances or subsidies can increase consumer choice and avoid the problem of stigma that has burdened occupants of public housing, they are not a substitute for ensuring an adequate supply of decent, safe, and accessible housing. In a situation of housing shortage, housing allowances may simply result in rent increases, as owners find that they can charge higher rents for the same units, because there is more money available (through the allowances or subsidies) to pay the rent. Indeed, this has been the experience in some cases with the federal housing voucher program.[40]

Proposal: Subsidies for Those in Need

There are numerous families in the United States who simply do not have enough income to pay for all of their nonhousing needs in addition to their housing needs. As long as there are the unemployed, the poor, and those who are unable to work, such persons will need housing assistance.

Presently in the United States, direct housing subsidies are based on the assumption that families can pay a certain percentage of their net income toward housing. Thus, families are expected to pay 25 to 30 percent of their income for rent (often more in the housing voucher program), regardless of how little income they have, with the subsidy covering that part of the rent charge that is not paid by the family. As Michael Stone has pointed out (see Chapter 1), many families cannot afford to pay even 25 percent of their income for rent and still have adequate funds for their other needs. Thus, a housing allowance program should not be based on a percentage of the family's income but rather on the sum that the family needs to meet its housing costs after it has met its minimum nonhousing needs.

In addition, tenant allowances should be coupled with rent control. The present housing subsidy programs, except in the case of public housing, subsidize the profits of landlords or financial institutions. They either pay directly to the landlord or financial institution whatever portion of the rent or mortgage payment that is not paid by the family, or else give to tenants the money to pay the difference between 30 percent of the tenant's income and the fair rental value of the unit. Rent control should be imposed on any units with subsidized tenants to ensure that superprofits are not being made off the subsidy program.

Low- and moderate-income home buyers who are in default on their mortgage loans because of unemployment, disability, illness, or other circumstances beyond their control, should be able to obtain allowances, or else low-interest loans from the Housing Bank to bring their mortgages current. Should the homebuyer wish to retain the home in the private sector, free to sell it for a profit, then the loan should be amortized and payable in monthly installments as any other mortgage loan. However, if the homebuyer agrees to sell the house to the Social Housing Sector at such time as the homebuyer no longer wishes to live in the house, then the loan should be a lien on the property, with the principal and accrued interest payable only upon foreclosure of the property (should the homebuyer fall into default again) or upon sale of the property to the Social Housing Sector.

As the experience of Norway and Sweden demonstrates, a change in the finance system, coupled with housing allowances or subsidies for those unable to afford even low-cost housing, can result in a substantial improvement in housing conditions in a relatively short period of time. Redesigning the housing finance system is a first priority in solving our housing crisis.

Chapter 5

Production, Preservation, and Allocation

At the present time in the United States, public and subsidized housing production have ground virtually to a halt. The housing that is built is produced privately, primarily for middle- to upper-income persons. More and more first-time homebuyers are getting squeezed out of the market, leaving those who are upper income or who already have equity in a home being the ones primarily able to buy the housing that is being produced. Tenants face not only an increasing shortage of housing but a deteriorating quality of that which is available. Thus, issues of production and allocation are critical to a resolution of the housing crisis. Necessarily, the issues of finance discussed in Chapter 4 are linked with production; as housing costs decrease and people can better afford housing, more will tend to be produced.

To produce an adequate amount of housing requires planning, so planning is the focus of the first part of this chapter. After discussion of alternative planning models and presentation of proposals regarding planning and zoning, the chapter discusses methods of producing an adequate supply of affordable housing in the second portion of the chapter. A necessary component of providing an adequate supply of housing is, of course, preservation of the existing supply of lower-priced housing; this is the focus of the third part of the chapter. Finally, since the supply of housing that is affordable to lower-income people is limited and will continue to be so for the foreseeable future, criteria for allocating the limited supply of low-priced housing is discussed in the last section of this chapter.

PLANNING

At present, housing is produced with little governmental planning. The amount of housing produced depends on the vagaries of the economy and is particularly sensitive to the interest rate. The result has been the ebbs and flows of housing construction discussed in Chapter 2. This method of producing housing is anarchic and chaotic and must be replaced with a system of planning, as a necessary precondition to ensuring a steady supply of new construction and rehabilitation.

Planning Models

There are a variety of methods that have been used to plan housing production. These include central planning, municipal planning, negotiated planning and housing needs assessments. The Soviet Union and Poland provide examples of different degrees of central planning, Sweden an example of municipal planning, Yugoslavia an example of planning by negotiations between different interest groups, and California an example of housing needs assessment.

Soviet Union. In the Soviet Union before Gorbachev, economic planning was highly centralized.[1] Thus, instead of housing being produced according to the vagaries of the market, as in the United States, with resulting ebbs and flows of housing construction, housing was produced according to plan. The plans themselves were developed by professional planners with input by scientific organizations. To plan consumption of housing, planners used norms as to the amount of living space per person, as well as forecasts of consumer behavior, with the amount of a consumer good to be produced determined in relation to other planning priorities. For example, if development of industrial capacity was the primary goal set by the government (as it was for most of the early years of Soviet society), then consumer goods production, including housing production, took second place, and fewer national resources were devoted to the production of housing. A key principle was that planning should be "imperative," meaning that plans were binding instructions to those below. Those in the organizations and enterprises that were below the planners were expected to carry out production in accordance with the plans designed by those at the top. (By contrast, indicative planning, used by most private companies in the United States, involves the company making forecasts and using plans to meet certain projected goals; planning targets are not imposed from above by the government.)

Poland. After World War II, Poland initially followed the Soviet model of central planning. In 1956, however, a less centralized type of planning was adopted. While central planning in housing continued to exist, it became less imperative and more of a combination of imperative and indicative planning. The state-owned sector of housing continued to be subject to imperative planning, with the central plan setting out specific directives as to the amount of materials and financing to be provided for housing on a national basis, as well as directives as to the regional distribution of housing. The specific housing development plans, as well as the construction of the housing, were, however, carried out by local authorities, who also managed the completed projects. Such housing was subject to minimum and maximum space norms per person. In addition, certain minimum amenities were required.[2]

Private construction, however, which became more permissible after 1956, was not subject to imperative planning; instead, the plans could only estimate the amount of private housing construction that was expected. Moreover, construction undertaken without any state aid was not subject to the space norms that governed state-owned housing, unless the housing was more than a certain number of square feet in size.[3]

Sweden. In the late 1930s and early 1940s Sweden established a comprehensive system of housing planning. Municipalities draft five-year plans of their housing needs; they are also responsible for receiving and evaluating applications for housing loans and subsidies and forwarding them to the central government. The central government consults with municipalities and labor market boards to determine the percentage of national investment that will go into housing over the following three years. The central government then tells the local authorities the maximum number of dwelling units for which state loans (described in Chapter 4) will be available, and the number of building permits that can be issued for private construction.[4]

Local governments control local land-use planning, having the power to decide where, when, and what type of building to permit. A municipality has the first right of refusal to buy any land that comes on the market, provided that it exercises its right within three months. It also can acquire land for community purposes through eminent domain powers, if approval is obtained from the central government. Once the municipality obtains the land, it must be leased rather than sold, to owners of the housing that is built on the land. Municipalities also have the right to expropriate, with compensation, rental housing that is below building standards. State-subsidized mortgage loans are available only for building or rehabilitation of property on land owned by a municipality, thus strengthening the planning powers of municipalities.[5]

Yugoslavia. Yugoslavia has a decentralized system of government, which leaves the primary responsibility for housing planning to each of the republics and autonomous regions that comprise Yugoslavia. Its planning process is more complex, and, in theory, more democratic, than the planning processes in any of the previous three countries discussed. The Federal Assembly (the national legislative body) sets policy only in broad outlines, leaving the planning and financing of housing to the communes, which are territorial units into which the country is divided, usually having from fewer than 5,000 to up to 100,000 residents.[6]

In very brief outline, the planning process for housing development on nationalized land (private housing development on private land is not subject to this planning process) involves interaction between various levels of decision-making bodies. Within a commune, the Communal Assembly (the legislative body for the commune) sets down general guidelines and makes decisions, such as the percentage of allocations to be used for housing construction. Local community assemblies, which consist of delegates from both workers and residents in a local community, come to agreement on the goods and services to be produced over a five-year period. This agreement is then sent to a self-managing housing interest group, which is an assembly composed of delegates from both producers and consumers of housing. This housing interest group is expected to negotiate and resolve conflicts between the producers and consumers of housing, and to determine housing needs and the location of housing to be built over a five-year period. This housing interest group assumes the role of both the market and the state in setting housing policy. Self-management agreements between the producers and consumers in the housing interest group set prices for a five-year period, rather than prices being set either by a free market or by a central government. This agreement is then sent to the commune, where any unresolved conflicts that have arisen in the various levels are resolved, and the agreement is adopted as a social compact.[7] To carry out the plans, the communal government acquires the necessary land and does the project planning for the particular housing projects.[8]

The planning process in Yugoslavia has a significant element of citizen participation that is not usually present in other countries. The delegates to the various assemblies are not merely representatives elected at periodic intervals but are delegates who are expected to solicit the views of their constituents on every pertinent topic before a decision is made, to report their constituents' views to the assembly, and to report back to their constituents. They are expected to be from the same socioeconomic background as their constituents and can be recalled at any time by their constituents. In addition, decision making in the assemblies is expected to be by consensus whenever possible, and a process of bargaining between the various parties in the assembly or interest group is the expected process for arriving at a decision. Planning is a continual process at the different levels, with information exchanged and annual assessments made of the progress on the plans. When plans conflict at different levels, then a process of negotiation takes place between the various levels to resolve the differences, before the social compact is finalized.[9]

California Planning Statute. In 1980, the State of California adopted a law that requires municipalities to prepare a "housing element" at least every five years. This housing element must provide an assessment of the housing needs and resources in the community. This assessment must include an analysis of population and employment trends and projections (based on the locality's share of regional housing needs), household characteristics and housing stock condition, land suitable for housing development and constraints on housing development, and special housing needs of different types of households (elderly, handicapped, large families, farmworkers, families with female heads of household, and those needing emergency shelter). The housing element must state the municipality's goals over a five-year period for the production and rehabilitation of housing, and a list of actions that the locality plans to take over the five-year period to achieve its goals. These actions must include removal of government constraints to housing development, assistance in developing adequate housing to meet the needs of low- and moderate-income households, identification of sites that will be made available for housing development, preservation of the existing affordable housing stock, and actions to combat discrimination. The city must also zone its vacant land so as to meet its housing needs. The housing element then is submitted to the state's Department of Housing and Community Development for review, and that department prepares statewide and regional housing needs assessments. The law does not require the locality, however, to spend any municipal funds on housing construction or subsidies.[10]

Critique of Planning Models

Both the Soviet and Polish systems have merit in the fact that there is national analysis and planning of housing needs. This, in theory, allows housing needs to be anticipated and planned for, rather than the after-the-fact adjustments that characterize the housing production system in the United States. The Soviet system of centralized imperative planning, however, is known for its bottlenecks and unwieldy character, as it requires bureaucrats at the national level to coordinate all the many components of a particular consumer good. Moreover, although it makes sense to have certain minimum housing standards set at a national level, the details of housing standards are best left to local authorities, who are more familiar with local living standards. The Polish system of some centralized planning, with local implementation and management, reduces the degree of top-down administration and therefore is an improvement on the Soviet system. But leaving it to a centralized bureaucracy, as in Poland, to plan the details of the amount of materials to be provided for housing is unnecessary.

The Swedish system of planning is much more decentralized than the Soviet or Polish systems. Its strength lies in the legally mandated municipal plans for meeting housing needs, combined with central government evaluation of municipal plans to determine and plan for the amount of national investment that must go into housing. By combining municipal planning with strong powers to regulate building, Sweden has provided teeth in its decentralized planning system.

The strengths of the Yugoslav method of planning are its participatory nature, the detailed exchange of information that is part of the planning process, and the emphasis on consensus through negotiation. The problems with the Yugoslav method of planning are three. First, a tremendous amount of time is involved in the planning process. Second, although the housing interest group was designed to give equal weight to both producer and consumer viewpoints, in fact, construction companies have a dominant voice in housing policies and housing location. Third, because there is no regional planning, there is no mechanism to coordinate communal plans.[11]

The California planning code provides an excellent model for development of local, regional, and statewide data. Its primary drawback is the fact that there is no legal mechanism provided to ensure that housing needed is, in fact, built.

Proposal: Planning

While imperative planning should be avoided, it certainly would be useful for the United States to have a national agency that provided up-to-date information on population and housing trends for use by Congress, the states, and local municipalities. At a minimum, local, state, and federal housing planning should be established to project present and future housing needs at the local, state, and national levels. Such a system of housing planning should not be difficult to set up. Most cities already have planning departments that gather data on their housing needs. Moreover, any city that applies for federal Community Development Block Grant (CDBG) funds must present data to the federal government on its housing needs through its Housing Assistance Plan. The Census Bureau does housing surveys on a regular basis (although there is a delay of three to four years in publishing the figures after the housing surveys are completed). Thus, the data exist as to what the housing needs are in each urban area and they are already in use by local governments. The delays encountered in obtaining Census Bureau survey results could be eliminated by providing additional personnel at the Census Bureau to ensure that results of the surveys are available within a year after the completion of the survey.

This existing raw data on current needs should be supplemented through the use of demographers to project anticipated need in future decades. These projections should include not only anticipated population growth in the locale but also the possibility of changing life-styles necessitating different types and quantities of housing. As unexpected changes occur, the projections would have to be revised. The projections should include the numbers of low- and moderate-income persons that could be expected to reside in the community if adequate low- and moderate-income housing were available.

Once present and future needs are established, local governments should develop concrete programs to meet these needs, setting specific annual, five-year, and ten-year goals for the number, types, and price range of new housing to be produced and existing housing to be rehabilitated. Estimates of the cost of producing the housing should be calculated, including the cost of any infrastructure development needed. Sources of funding for such costs should be spelled out, including the projected need for state or federal funds.

To prevent planning from becoming a bureaucratic exercise removed from the needs of those living in the community and the surrounding area, the local planning agency should have the following people as members of its board: representatives from the local legislative body; housing specialists elected from the community; representatives from minority, handicapped, and women's groups; and representatives from low-income housing advocacy groups. These representatives should all have a vote in setting recommended policy. The representatives from minority and low-income housing advocacy groups could include those from such groups in the surrounding metropolitan area if none exist in the municipality. This would ensure that municipalities that have excluded minorities and lower-income groups in the past would have input from the excluded groups in developing their housing plans. The paid staff of the planning agency would be the ones who develop the statistical data, while the planning board would set policy based on the data developed by the staff.

As in Yugoslavia, the planning process should be an interactive process with higher levels of government. Thus, housing-need projections of local municipalities should be amalgamated into housing-need projections for the entire state, and then state totals should be used to derive national needs.

Proposal: Changes in Zoning Laws

Planning can, of course, be a means of excluding low-income and minority households from a community. States therefore should amend their state zoning laws to require that each municipality in the state that does not have its fair share of housing for low- and moderate-income persons amend its zoning code to provide a realistic opportunity for low- and moderate-income housing to be built within the municipality. While changes in zoning laws will not, per se, ensure that low- and moderate-income housing is built, these changes are a necessary precondition for such construction. (See Chapter 6 for further discussion of exclusionary zoning and fair share housing.)

PRODUCTION

Historical Background

Until the Depression, the dominant approach to the persistent problem of housing shortages and dilapidation in the United States was to rely on private enterprise to provide the solution, with local government adopting only minor restrictions, in the form of housing codes, on realtors' ability to exploit the housing market. The only government support for housing was in the indirect form of mortgage interest and real estate tax deductions. (These deductions were in the Internal Revenue Code almost from the beginning of federal income taxation and were not specifically adopted as housing measures.) While direct government production of housing occurred during World War I, this was justified by the need to house war-industry workers; the housing, however, did not remain under public control after the war, instead being sold to private persons. The only post-war efforts to help housing consisted of tax breaks to the construction industry.[12]

It took the trauma of the Depression to bring the government into the housing production picture. The major type of government involvement was indirect support for the production of housing, through the restructuring of the financial market that was discussed in Chapter 4, and through continuation of the mortgage interest and property tax deductions. Public housing, though also started during the Depression, was a much smaller portion of the government's involvement in housing production. Indeed, public housing has never been more than a tiny fraction of housing construction, a far lower percentage than in Europe; by contrast, one-third of housing in Great Britain is publicly owned council housing.[13] Opposition to public housing led, in the late 1950s and early 1960s, to various subsidized housing construction programs.

Public Housing. The first major public housing program began in New York City in 1934. Between 1934 and 1938, 35 percent of new housing in New York City was public housing for working class households (tenants had to be employed to qualify).[14] The federal Housing Act of 1937, establishing the United States Housing Authority, began the federal public housing program. Because of opposition to public housing by national real estate and business interests, as a threat to private control of real estate, the public housing that was authorized by the 1937 Housing Act had two significant limitations, designed to minimize any threat that public housing might pose to private real estate profits. First of all, the act prohibited the income of a family in public housing from being more than 80 percent of the income necessary to afford housing on the private market. Second, the act required that one unit of substandard housing had to be demolished for each unit of public housing built.[15] These restrictions were followed, in 1940, by a provision in congressional legislation authorizing the construction of war housing (the Lanham Act) that none of the war housing could be used after the war to provide subsidized housing to poor people without special congressional approval; such housing was to be sold after the war at market value to private persons.[16]

World War II brought a virtual halt to the public housing program, which was not renewed until the 1949 Housing Act revived federal expenditures for public housing. The act followed the same basic structure that the 1937 act had established, although it did eliminate the requirement that one unit of housing had to be demolished for each public housing unit built. It authorized, however, only 810,000 units (one-tenth the total need); limited appropriations thereafter caused it to take until 1972 before the originally authorized 810,000 units had all finally been completed.[17]

The act also contained serious weaknesses. The federal government was authorized to pay only the capital costs of building the projects, while the local housing authorities had to pay all the operating and repair costs out of rental income. In addition, local housing authorities had to pay 10 percent of their rent receipts to the local government in lieu of taxes. Any tenants whose incomes increased beyond the allowed maximum income for public housing had to be evicted. The shoddy construction of many of the housing projects, as well as their poor design, resulting from inadequate funding by Congress, guaranteed that they would need repairs sooner than most other housing. Yet Congress prohibited local housing authorities from accumulating more than 50 percent of one year's rent receipts as reserves toward future repairs. Any money accumulated beyond the 50-percent limit had to be used to pay off the capital costs of the project, thereby reducing federal expenditures for capital costs.[18] Thus, it was virtually inevitable that housing authorities could not maintain their projects adequately on the limited rents they could collect.

While public housing rent receipts rose only 25 percent during the period from 1950 to 1958, expenses rose 52 percent.[19] The increasing financial pressure on local housing authorities finally led Congress, in 1961, to amend the 1949 act so as to allow families whose income increased above the maximum permissible level to remain in public housing, *if* they could not find decent, safe, and sanitary housing elsewhere within their financial means.[20] Moreover, subsidies from the federal government of $120/year for each unit of public housing rented to elderly persons were authorized. In 1969, because of increasing financial pressures on tenants, Congress passed the Brooke Amendment, which limited rent paid by tenants to 25 percent of their household income (this was increased to 30 percent in the 1980s). This restricted total income that could be received by the local authority, yet not until the early 1970s was money for modernization, as well as significant regular operating subsidies, authorized for public housing.[21]

By the mid–1980s public housing was facing threats to its very existence, with cutbacks in funding and proposals to sell it off or demolish it. In all, about 1.5 million units of public housing have been constructed since the beginning of the federal public housing program in 1937.[22]

Subsidized Housing. In the late fifties and early sixties, federal programs began to shift to various interest-subsidy programs as a means of stimulating the production of low-income housing. The Section 202 program, established in 1959, provided federal loans at low interest rates to nonprofit developers of elderly and handicapped housing, although after 1974 the interest rates were raised to approximately market rates. The Section 221(d)(3) program, instituted in 1961, subsidized the mortgage interest rate for construction of low-rent housing. The Section 312 loan program, established in 1964, provided low-interest loans to owners and tenants in urban areas to pay for rehabilitation required to conform to urban renewal plans or insurance underwriting requirements of Fair Plans. The Section 235 program, established in 1968, subsidized the interest rate on home mortgage loans for lower-income households, while the Section 236 program, established at the same time, subsidized the interest rates on mortgages for private developers of rental housing projects, provided that the apartments were rented out to lower-income tenants. The Section 8 New Construction program, which replaced the Section 236 program in 1974, guaranteed rent subsidies for 20 to 40 years to developers of low- and moderate-income rental units. Together, these programs resulted in the construction of almost 2 million units of low- and moderate-income housing.[23] Today, virtually no new construction of low-income housing is occurring under any of these production subsidy programs, or through public housing.

Other Production Models

Eastern Europe. Housing production in the socialist Eastern European countries is a mixture of public and private construction. Construction by enterprises (i.e., employers) and by cooperatives is a significant percentage of total construction in Eastern Europe. For example, in the Soviet Union, 35 percent of urban housing is built by enterprises and 11 percent by cooperatives, while 45 percent is built by local soviets (comparable to local government in the United States), and only 9 percent by private persons.[24] Moreover, the role of the cooperative sector in construction has been increasing; in Poland by 1975, for example, between 45 percent and 75 percent of new housing was built by cooperatives.[25] One of the major methods used to increase production in the Soviet Union was industrialization of the production of housing through prefabrication and development of standardized building components that are interchangeable between buildings. Such techniques have also been adopted by other Eastern European countries, particularly for the construction of apartment buildings.[26]

Those who wish to build housing cooperatively in the Soviet Union must submit an application to the local soviet or enterprise. If the application is approved, the houses built by the cooperative belong to the cooperative, with members having the right to own and use the housing. However, individual members of the cooperative cannot sell, give, or bequeath their housing; only the cooperative can transfer title. Cooperatives are able to get 0.5 percent loans from the state for 70 percent of the construction cost, payable over a twenty-five-year period. Most cooperatives are formed around the workplace in large cities.[27]

Eastern European countries have supported construction of housing by enterprises in a variety of ways over the years. In the Soviet Union, as part of the central plan, the state bank gave money to enterprises to finance the construction of housing during the period from 1937 to 1956. After 1956, decision making was decentralized, and enterprises were allowed to use some of their profits to build housing for their employees. In 1979, enterprises were given the right to use some of their profits to partly repay bank loans for cooperative and private housing for their employees. In general, workers living in enterprise-owned housing will lose their housing if they leave their jobs or commit a crime.[28] In Poland, when enterprises construct housing, the funds for such construction come primarily from surplus funds of the enterprise. Employees who leave their jobs with good records cannot be evicted. In Czechoslovakia, on the other hand, industrial enterprises faced such a problem of workers leaving their jobs and remaining in homes that had been provided free as part of their employment, that free housing for workers was eliminated in 1963. Instead, the enterprises began to lend its workers money for the down payment to get into a cooperative. If the worker stayed at his or her job a sufficient length of time, 90 percent of the loan would be forgiven, whereas those who left their jobs before the minimum time period had elapsed could keep their homes only if they repaid the loan in full.[29]

Britain. Britain has the largest stock of publicly owned rental housing units in Western Europe. In 1985, 30 percent of all dwelling units was council housing (public housing in Britain is called "council housing"), 63 percent was owner-occupied, and only 7 percent was privately rented.[30] Although council housing began to be constructed in 1919, it was not until after World War II that it became an important feature of British housing policy. While Britain under the Thatcher government has switched toward a policy of primary support for private owner-occupancy and has begun selling off council housing, British policies immediately after World War II with regard to housing production provide a useful model for the United States.

During the heyday of council housing, from 1945 to 1954, the goal was to provide council housing to a wide range of working-class people. The construction of private housing on a speculative basis was banned, except for those who wished to build a private house for their own use. Both building materials and construction were licensed. The maximum proportion of privately built owner-occupied housing in a local area was limited to 20 percent (increasing to 50 percent in 1951), and the remaining building permits were reserved for council housing. The central government paid for three-fourths of the total costs of council housing; moreover, council housing tenants whose incomes were too low to pay the rent were given rent and other subsidies.[31]

The actual production of council housing was done by private builders. Municipalities let contracts to build council housing in one of four ways: open bids, selective bids, negotiations, and package deals. Under open bidding, any firm can bid to do the construction. Problems with workmanship under this system led some authorities to adopt a selective bidding system, used by a majority of housing authorities, under which only firms capable of doing the job right were allowed to bid. Other authorities approached one builder and negotiated the contract price with that one builder, while package bidding involved a contract negotiated with one firm not just for construction but also for design.[32]

Critique of Production Models

Public housing generally has received a bad name in the United States. That is in large part because public housing has not had the type of support that would have enabled it to thrive. Poor design and shoddy construction ensures that property, whether public or private housing, will not meet the needs of its residents adequately and that it will deteriorate. Lack of funds for maintenance ensures that the property will not be able to be repaired when it does deteriorate. The British experience with council housing, as well as those public housing projects in the United States that have been successful, demonstrates that public housing need not mean poor-quality housing. The British system of selective bidding, where only qualified contractors are allowed to bid for construction of public housing, is a bidding system that appears to be the one most likely to ensure good-quality construction at competitive prices. There is the danger, however, if standards for determining who is qualified are based on factors such as length of time in business, size of company, and past government contracts, that such standards will result in discrimination against minority- and women-owned construction companies, which tend to be younger and smaller.

Most of the subsidy programs in the United States that were designed to stimulate the production of housing for lower-income households had two major flaws. First, most of the programs accepted the prevailing interest rate, and sought merely to reduce the price to the contractor or homebuyer of the housing, by subsidizing the interest rate. (See Chapter 4, "Proposal: Housing Bank.") Second, the subsidy programs adopted in the United States did not require that the property constructed under the programs remain permanently lower-priced. Consequently, many lower-income residents of subsidized housing units are now facing conversion of those units to market rate rentals. (See "Proposal: Preservation of Existing Subsidized Housing.")

While the concept of employers building housing for their workers is an attractive one, the pitfalls with such a program are apparent in Eastern Europe. If the right to housing is tied to a job, as in the Soviet Union, then workers have strong incentives to conform to the demands of the workplace, to avoid losing their jobs, and, hence, their homes. Certainly the experience of company towns in the United States in this respect has not been enviable. Letting workers remain in the housing even if they no longer work for the company, on the other hand, can result in workers taking jobs simply to get housing, with no intention of remaining on the jobs. The Czechoslovak solution—employers lending money to their workers for housing, with repayment obligations based on the length of time the worker remains on the job—provides a compromise solution.

The Soviet experience with prefabricated housing demonstrates that such housing is both feasible and cost-effective. Concerns over quality of such housing can be met by setting certain minimum standards.

Proposals: Production

Both the proposal for a Housing Bank that would make low-interest loans for housing construction and the proposal for land price controls, both made in chapter 4, will help to increase housing production by decreasing the costs of such production. There are several additional measures that will also help to increase the production of lower-priced housing. Municipal regulation of building permits to help ensure that lower-priced housing is built before higher-priced housing, coupled with municipal liability for faulty work on new construction and rehabilitation projects to ensure good quality construction, are first steps that can be taken. Municipalities can also reduce housing development costs by removing excessive site improvement requirements, permitting clustering and higher density of units on a site, and eliminating the sales tax on building materials sold to entities in the Social Housing Sector. Congress can assist by funding research and development of prefabricated housing components. Finally, building by the city itself if insufficient lower-priced housing is built by private or Social Housing Sector contractors is an important back-up measure to ensure that lower-priced housing is built.

Regulation of Building Permits. As Britain did after World War II, localities should regulate the issuance of building permits to assure the construction of low-and moderately-priced houses and apartments. The locality's housing plans should include the location of new housing to be built in the community as well as the price range for that housing. No building permits should be issued for the construction of more expensive housing until building permits have been taken out for the construction of all the low- and moderately priced units that had been given as the goal in the production plan for the year. The only exception would be in those cases where the applicant's building plans included provision for a certain minimum percentage of low- and moderate-priced units in the development plans.

The criteria for issuance of building permits should include not only the type of housing planned but the type of builder (preference being given to limited equity cooperatives and community land trusts), the extent to which the builder is nonracist and nonsexist in hiring practices, and the builder's past track record with regard to the quality of construction.

Municipal Responsibility for Construction Quality. The Swedish system of liability should be adopted to ensure that local building departments adequately supervise the quality of construction.[33] Under this system, the local government is liable to purchasers of new property for any defects in workmanship. The homebuyer can sue the city directly for defects, with the city then looking to the builder to reimburse the city for payments it has made to the homebuyer. This system would provide protection for homebuyers, by providing city building departments with powerful incentives to ensure that builders do the job right. Homebuyers would be assured that they can obtain compensation for the cost of repairing the defects that city inspectors should have caught. This same system should also be applied to rehabilitation, whenever the contractor must get a permit from the city to do rehabilitation.

Reduction in Development Costs. Municipalities can also take measures to reduce the cost of development. Housing development costs consist of costs for the land, site preparation, construction, interest costs, and fees and permits. Measures to reduce land and interest costs have already been discussed in Chapter 4 (land price controls and the establishment of a Housing Bank). Interest costs can be lowered further by reducing the time from start to completion of the development, through a reduction in the amount of time needed to obtain permits and reviews, for example. To reduce site preparation costs, municipalities can reduce excessive site improvement standards and can allow developers to cluster their units on the development site (referred to as higher net density)—such clustering can result in substantial savings even if the total number of units per acre is not increased. Communities can also allow for increased density per acre (referred to as higher gross density) as another way of decreasing development costs per unit.[34]

To reduce construction costs even more, several steps can be taken. Congress should appropriate funds for research and development of more prefabricated housing parts. Moreover, the sales tax on building materials purchased by entities in the Social Housing Sector should be eliminated. Since construction costs are about half of the total unit cost of construction, and since sales taxes are 6 percent or higher in many municipalities, the elimination of the sales tax on building materials could decrease unit costs by 3 percent.[35] Other reductions in per unit construction costs can be achieved by redesigning housing so that a smaller amount of space will be adequate, by using standard components and modules, and by using manufactured housing components for small projects.[36] Reduction in housing construction costs should not be achieved, however, by requiring the use of non-union labor.

Construction by the City. If insufficient numbers of builders apply for building permits to construct low- or moderately priced housing, then the local government itself should have the obligation to construct the housing. Municipalities can landbank vacant or abandoned land as a resource for such construction. Any housing constructed by the local government should be retained by the local public housing authority or else sold to other entities in the Social Housing Sector. Construction should be done by the selective bidding system used by Britain in building council housing. The criteria for determining which builders would be able to bid for a project should include not merely quality of workmanship in past projects but also a commitment by the builder to training and employing unemployed or underemployed men and women, and minorities, in the construction of the housing. This will accomplish several goals at the same time: constructing low- and moderate-income housing, training persons who were formerly unskilled in the construction trades, combatting discrimination, reducing of unemployment, and increasing the number of taxpayers.

PRESERVATION AND REHABILITATION

In many cities, there is a housing crisis for lower-income persons at the same time that there are vacant housing units. Preservation of these vacant housing units could be a significant step toward addressing the needs of low- and moderate-income persons. In addition, there are other properties that could become a resource for lower-income households, or that already are a resource for lower-income households and should remain so. These include deteriorated property that has not yet become abandoned, tax-delinquent property, property owned by the FHA and VA as a result of foreclosures under the FHA mortgage-insurance and VA mortgage-guarantee programs, property owned by HUD as a result of foreclosures on HUD-subsidized projects, and existing subsidized housing units that are presently occupied by lower-income households. A top priority should be the preservation of this housing stock as a resource of lower-income persons, and its transfer into the Social Housing Sector.

Proposal: Demolition Controls

To prevent landowners from simply demolishing properties that they no longer wish to maintain as rental housing, and converting the land's use to commercial, demolition of a residential apartment building should be prohibited except when necessary for health or safety. If an owner applies for a demolition permit for residential property, and demolition is not warranted for health or safety reasons, then entities in the Social Housing Sector should have the first option to buy the property at its fair market value as residential property. If no entity wished to bid on the property, then the municipality should have the obligation to buy the property at its fair market value as residential property. The municipality could either continue to rent the property out to residential tenants through the local housing authority, or, if the property is uninhabitable, preserve the building until funds are available to repair it.

Proposal: Take Absentee-Owned Deteriorated and Tax-Delinquent Property

Local governments should take, by eminent domain, any absentee-owned building that does not meet minimum housing codes, when the owner has failed to make repairs after being given notice and adequate time to do so. In addition, when back taxes are owed for more than one year on any absentee-owned building, the property should be taken by eminent domain. The cost of repairs to bring the building up to minimum housing code and the amount of any back taxes due should be deducted from the compensation to which the owner is entitled under eminent domain. Once the building is brought up to minimum code standards, it could then either be retained under the control of the local housing authority as public housing, or else sold at cost to an entity that agrees to retain the housing in the Social Housing Sector. The building should not be sold to a private owner, for then the private owner could make a profit off the rehabilitation work done by the city.

Proposal: Low-Interest Loans for Poor Owner-Occupants

For owner-occupants of deteriorated housing who cannot afford to do the repairs necessary to bring their housing up to minimum code standards, low-interest loans should be available from the Housing Bank. If the owner is willing to transfer the property to the Social Housing Sector, then the owner should receive a lifetime right to remain in the housing unit, and should not be required to repay the loan. Instead, the entity in the Social Housing Sector that acquired the property would pay off the loan. If the owner wished to retain the property, then he or she would repay the loan on an amortized basis.

Proposal: Preservation of Existing Public Housing

Since many of the 40-year bonds that were floated to finance public housing projects are starting to be paid off, public housing authorities now are beginning to have the legal right to sell off their public housing projects, and the Reagan administration encouraged this. Public housing is one of the largest sources of social housing in the United States (1.3 million units) and provides much needed housing for low-income families and the elderly. The sale of public housing to private realtors or to tenants, with no requirement that the unit remain a low-income resource, would have a disastrous impact on low-income people and would exacerbate tremendously the already serious problem of homelessness. Accordingly, any proposals to sell public housing, whether to tenants or to private developers, should be vigorously opposed. Instead, such housing should remain in the Social Housing Sector and should be rented on a cost-rental basis, modified to take into account different amenities in different units.

Proposal: Preservation of FHA-, VA-, and HUD-foreclosed Property

Both HUD and VA acquire substantial numbers of units through foreclosures each year. From 1981 to 1987, HUD acquired over 245,000 housing units through foreclosures and resold most of them into the private market at auctions. The VA has sold over 125,000 foreclosed units at auctions since 1981.[37] Most of the property is purchased at auctions by speculators. Federal legislation should be passed mandating that, upon default and foreclosure on an FHA- or VA-insured property, entities in the Social Housing Sector should have first right of refusal to purchase the property at a price equal to that calculated in accordance with the resale price control proposal made in Chapter 4. Similarly, those fore-closed properties already held by FHA and VA should be offered for sale first to entities in the Social Housing Sector for a price equal to the out-of-pocket costs of the agency in the foreclosure process. By selling foreclosed property for an amount equal to its costs of acquisition, FHA and VA will recoup their out-of-pocket costs, but they will not make a profit from any increase in the market price of the property while it is being held by FHA or VA. Any increase in the value of the property will, in essence, remain in the community, since an entity of the Social Housing Sector will own the property and will hold it outside the spec-ulative housing market. Moreover, the current FHA practice of requiring that the property be vacated upon foreclosure should be ended, as this merely results in the displacement of a household, and, in addition, renders the property susceptible to vandalism. Instead, the household, if it wishes to remain in the property, should pay rent.

Proposal: Preserve Existing Subsidized Housing

The 645,000 subsidized housing units built between 1961 and 1973 that receive mortgage interest subsidies (and, in most cases, mortgage insurance) under the Section 221(d)(3) and Section 236 programs are at risk of loss as housing for low- and moderate-income households. De-velopers that constructed projects with these subsidies were obligated to rent the units to tenants with moderate incomes; tenant rents in such projects were limited to 25 percent (now 30 percent) of income, with rent supplements helping to subsidize the rents.[38] The for-profit owners of 367,400 of these 645,000 units (57 percent of the total) are eligible to convert the projects to market-rate rental units any time after 20 years from the beginning of the project, by prepaying the mortgage and ter-minating its contract with the government. These 367,400 units will be eligible for removal from the low-income housing stock during the period between 1986 and 2001; the largest number of units will be at risk of loss between 1991 and 1995, during which time about 235,000 units will pass the twenty-year mark. A study by the National Low Income Hous-ing Preservation Commission predicts that owners of 243,000 of the 367,400 units will prepay through 2001, meaning that these units will be converted to non-subsidized housing.[39] Owners of the remaining 43 percent of Section 221(d)(3) and 236 units (277,600 units) must maintain the projects as subsidized ones for forty years rather than twenty years;

these units then too will be available for conversion to market-rate housing, unless there is a change in the law.

Another timebomb is the impending loss of subsidized units constructed under the Section 8 program. Between 1974, when the program began, and 1985, when the program ended, 840,000 Section 8 housing units were constructed. Developers were guaranteed a subsidy covering the difference between 30 percent of the tenant's income and the market rent. By 1995, however, owners of up to 200,000 units will have the option of terminating their Section 8 contracts with the government, while by 2002, contracts will expire on an additional 496,000 units. Once the contracts terminate, owners are free to convert the apartments to market-rate units.[40]

Measures need to be taken to ensure that all of this subsidized housing is preserved as housing for lower-income people. The Emergency Low Income Housing Preservation Law, effective February, 1988, imposed a two-year moratorium on the prepayment of mortgages on subsidized housing.[41] While the moratorium is an important first step, it should be followed up by a permanent law regulating prepayment of mortgages. Such a law should require that, if any owner of a subsidized housing project wishes to prepay his or her mortgage and terminate his or her contract to maintain the property as low- and moderate-income housing, then the owner will be required to sell the property to the Social Housing Sector for a price equal to the cash invested by the owner in the property (down payment, payment on principal, and value of improvements), plus a fair return on the investment.

ALLOCATION OF SOCIAL HOUSING

Allocation in the United States has, with the exception of subsidized and public housing, been through the price mechanism. For housing that remains outside the Social Housing Sector, price will continue to be a major mechanism of allocation. As the Social Housing Sector develops, however, a variety of methods of allocation for the Social Housing Sector will need to be developed, tailored to the type of social housing that is involved. For example, a limited equity cooperative would likely have criteria for its members that would differ from a nonprofit corporation, since a cooperative would be interested in persons who are able and willing to live cooperatively and who are willing to agree to limit their equity. An employment-related nonprofit corporation is likely to give first preference to employees of the organization. Other nonprofit corporations that manage apartment buildings are likely to operate in a fashion similar to that of a traditional landlord, selecting tenants from the public at large.

Alternative Methods of Allocation

Those entities that have had experience in the administrative allocation of housing can best provide us with possible models. Such entities include council housing in Britain, public housing in the United States, and cooperative housing in the Soviet Union.

Council Housing. Council housing is allocated based primarily on need, with a point system used to determine one's place on the waiting list.[42] Points are given based on the number of children, the condition of and degree of overcrowding in the present dwelling unit, mental and physical disability, and other factors, with the primary consideration being the physical condition of the present housing of the applicant. In order to get on the waiting list, a person has to register but normally cannot do so until he or she has lived in the community for two or three years. Other persons eligible for council housing, if accommodation is available, are those displaced by urban renewal, and the homeless. Many housing authorities exclude single persons, single-parent families, and owner-occupants. Blacks tend to be under-represented in council housing.

Public Housing. Public housing in the United States generally is allocated by use of a waiting list. While each housing authority writes its own policies, these policies must comply with federal regulations, which require that preference be given to those who have been displaced involuntarily, those living in substandard housing, and those paying more than 50 percent of their income on rent. The federal regulations prohibit housing authorities from requiring applicants to have lived in the area for a certain period of time, although they can give preference to local residents. The regulations also prohibit exclusion of groups of people (e.g., unwed mothers).[43]

Soviet Cooperative Housing. To become a member of the cooperative, a family must live in the district where the cooperative is located and must have per capita dwelling space below the average in the area. In addition, preference for cooperative membership is given to the following categories of people: those who had lived in housing demolished by urban renewal, young specialists, those on waiting lists for housing, young workers in hostels, tenants in the private sector, large families, those in poor quality housing, those who have worked for a period in inhospitable areas (e.g., Siberia), and those with connections to the military.[44]

Critique of Methods of Allocation

While some countries have used social or political criteria for admitting persons to socially owned housing, such criteria have too much potential for housing being used as a political weapon against those who are not in favor with the current power structure. Thus, the Soviet system of giving priority to favored workers (e.g., young specialists) should not be used. Moreover, such a system rewards those who are already likely to receive higher-than-average salaries and therefore have less need of housing assistance.

An allocation system based on waiting lists and need, which is the type of system used in council housing in Britain and public housing in the United States, would appear to be the most equitable type of system of allocation. A detailed study of the Boston Housing Authority by Jon Pynoos, however, revealed that such systems have their own problems.[45] Measurement of "need" often tends to be subjective. This is because the prospective tenant's own perception of need is subjective, as are the perceptions of the housing authority staff. The fewer the standards for measuring need, the more subjective the assessment. Where the supply of housing is inadequate and the waiting lists long, staff members inevitably are subjected to pressure (whether from politicians, social workers, or the applicant himself or herself) to move certain applicants up to a higher spot on the waiting list. Since some of the reasons for moving someone upward on the waiting list are legitimate (e.g., the person was just burned out and has nowhere to go), it inevitably leads to adjustments in the waiting list based on the amount of pressure the applicant can bring to bear, and on the sophistication of the applicant. An applicant who is not knowledgeable, or who does not have someone to advocate for him or her, may remain far down on the waiting list even if he or she has good reason to move up on the waiting list.

To reduce the problems inherent in any large bureaucratic allocation of housing, Pynoos recommends several steps: (1) Make sure that applicants have access to the rules and procedures, so that they will know their rights. (2) Provide advocates for applicants. (3) Increase the efficiency of the allocation system (for example, through computerization of applicant information). Inefficient systems (i.e., ones in which information is not easily retrievable) tend to result in public housing workers allocating housing on an ad hoc basis, based on whoever is giving them the most pressure, rather than according to the rules. (4) Have professionals in the system make the decision as to when and whether to bend the rules, so that the caseworkers are not subjected to the pressure. (5) Decentralize decision making to project managers and tenant organizations, provided that they adhere to nondiscrimination rules. This will empower managers and tenants at the local projects. (6) Have an outside organization monitor the system to make sure the rules are being followed. (7) Review the rules periodically to make sure that they are still appropriate.[46]

Proposal: Allocation by Modified Waiting List

For newly constructed or rehabilitated units in the Social Housing Sector, a lottery of eligible households should be used to select the initial tenants. Thereafter, a waiting list system should be used to select persons for admission, with the list consisting of those persons who meet the minimum criteria for each type of housing. The waiting list should be modified, however, to give priority to three groups: (1) to those who have been displaced due to redevelopment, condominium conversions, or rent increases that forced them out of their privately owned dwelling units; (2) to those who are homeless; and (3) to those who are lower-income. To prevent these persons from overwhelming a new Social Housing Sector project, this priority system could require that every Social Housing Sector project set aside a certain minimum percentage of its units for displaced, homeless, and lower-income persons. As units opened up, the project would offer the vacancy first to those who have been displaced, are homeless, or are lower-income, unless the project already had met its minimum percentage requirement for such households. This would prevent any one project from carrying the entire burden of the housing crisis, a burden that would likely force a project quickly into bankruptcy.

To help to eliminate discrimination in housing, all Social Housing Sector entities should also be required to prohibit discrimination based on race, color, national origin, sex, age (except exclusively elderly projects), marital status, source of income, disability, health-related condition, religion, or sexual orientation. When vacancies arise, if the project has no waiting list, the social housing organization should be required to advertise the vacancy in minority publications, and to notify social service agencies of the vacancy, to ensure that they affirmatively market to racial minorities.

Redesigning the systems of housing finance, production, and allocation will go a long way toward resolving the current housing crisis. Simply providing adequate affordable housing does not, however, ensure that such housing will be made available on a nondiscriminatory basis. It is the problems posed by the nation's long history of discrimination to which we now turn.

Chapter 6

Discrimination

Developing policies to finance and produce housing for low- and moderate-income households are important measures to end the housing crisis. However, racism is a deeply ingrained aspect of American history and is imbedded within our culture and institutions (in part because racial minorities cannot "pass") and strategies to deal with racism must be included in proposals to reform the housing system. Racism also intertwines with class, to result in an intensification of both race and class segregation, since racial minority populations tend, on the whole, to have lower socioeconomic status than the white majority. Racism and classism are so interlocked that it is often impossible to tell which tendency predominates in a particular situation. Racial, ethnic, and class segregation must be attacked. Minority and working-class persons must have access to housing located near employment opportunities, which are now primarily found in the suburbs. Integrating the suburbs will not only bring housing closer to the types of employment opportunities that are important to working-class people but will also provide minorities with access to suburban school systems and promote the integration of our school systems.

There are, of course, other types of discrimination in housing, in addition to discrimination based on race, ethnic origin, or class: discrimination based on handicap and discrimination based on family composition (discrimination against families with children and against gay and nonnuclear families).

Those who suffer from handicap have experienced widespread discrimination, often because of building designs that make housing inaccessible. An important step in combatting such discrimination occurred in 1988 with the passage of amendments to the Fair Housing Act to prohibit handicap discrimination. (See "Handicapped Accessibility.")

Discrimination against children has also been widespread throughout the United States. A 1980 HUD study found that 26 percent of all rental units did not allow children, and another 50 percent had policies restricting the ability of families with children to rent. Until the mid–1970s the federal government did not require new federally subsidized rental units to provide units for families.[1] In 1988, Congress made a welcome amendment to the 1968 Fair Housing Act, by prohibiting discrimination against children under 18 years of age in rental housing, except in elderly housing complexes.[2]

As for discrimination against unmarried heterosexual couples and against gay men and lesbians, few states or localities have laws that prohibit such discrimination. This type of discrimination is focused, however, in the rental market. In the for-sale market, such discrimination is much less widespread than discrimination against racial and ethnic minorities, except in communities that have anticohabitation laws restricting the number of unmarried people that can live together (or prohibiting such cohabitation altogether), or limiting residency in a single housing unit to nuclear families. Such anticohabitation laws discriminate not only against unmarried heterosexual and gay and lesbian couples, but also against racial and ethnic minorities that have a tradition of living in extended families, and against poorer and elderly people who may need to share housing for financial reasons or for companionship. Repeal of such laws, proposed below, will benefit a wide variety of groups—unmarried heterosexual couples, gays and lesbians, racial and ethnic minorities, the elderly, and lower-income households.

The most obvious types of discrimination are those that are overt—outright refusals to sell or rent to certain categories of persons. As laws prohibiting overt discrimination have been passed, however, discrimination now is more often subtle and indirect, or disguised behind laws and policies that do not appear discriminatory on their face. For example, in a city that prohibits apartment construction, tenants simply cannot find an apartment to rent. In a locale where there are only one-bedroom apartments, households with children cannot find a place to rent. In suburbs that have no houses for sale under $150,000, moderate-income and many middle-income persons cannot afford to buy homes; such suburbs also effectively exclude the vast majority of blacks and Hispanics. Households with a member in a wheelchair cannot live in a dwelling unit with doorways too small to allow a wheelchair to pass. Unmarried couples cannot live in suburbs that prohibit nonrelatives from living together.

Because of the particularly entrenched role of racism and classism in urban American culture and the important relationship that housing location bears to opportunities for better education, jobs, and services, the historical focus of this chapter will be on racial and economic segregation. Handicap and household composition discrimination will be discussed briefly in proposals made at the end of the chapter.

HISTORICAL BACKGROUND

The pervasive racial and economic segregation evident in American cities today reflects the various discriminatory practices, some of which are continuing, pursued by realtors, financial institutions, local governments, and the federal government during this century. It also reflects the economic inequality between different classes and races of citizens, brought on by unemployment, wage discrimination, and unequal educational opportunities. It is to the discriminatory practices in housing that we now turn.

1900 to 1948

Associations of real estate brokers and agents played a key role in ensuring both racial and economic segregation of neighborhoods. During and after World War I, as the black migration swept into the cities, real estate boards established policies designed to ensure segregation.[3] The National Association of Real Estate Boards (NAREB), formed in the early 1900s, and its affiliated local real estate boards and members believed that realtors must protect property values and that the way to do this was to maintain the social and economic homogeneity of neighborhoods. NAREB therefore published a Code of Ethics in 1924 reflecting this racial and class bias. Even realtors who did not belong to a real estate board rarely violated NAREB's Code of Ethics. The Code of Ethics stated: "A Realtor should never be instrumental in introducing into a neighborhood a character of property or occupancy, members of any race or nationality, or any individuals whose presence will clearly be detrimental to property values in that neighborhood."[4] This provision remained in the code until 1950, when it was replaced by a less explicitly racist provision that, however, had the same goal of segregation.[5]

Cities and suburbs also sought to ensure segregation by enacting racial zoning ordinances that prohibited blacks from purchasing homes in white areas. When these were struck down by the Supreme Court in 1917, and again in 1926 and 1930,[6] cities, suburbs, and realtors turned to another means to enforce segregation: racially restrictive covenants. Not until 1948, in the case of *Shelley v Kraemer*, did the United States

Supreme Court hold that state courts could not *enforce* such restrictive covenants. However, that court decision did not prohibit property owners from themselves voluntarily adhering to restrictive covenants.[7]

The federal government also played a substantial role, through the FHA and public housing programs, in the development of residential apartheid. The FHA insured only those loans that it believed were economically sound. It adopted the prevailing racism in the real estate industry and therefore suggested in its 1936 underwriting manual, used by its employees who made the decisions as to which mortgage loans would be insured by FHA, the use of restrictive covenants on deeds as a protection against "inharmonious racial groups." Likewise, it recommended assigning a lower rating to a piece of property if it were located in a neighborhood with "incompatible" racial groups. While FHA omitted a direct reference to race in 1947, that edition of the underwriting manual continued to emphasize the need for homogeneity in neighborhoods.[8] FHA not only refused to insure mortgages in many areas of the central cities but routinely insured property being sold exclusively to whites in the suburbs. FHA's influence on the subsequent development of neighborhoods was substantial: its policies set and reinforced trends in the real estate market, as realtors would not market homes in areas where they knew that FHA would deny insurance.[9]

The federal public housing program similarly adopted a racist policy. Segregated housing projects were the norm established by the agencies administering public housing, with segregation policies lasting until the early 1970s. Not merely were particular complexes segregated but the federal government used discrimination in selecting the site for a particular public housing project. Thus, even when there were vacant sites available in the outlying areas of metropolitan areas, the federal government refused to build public housing there for minorities.[10]

1948 to 1968

After the Supreme Court struck down enforcement of restrictive covenants in the 1948 *Shelley v Kraemer* decision, communities turned to a variety of zoning and building restrictions to keep out minorities and working-class people. Since communities could no longer enforce overt racial exclusion through restrictive covenants, they began using exclusionary zoning to indirectly keep minorities out of suburbs. Common zoning restrictions, all of which continue today in one community or another, include the following:

• limits on the number of bedrooms allowed

• regulations that make the construction of apartment buildings uneconomical

• temporary moratoria on apartment construction

- bans on apartment building construction
- requirements that houses be of a minimum size or be built on lots of a minimum size
- establishment of detailed construction standards
- requirements of extensive infrastructure construction by the developer.

Thus, tactics range from outright prohibition of certain types of construction to requirements that unnecessarily increase the cost of housing development projects.[11] In addition, suburbs have adopted requirements that voters approve zoning changes, have delayed the efforts of developers wishing to build lower-income housing in the suburb so as to make the project financially unfeasible, and have withdrawn from participation in federal housing programs designed to help the poor.[12]

In the early years of exclusionary zoning, the courts generally upheld local zoning laws as within the police power to provide for the local welfare. Not until the end of the 1950s did a few scattered courts question such zoning laws. Not until the 1970s did a number of courts strike down a variety of exclusionary zoning laws, and mandate states to take affirmative steps to plan for low- and moderate-income members of the population.[13] (See "Class Discrimination.")

Meanwhile, after the 1948 *Shelley* decision, realtors turned to block-busting and steering as mechanisms to ensure continued racial segregation. The block-busting and steering by realtors meshed with redlining by financial and insurance institutions to ensure segregation. Financial institutions often refused to lend money in minority neighborhoods, while insurance companies often refused to insure homes in minority or mixed neighborhoods, on the grounds that such homes were not good risks. Both of these redlining practices, which still exist, were based on the inaccurate premise that property values fell when minorities moved in.[14] Appraisers also routinely devalued property in minority neighborhoods. The widely used textbook of appraisers, *The Appraisal of Real Estate*, stated in 1938 that the "infiltration" of "inharmonious racial groups" led to the decline in property values. In 1960, it referred to people of a "lower economic status and different social and economic background" as causing property values to fall, while in 1975 it referred to shifts in "the economic, social and physical forces creating the environment" as the cause of decreases in property values. Training materials used for appraisers in 1977 continued to use 100 percent "Caucasian" as an example of a neighborhood without adverse effects from minorities.[15]

The redlining practices of financial institutions, in turn, gave further encouragement to the block-busting and steering practices of realtors, for it made such practices even more profitable. For example, when the demand for homes by moderate-income blacks increased in the 1960s, mortgage institutions refused loans to blacks. As a result, the land-installment contract developed. In this type of contract, in contrast to a mortgage loan, the purchaser acquires no equity in the home during the years that he or she is paying on the note, instead acquiring title only upon final payment of the last month's installment. If the purchaser defaults on the loan, the home can be lost, with the purchaser receiving nothing since he or she has no equity. Furthermore, since the purchaser has no title to the home, he or she has no legal interest in the real estate that can be mortgaged to get a home improvement loan. Sellers of land installment contracts in the 1960s often got around state usury laws (which placed limits on the interest that could be charged on loans) by deliberately inflating the value of the property. Because of the difficulty that blacks faced in obtaining mortgage loans, speculators were able to sell homes to blacks on the land installment contract at a great mark-up. Furthermore, savings and loan associations, rather than giving mortgage loans to blacks, were using their funds to finance these land installment contracts. Realtors then engaged in block-busting to get middle-class whites out of neighborhoods, steered whites to the suburban fringe where new homes were being sold with FHA insurance, and sold the homes formerly owned by whites at a mark-up on land installment contracts to blacks.[16]

The federal government continued to allow and encourage racism to proceed, through both the urban renewal and FHA programs, even though overt government enforcement of racial discrimination had been prohibited by the *Shelley* decision. Cities often targeted urban renewal programs, instituted after passage of the 1949 Housing Act, at black and integrated communities. The slum clearance portions of urban renewal projects became a vehicle for black removal in many cities, while in the South and border states, urban renewal was used to wipe out integrated communities. Nationally, by 1963, over 60 percent of persons displaced by urban renewal were blacks, Puerto Ricans, and members of other minority groups, who were usually replaced by whites.[17] Less than 3 percent of the 400,000 housing units destroyed by urban renewal, many of which had been occupied by minorities, were replaced by new public housing during the 25 years of urban renewal.[18]

As for FHA, it was two years after the 1948 *Shelley* decision before FHA reversed its policy on restrictive covenants. Yet, realtors still found that FHA did not object to "gentlemen's agreements" to exclude blacks, or to covenants requiring that a group of neighbors had to approve any real estate sales in the neighborhood, or to similar covenants.[19] The 1955 edition of the FHA underwriting manual continued to refer to the desirability of maintaining neighborhood "homogeneity." Not until 1962, when President Kennedy signed Executive Order 11063 prohibiting discrimination in federal housing programs and ordering all departments of the federal government to take steps against racial discrimination, did any official change occur in FHA's policies. Enforcement of this order was extremely weak, and furthermore, the order applied only to federal housing programs, not to private housing.[20]

THE MODERN ERA: 1968 TO THE PRESENT

Substantial change in federal policy began to occur in 1968, as a result of the massive Civil Rights movement and Martin Luther King's assassination, which forced the adoption of the federal Fair Housing Act (Title VIII) in 1968. The Fair Housing Act made it illegal to discriminate on the basis of race, color, religion, or national origin, in virtually all housing and housing-finance transactions. (Sex discrimination was added in 1974.) Congress followed up with two additional antidiscrimination laws in the 1970s: the Home Mortgage Disclosure Act (HMDA) of 1974, and the Community Reinvestment Act (CRA) of 1977. The courts also began attacking the problem of discrimination, starting with the historic decision by the United States Supreme Court in 1968, in the case of *Jones v Alfred H. Mayer Co.*, that a post–Civil War statute (Section 1982) outlawed private racial discrimination in housing.[21] More recently, some state legislatures, as well as courts, have begun addressing the practice of exclusionary zoning.

While the 1968 Fair Housing Act and the *Jones v Mayer* decision gave minorities two legal tools for suing those who discriminated against them, and certainly led to some success in eliminating the most blatant types of housing discrimination, neither has had nearly the impact on segregation as had been anticipated. Likewise, the Home Mortgage Disclosure Act and the Community Reinvestment Act, while providing important tools to community organizations in attacking the problem of redlining, have had serious restrictions that have hampered their effectiveness. Attacks on exclusionary zoning are of more recent vintage, and are limited to particular states and localities, but, where exclusionary zoning has been challenged successfully, there has been benefit for low- and moderate-income households. Each of these approaches since 1968 is discussed below.

Fair Housing Act of 1968

The Fair Housing Act did not have the impact on discrimination and segregation that had been expected for several reasons: lack of strong enforcement provisions, failure to address the systemic nature of housing discrimination, government and court interpretations of the law that have justified discrimination against minorities in the name of integration, and lack of enforcement by the executive branch. Each of these problems is discussed below.

Lack of Strong Enforcement Provisions. Title VIII did not contain strong enforcement provisions. Individuals who sued could recover their actual damages but were limited to $1,000 in punitive damages, and attorney's fees were recoverable from the defendant by the successful plaintiff only if the court found that the plaintiff did not have the financial ability to assume the fees. (In contrast, attorney's fees in other civil rights cases automatically must be paid by the losing defendant.) While plaintiffs could recover damages for humiliation and loss of civil rights, the restrictions on punitive damages and attorney's fees limited severely individuals' abilities to find lawyers willing to take housing discrimination cases.

In addition, it was difficult for individuals to bring and win the lawsuits. First, except in cases of blatant racism, it is often difficult for a person to know that he or she has been lied to (for example, as to availability of a housing unit) or steered for racial reasons. Second, where realtors play on white racism, such as in a blockbusting situation, the whites involved are unlikely to bring suit, as they simply flee in panic. Third, lawsuits are extremely expensive, particularly where the discrimination is subtle and hard to prove. Fourth, even when the plaintiff is successful, the particular house or apartment that he or she sought is likely to have been sold or rented to another during the long pendency of the lawsuit, unless the plaintiff filed suit immediately upon experiencing discrimination and obtained a restraining order from the court to prohibit disposition of the unit during the pendency of the lawsuit.

Underlying Premises. In passing the Fair Housing Act, Congress assumed that the housing market was basically nondiscriminatory, that all that was needed was to punish those aberrant individuals who discriminated. The law therefore focused on compensation to individual victims of discrimination, with each case of discrimination being considered separately from other cases of discrimination. Only in a class action "pattern and practice" lawsuit will the court look at the practices that a realtor has used toward a number of individuals. Accordingly, each plaintiff has to reinvent the wheel, so to speak, in each case—a very expensive way of trying to eliminate the racism that has pervaded this society for over 300 years.

The law failed to address the strong motivations to discriminate that exist in the real estate world, motivations that will not be eliminated by a few housing discrimination lawsuits. A real estate agent's social and personal reputation in the community is his or her primary business asset. The real estate business is very local in nature, and listings are obtained primarily from referrals, repeat sales, and solicitations for listings. Most realtors see their success being based on their ability to select the "right" neighborhood for prospective buyers, and, accordingly, feel pressure to respond to what they perceive (not totally without reason) to be white preference for all-white neighborhoods. Most realtors try to sell housing only to whites, and most apartment house owners, as well as builders, are unwilling to affirmatively market to blacks.[22] That is, most realtors, apartment owners, and builders do not make special efforts to attract blacks and other minorities to their housing, whether through advertising in minority communities, hiring minority agents, or training minority personnel to have high level positions in their companies.

Moreover, blockbusting can be extremely profitable, as realtors earn their living from commissions on sales—the more sales, the more commissions. Even a realtor who does not appeal to racism through blockbusting is likely to steer blacks away from white neighborhoods, and whites to all-white neighborhoods. It is difficult to maintain integrated neighborhoods in the face of such steering, for blacks are steered to black and integrated neighborhoods, while whites are steered away from integrated neighborhoods, thus putting enormous pressure on an integrated neighborhood to become a largely or totally minority neighborhood.[23] Finally, with racism as imbedded as it is in this society, many realtors will discriminate without even being consciously aware that they are being racist.

Discrimination in the Interest of Integration. Ironically, as a result of court interpretations, the Fair Housing Act became a means of denying blacks needed housing. As discussed below, not only were HUD site selection criteria designed to prevent the construction of public housing in minority neighborhoods, but courts also upheld the denial of housing to blacks in the interest of integration.

Title VIII required HUD to "administer [its] programs and activities . . . in a manner affirmatively to further the policies of this [act]."[24] Interpreting this provision, the Third Circuit in its 1970 *Shannon* decision held that HUD had to take into account the effect that subsidized housing projects would have on racial concentration in a neighborhood.[25] This resulted in HUD changing its site selection policies for public and subsidized housing. While HUD previously had located public and subsidized housing primarily in segregated neighborhoods, now HUD adopted site selection regulations that favored dispersing poor black populations. HUD viewed the proper racial mix in an area to be no more than 10 to 30 percent minority and the rest white. Therefore, it was reluctant to build or approve public or subsidized housing projects in areas where there was a significant minority population, even if a majority of the population was white.[26] Congress reenforced this interpretation of the Fair Housing Act by providing in the 1974 Housing and Community Development Act that one of the goals of federal housing policy should be to spatially deconcentrate lower-income persons (read: blacks) and to revitalize deteriorating neighborhoods by attracting persons of higher income (read: whites).

In 1973, the Second Circuit took the *Shannon* decision one step further, in *Otero v New York City Housing Authority*.[27] In that case, the New York City Housing Authority had built two large apartment buildings for low-income tenants as part of an urban renewal project, displacing 1,852 households (60 percent nonwhite) from the project area prior to construction. Although the Housing Authority had given written assurances to the displaced households that they would be given first priority to return to the new apartments, when the displaced households applied to return, the Housing Authority reneged on its promise to give first priority to all displaced households. It refused to honor the applications of a group of mostly nonwhite households that had been displaced, in favor of another group that was predominantly white. The appeals court upheld the New York City Housing Authority's discrimination against nonwhite former residents of an urban renewal area. It adopted the Housing Authority's argument that if they were to accept applicants for the new low-income housing project on a nondiscriminatory basis, the project would become majority black and would cause "white flight" in the surrounding community. Thus, the court used the racism of whites (evidenced by the phenomenon of white flight) to authorize discrimination against blacks. The 1968 Fair Housing Law became an excuse not to build housing for minorities.

Not until the 1980s did some change occur in this use of Title VIII. First, because of protests by black leaders regarding the denial of needed housing that resulted from the new site selection criteria of HUD, and the dilution of black political strength implied by a dispersal strategy, Congress amended the Housing and Community Development Act in 1980. The amendment provided that HUD was not to exclude a project from its consideration for financial assistance under federally assisted housing programs simply because the project was proposed for a minority area. HUD responded by making its site selection criteria more flexible than they had been during the years of spatial deconcentration.[28] This became, however, a Pyrrhic victory for minorities, as the Reagan administration successfully slashed direct federal housing subsidy programs to the bone, resulting in little new subsidized housing being built in any neighborhoods, white or black. Second, in 1988, in the widely publicized *Starrett City* case, the Second Circuit Court of Appeals, the same court that had issued the *Otero* ruling, struck down racial quotas that had been justified on the grounds that they were necessary to assure the maintenance of integration.[29] In that case, the management of Starrett City had established a quota of 64 percent white, 22 percent black, and

8 percent Hispanic residency for its subsidized housing project, opened in 1973. It based its quotas on the argument that they were necessary to maintain the integrated nature of the project. The court held that, because of the fact that the quotas in Starrett City were not time-limited, the integration management program was invalid. The court did not, however, state that *all* integration management programs violate Title VIII.

Weak Enforcement. Enforcement of the Fair Housing Act by the federal government, which has resources that are unavailable to most individuals, was extremely weak. This was due both to limitations in the 1968 Fair Housing Act, and to lax government enforcement. Under the 1968 act, HUD, which was authorized to take complaints, had no authority to file suit against a party that discriminated. While the Justice Department was permitted under the 1968 act to file suit, it could only do so when there was a pattern or practice of discrimination (i.e., when it could be shown that a number of people had been discriminated against by one defendant). Moreover, HUD refused to do testing for housing discrimination, except for research purposes, although testing has proven to be the most effective way to show that discrimination is occurring.[30] (Such testing not only is helpful for establishing individual cases of discrimination but also is useful for showing that a pattern or practice of discrimination is occurring, thus setting the stage for Justice Department involvement.) Finally, under the Reagan administration, enforcement of all civil rights laws, including the Fair Housing Act, was particularly weak. Indeed, the major Reagan initiative in housing discrimination was to intervene in the *Starrett City* case after a settlement had been reached by all the parties and approved by the court, in order to challenge racial quotas in that project's integration management programs. While this author agrees that racial quotas that are used to deny housing to minorities should be held to be illegal by the courts, she also agrees with Robert Lake that it is an insufficient approach to housing discrimination for the executive branch of the government to challenge integration quotas without at the same time vigorously attacking racial and ethnic discrimination.[31]

1988 Amendments to Fair Housing Act

As a result of the lack of effective remedies and weak enforcement of the Fair Housing Act, Congress amended the act in 1988, effective March 1989.[32] It gave HUD the ability to initiate suits for restraining orders to hold the affected unit during the pendency of the complaint, gave the Department of Justice the right to file suit in cases of individual as well as "pattern and practice" discrimination, and required HUD to give Congress annual reports on its progress in eliminating housing discrimination. It also required HUD to make data publicly available on the characteristics of persons eligible for and assisted by HUD programs. In addition, it increased the recovery possible by those who have suffered discrimination.

Under the 1988 amendments, if HUD finds reasonable cause to believe that discrimination has occurred or is about to occur, the victim of discrimination may choose to proceed in an administrative hearing within HUD, on an expedited basis, rather than proceed into court. The Administrative Law Judge, upon making a finding of discrimination, may award actual damages, injunctive relief, and attorney's fees to the complainant. In addition, the administrative judge can impose civil penalties on the defendant ($10,000 for the first violation, $25,000 for a second violation within five years, and $50,000 for two or more violations within a seven-year period). The decision of the Administrative Law Judge is appealable to court. If the victim chooses to proceed into court, federal judges can, in addition, award punitive damages to the plaintiff. Moreover, the Justice Department is *required* to file suit on behalf of individuals who elect to proceed directly into court rather than through the administrative procedure. In pattern and practice cases brought by the Justice Department, the court may order civil penalties against the defendant of $50,000 for the first violation, and $100,000 for subsequent violations. While these amendments have the potential to make a substantial improvement in the enforcement of the Fair Housing Act, it remains to be seen whether or not the executive branch chooses to enforce the new law vigorously.

Home Mortgage Disclosure Act

In response to the problem of redlining, Congress passed, in 1975, the Home Mortgage Disclosure Act (HMDA).[33] The purpose of the act was to provide community groups with information as to where federally chartered lending institutions are making mortgage loans. Under the act, lending institutions must keep records as to the number and total dollar amount of mortgage loans and home improvements loans made or purchased by the institution each year by census tract. While the act provides some information as to where institutions are lending their money, it does not require that the information be broken down by neighborhood or street, nor that the dollar amount of each mortgage loan be revealed, nor that the number of requests for loans be disclosed. Thus, a lending institution can report that it is lending money in a particular census tract, but if the census tract contains both higher-priced and more moderate-priced homes, the public does not know whether the lending institution is providing money to buyers of the higher-priced or the more moderate-priced homes within the census tract. Moreover, in census tracts that are undergoing redevelopment, the mortgage loans may simply be helping upper-middle-class persons to move in, at the expense of the existing working-class or poor residents. Yet the data provided will not reveal details as to exactly which blocks are receiving the mortgage loans. Because the federal HMDA preexempts state regulation in the area, states cannot pass laws requiring more detailed disclosure by federally chartered banks (although states can regulate *state*-chartered financial institutions).[34]

Community Reinvestment Act

A second act passed by Congress that was intended to help combat mortgage redlining was the Community Reinvestment Act (CRA) of 1977.[35] The purpose of the law was to ensure that federally regulated financial institutions provide credit to the community in which they are located. Prior to the passage of the CRA, financial institutions, with the encouragement of federal regulatory agencies, used the rate of return as their primary lending criteria; they did not consider the effects on neighborhoods of refusals to give mortgage loans.[36]

Under regulations adopted to carry out the law, financial institutions must publish a CRA statement describing the institution's lending community and how their lending practices help to meet the credit needs of the community; in addition, they must make available a CRA public comment file, for public inspection and input. Federal regulatory agencies are required to "assess the institution's record of meeting the credit needs of its entire community, including low- and moderate-income neighborhoods, consistent with the safe and sound operation of such institution."[37] This assessment occurs about every year to year and a half, and involves, among other items, an evaluation of the institution's efforts to determine the credit needs of the community; the distribution of the institution's credit applications, extensions, and denials; any practices intended to discourage credit applications; any evidence of discrimination; the institution's record of opening and closing branch offices; the location of mortgage and home improvements loans made or purchased by the institution; and the institution's participation in federally insured, guaranteed, or subsidized housing programs. The results of that evaluation are not, however, made available to the public, a significant weakness in the administration of the act.

The public has been able to use the CRA when there have been mergers, acquisitions, or branch openings or closings of financial institutions. Whenever a federally insured bank or savings and loan institution applies to its regulatory agency for permission to establish a branch office, to relocate any office, or to merge with or acquire assets of another insured institution, the regulatory agency must use the information gathered in its CRA assessments to evaluate the institution's application. Community groups have used this provision of the law to their advantage, by filing protests to proposed mergers, acquisitions, or branch openings or closings, if an institution has not been making credit sufficiently available to low- and moderate-income communities in its service area. To make their case, they have used data available under the Home Mortgage Disclosure Act. As mergers and acquisitions in the lending industry mushroomed after 1985, due to a favorable Supreme Court decision on regional banking pacts,[38] the CRA has become a tool that community groups can use to pressure a financial institution to establish programs to increase lending in the community, in return for the community group dropping its opposition to the merger or acquisition.

Despite the leverage the CRA gives to community groups when a financial institution is planning a merger, acquisition, or branch office opening or closing, there are three significant problems with the act. First, while the CRA was passed to prevent redlining, the CRA has resulted in displacement of lower-income households, as financial institutions provide loans for middle- and upper-class in-movers into redevelopment areas.[39] Second, the public is denied the information that the federal regulatory agencies acquire concerning financial institutions' lending activities. Instead, in protesting an institution's practices, community groups must rely on the more limited information obtained through the HMDA concerning the mortgage practices of the institution. Third, the public must rely on the federal regulatory agencies to enforce the law. Even when there are *state* laws prohibiting redlining, only *federal* regulatory agencies have the legal authority to enforce such laws.[40] Courts rarely will overturn the decision of a regulatory agency as to a financial institution's compliance with the CRA. Instead, they will uphold the agency's decision so long as there is some evidence (even if that is contradicted by other evidence) to support the agency's action.[41] Regulatory agencies rarely have sanctioned financial institutions, although they have at times denied applications for branch offices and mergers, or have conditioned approval on the financial institution taking steps to comply with the CRA. Of the four agencies involved in enforcing the CRA (Federal Home Loan Bank Board, Office of Comptroller of the Currency, Federal Deposit Insurance Corporation, and Federal Reserve Board), the Federal Reserve Board has demonstrated the most resistance to enforcement of the CRA.[42]

Class Discrimination

In the 1960s and 1970s pressure developed to open up the suburbs to minorities, due to the 1970 *Shannon* decision (see "Fair Housing Act of

1968"), the movement of jobs to the suburbs, and the creation of federal subsidized housing programs. In response, suburbs used the zoning techniques developed after 1948 (see "1948 to 1968") to prevent federally subsidized housing projects from being built in their communities.[43] For decades, federal courts had struck down zoning laws that could be proven to be based on racial discrimination. Yet litigants found federal courts much less willing to strike down laws that are based on class discrimination, even when racial minorities are the ones who suffer from the laws. Legal challenges to such zoning laws have faced several major hurdles in the federal courts: proof requirements, judicial deference to local decisions, and the time required for litigation.

Under Supreme Court interpretations of the Equal Protection Clause of the Fourteenth Amendment (applicable when there is government involvement in discrimination, as in enactment of zoning laws), a plaintiff suing a municipality under the Equal Protection Clause must prove that the defendant *intended* to discriminate.[44] With over two decades having passed since the passage of various civil rights laws, most suburban governments are not stupid enough to be blatantly racist in their resistance to the construction of low-income housing.[45] Therefore, it is extremely difficult for most plaintiffs to win lawsuits challenging a denial of equal protection under the Constitution (for example, cases challenging zoning decisions that are alleged to have been racially motivated), because of the requirement that the plaintiff show that the defendant intended to discriminate.

Second, federal courts generally are loathe to interfere with local decisions pertaining to housing. In 1971, for example, the Supreme Court upheld a state law requiring voters to approve public housing projects before they could be built.[46] In 1976, the Court upheld a suburb's charter provision that conditioned all zoning changes on approval of the changes by a 55 percent referendum vote.[47] Thus, so long as municipalities avoided blatant racism in their zoning decisions, they could keep minorities and disfavored groups out under the guise of a "devotion to democracy" (giving residents a right to vote on public housing) or "power to the people" (requiring 55 percent referendum vote to approve proposed zoning changes).

Finally, the time period involved in contested litigation is extremely long, generally running into several years, if not a decade. Consequently, a suburb can cause such a delay in a project by forcing the developer of a proposed low-income housing project to go to court, that any victory by the developer may be an empty one—by the time the suit is won, the financing for the project may have long since run dry.

At the state level, some legislatures and courts began recognizing the need to confront exclusionary zoning. In the late 1960s and early 1970s, New York, Massachusetts, California, and Oregon passed statutes that permitted challenges to local restrictions on low-income housing or that required localities to prepare plans to meet the housing needs of all economic segments of the community.[48]

But it was the New Jersey *Mount Laurel* decisions in 1975 and 1983 that propelled the problem of exclusionary zoning to the legal fore. In 1975, in its first decision (called *Mt. Laurel I*), the New Jersey Supreme Court held that, in carrying out their police powers for the general welfare, local municipalities had a *constitutional* obligation to consider regional, not just local, welfare in making zoning decisions. Specifically, it held that every "developing" community had to use its zoning powers affirmatively to afford the opportunity for the construction of low- and moderate-income housing and had to consider the needs of nonresidents employed in its community in making zoning decisions.[49] The *Mt. Laurel I* decision influenced courts throughout the country.

Eight more years of recalcitrance by the town of Mount Laurel, however, led the New Jersey Supreme Court in its 1983 *Mt. Laurel II* decision to note that Mount Laurel still remained "afflicted with a blatantly exclusionary ordinance."[50] In an effort to put some teeth into its 1975 decision, the court held that zoning restrictions that are not necessary for health and safety must be stricken, at least in part of the municipality. Thus, a municipality can have exclusionary zoning restrictions in some areas of the community only if it has eliminated such exclusionary restrictions in sufficient portions of the community so as to permit housing affordable to low- and moderate-income households to be built in the municipality. Moreover, municipalities must help developers affirmatively to provide housing for low- and moderate-income persons, where mere elimination of unnecessary zoning restrictions will not result in the construction of lower-income housing. Municipalities in such instances will have to cooperate with a developer's attempts to obtain housing construction subsidies and tax abatements. Zoning devices designed to include lower-income housing (referred to as "inclusionary zoning"), such as incentive zoning and mandatory set-asides, must be used. Incentive zoning involves either granting partial exemptions from density limitations to a housing developer or giving developers bonuses for each unit of lower-priced housing built. The extent of density exemptions is based on the number of lower-priced units to be built by the developer. Since the court noted that incentive zoning often is not enough to induce developers to construct lower-income housing, the court required municipalities to establish mandatory set-asides, if necessary to achieve their fair share goal. These are zoning requirements that a developer set aside a certain minimum percentage of a housing development for units affordable to low- and moderate-income households.

In order to prevent these units from later becoming unaffordable for lower-income persons, the court held that lower-priced housing had to be subject to resale controls, unless its market price was such that it was affordable to lower-income households without controls. To prevent a developer from building the market-rate units in its development first, and then reneging on its obligation to build lower-priced units, the court held that municipalities should require developers to include in every phase of the development the requisite percentage of lower-priced units.

If the preceding changes in zoning laws and affirmative steps by a municipality did not result in construction of low- and moderate-priced housing, then, the court held, zoning laws should be amended further to allow for mobile homes in designated portions of the municipality.

If, after a municipality had taken all of the preceding measures to meet its fair share obligations, it still did not have sufficient lower-priced housing in its community (because, for instance, of extremely high land prices in the community), then and only then would the court allow the municipality to meet its fair share obligation by providing for the building of the least cost housing possible in the community, up to the number of units required by its fair share obligations.[51]

The *Mt. Laurel II* decision is a landmark one and has produced results in New Jersey suburbs, although not as extensive results as would be desired. By the beginning of 1988, five years after the *Mt. Laurel II* decision, about 2,000 units of low- and moderate-priced housing had been built, and another 10,000 units were in the process of development. About half of the units have been affordable to low-income households and half to moderate-income households, despite the fact that most units were constructed without any public subsidy whatsoever. This reflects the fact that, in an area with a strong housing market (as is true of many suburbs), profits from the sale of higher-priced units are sufficient to enable a builder to sell housing to lower-income households within such households' price range, and still make a profit. The limitations of the implementation of the *Mt. Laurel II* decision are three: (1) it has been mostly white suburbanites who have benefited from the decision, not central city blacks and Hispanics; (2) few rental units have been constructed; and (3) the poorest households have not been able to benefit. Moreover, resale controls will expire on the units within six to twenty years, depending on the suburb.[52] The *Mt. Laurel II* decision thus shows both the potential and the problems in opening up the suburbs for both low-income and minority persons.

Summary

While the civil rights movement of the sixties was successful in getting fair housing laws passed, both at the national and local level, enforcement of the laws has been weak. Although the amendments to the federal Fair Housing Act have the potential of improving the situation, a great deal depends on the interest of the federal government in vigorously enforcing the new law. Moreover, few laws exist that attack the problem of class discrimination. Thus, many changes must occur before the problems of race and class discrimination are eliminated from our urban centers. It is to proposals for such changes that we now turn.

PROPOSALS

Racial and class segregation are widespread in U.S. cities, as is discrimination based on handicap and family composition, yet there are few models on which to draw for solutions to the problems. While there are countries that have developed alternative methods for financing and producing housing, few countries with a history of racism or ethnic conflict have managed to solve their conflicts.

While integration is important, increasing minority choice is even more important. Thus, integration management programs that seek to control the percentage of minorities in a community should not be pursued. Moreover, when minorities truly prefer living in a predominantly minority community, not because of the hostility they might face in other communities, but because it is a way of increasing minority political power and representation in local, state, and federal legislative bodies, that choice should be supported. Thus, the focus should be on eliminating discrimination in housing, rather than trying to manipulate the housing market to assure a certain percentage of whites and minorities in each neighborhood.

Eliminating discrimination in housing will require, of course, an attack on prejudice at all levels of society. The proposals presented in the following sections are only one facet of a broader attack on the problems of prejudice and discrimination that must take place through education, consciousness-raising, development of respect for cultural diversity, and vigorous enforcement of civil rights legislation by all levels of government. While the following proposals, therefore, cannot by themselves solve the problem of housing discrimination, they are an important step toward that goal.

Racial and Ethnic Discrimination

Vigorous Federal Enforcement of Title VIII. Title VIII was amended in 1988, effective March 1989, to provide HUD and the Department of Justice with significantly greater enforcement powers. The federal government should proceed immediately to take advantage of its broadened powers and should vigorously pursue claims against persons and institutions that discriminate.

This vigorous enforcement needs to have several components. First, there should be a widespread educational campaign in minority communities to inform people of their right to open housing and the enforcement mechanisms, for the number of housing discrimination complaints filed with HUD are far lower than the extent of discrimination that exists, particularly among Hispanics.[53] Second, HUD should regularly perform testing in urban areas to determine whether or not minorities are being treated differently than whites, or are being given less information as to the availability of housing, and to determine whether or not whites and minorities are being steered. Upon finding evidence of discriminatory practices, the Department of Justice should immediately proceed with suit. Third, HUD should provide free testing services to any minority person who suspects discrimination and requests testing, to establish whether or not discrimination is being employed by the realtor or landlord. HUD should make the availability of such testing known to minority communities through its educational materials on the Fair Housing Act.

Expansion of Antidiscrimination Tools. Title VIII should be further amended to provide additional tools to combat discrimination, by expanding the right of agencies to sue, by increasing penalties, and by providing funding for fair housing groups.

First, local and state agencies should be given the right to bring pattern and practice suits, rather than such authority being limited to the Justice Department.

Second, penalties for discrimination should be increased. At the present time, most realtors and landlords face only monetary penalties if they are found to have discriminated. Because of the strong incentives to discriminate that exist, such monetary penalties are not sufficient, particularly when the offending party is wealthy enough to absorb such costs into the expense of doing business and continues to be able to profit from the real estate that was denied to minorities. Where appropriate, the weapons of the criminal law, eminent domain, and/or administrative revocation procedures should be used to increase the penalties for discrimination, as explained below.

Criminal laws should be enacted that make it a crime to discriminate in the sale or rental of housing, with the further provision that, upon conviction, the property involved would be forfeited to the local or state government, and thereafter transferred to the Social Housing Sector. The precedent exists in the criminal law (under racketeering and drug laws) for property forfeiture provisions. While current forfeiture provisions in these laws are excessive, in that they allow for forfeiture *before* conviction, the concept of forfeiture of the property through which the defendant made a profit at the expense of minority persons is a good one. While it is likely that criminal prosecution will only rarely be initiated by local prosecutors, criminal laws should be enacted to permit criminal prosecution and forfeiture after conviction in particularly egregious cases of discrimination.

Moreover, any property owner found by a court in a civil lawsuit to have discriminated should have the property that was illegally denied to a homeseeker taken by the local government through eminent domain, with the property then resold to an entity in the Social Housing Sector. This will reenforce the concept that housing exists for the social good, not merely for private profit, and that those who violate the law do not deserve to be able to continue owning the property involved for profit-making activities. Eminent domain, however, differs from forfeiture, because in an eminent domain proceeding the owner is paid fair market value for the property; in forfeiture, the owner loses the property without compensation.

Realtors, homeowners' insurance companies, and financial institutions that are found by a court to have discriminated also should face consequences that impinge on their ability to make profits. Individual realtors should have their licenses to buy and sell residential real estate revoked for at least two years, and insurance companies should have their authority to sell homeowners' insurance in the state revoked for at least two years. Such administrative actions would not eliminate all avenues of business for such persons or institutions but would eliminate their ability to make profits off the residential real estate market for at least two years. Financial institutions that discriminate should be required to pay to the Housing Bank a certain percentage of their net worth.

Third, Congress should provide funding for local fair housing groups in jurisdictions where HUD offices are nonexistent or too small to be able to pursue effectively housing discrimination complaints. Such funding should also be provided to groups where local or state authorities have not been enforcing existing antidiscrimination laws, so that fair housing groups can provide needed testing and legal assistance to victims of discrimination.

Provide Public Information on the Availability of Housing.[54] Since minorities often receive less information than whites as to the availability of housing, urban areas should establish computerized housing referral and counseling services that have information as to all housing available for sale or rental in the metropolitan area. Owners and real estate agents should be required to file with the service a notice of intent to sell, and landlords should be required to file a notice of intent to rent. This would insure that information as to housing for sale and for rent is equally available to all racial and ethnic groups. Since municipalities may balk at setting up such services, particularly because realtors are likely to object to losing their monopoly on listing services, the federal government should fund nonprofit fair housing information services in any metropolitan area where the local governments refuse to set up such services or fail to fund such services adequately. Federal law should require that realtors, owners, and landlords be required to list with such services.

Support for Integrated Neighborhoods. Presently, enormous pressures are placed on integrated communities. Minorities often are steered to such communities, while whites are steered away. Even without the inducements of blockbusting realtors, many whites begin to leave neighborhoods when minorities move in. Much of this white flight could be halted through a variety of measures: government efforts to counteract white fears, maintenance or enhancement of community services in integrated communities, and public relations campaigns to attract residents of all races to the neighborhood. Eliminating the white racism that leads to white flight is, of course, a long-term process, involving efforts to eliminate prejudice from the earliest ages on up.

Although no community can expect to eliminate all white racism overnight, steps can be taken to at least reduce, if not eliminate, white prejudice. First, as soon as it appears that white flight may be starting in a neighborhood, the city should initiate neighborhood meetings to discuss what is happening and to lessen white prejudice and fears. Second, cities should maintain, or even improve, services to neighborhoods that are integrated or are beginning to have minority residents, so that community residents will see that there are positive economic benefits to integration. Third, public relations campaigns should be launched to promote integrated communities. Since people's perceptions of communities are based on what they hear, the potential of public relations campaigns to change perceptions should not be underestimated.[55] The danger, of course, is that such public relations campaigns will be directed only to whites, resulting in gentrification and displacement of existing minority residents, rather than in true integration. Accordingly, such campaigns should be coupled with strong anti-displacement measures, discussed in Chapter 7.

Racial Impact Studies. When any governmental or private body proposes to redevelop an area, the city should be required to do a racial impact study, similar to the environmental impact studies required in federally funded projects, before deciding whether or not to approve the redevelopment plan. At a minimum, such a requirement would provide information for community activists concerned about the redevelopment, so that they have the information necessary to lobby for or against the redevelopment, or to try to get it modified.

Measures against Redlining. The Home Mortgage Disclosure Act should be amended to require that financial institutions provide information by block concerning mortgage loans. This information should include the following:

- number of applications for loans
- the amount of each mortgage loan granted
- the race or ethnic origin of each household applying for and each household receiving mortgage loans
- sex of each borrower
- the approximate total household income of the borrower's household.

(To insure privacy for borrowers, the household income figures should not be specific but should be in ranges—for example: less than $15,000, $15,000 to $25,000, $25,000 to $35,000, $35,000 to $50,000, $50,000 to $75,000, above $75,000.) This will provide meaningful information to the community, so that it can adequately monitor where mortgage loans are being made, as well as the race and sex of the people receiving the loans. This will help community groups determine if loans in a particular area of the city are being made to white "incipient yuppies" or to moderate-income, minority, and female households.

The Community Reinvestment Act should be amended to provide that the information acquired by federal regulatory agencies concerning the credit practices of financial institutions be made available to the public. Moreover, federal regulatory agencies should be authorized to take corrective action against financial institutions any time they find that institutions are redlining, rather than limiting federal action to the point in time when a financial institution wishes to merge, acquire another, or open or close an office.

More fundamentally, the CRA should be amended to authorize state and local agencies to file suit against financial institutions that redline, with courts authorized to grant injunctions against institutions that are found to be discriminating on the basis of race, ethnicity, sex, or neighborhood. Such injunctions should include requirements that institutions that have redlined must allocate a certain percentage of the total value of their loans to minorities, women, and low- and moderate-income residents of neighborhoods that have suffered from redlining.

Both the HMDA and the CRA should be amended to provide that these federal laws do not preempt state laws against redlining.

Realtor Requirements. In metropolitan areas that have minority newspapers, realtors should be required to advertise their properties in at least one minority newspaper. Realty companies that have more than four agents should be required to advertise employment openings for sales and rental agents in minority publications.

Class Segregation

The proposed amendments to the Home Mortgage Disclosure Act and the Community Reinvestment Act discussed previously will help to at-

tack class, as well as racial, discrimination. In addition, two policy recommendations made in Chapter 5 will also reduce class discrimination:
fair share planning and regulation of building permits to ensure the
construction of lower-income housing.

Another necessary component of an attack on class discrimination is
inclusionary zoning. Municipalities should eliminate all zoning requirements that are not necessary for health and safety, and adopt inclusionary zoning laws of the type outlined by the court in *Mt. Laurel II*:
incentive zoning (partial exemptions from density limitations or density
bonuses), elimination of restrictions on the use of prefabricated housing
(provided that the prefabricated parts met minimal housing code standards), and authorization for a certain number of mobile homes, if necessary to meet inclusionary planning goals.

Because many municipalities are likely to refuse to repeal exclusionary
zoning laws, Congress should pass a zoning override law, to permit the
federal government to override exclusionary zoning laws in suburbs
where local municipalities have proven to be recalcitrant about meeting
their fair share. Alternatively, states can enact laws requiring elimination
of exclusionary zoning laws to the extent they keep out low- and moderate-income households, and laws requiring communities to provide density bonuses or other financial benefits to developers willing to construct
a certain percentage of low- and moderate-priced housing as part of a
proposed development.[56]

Voluntary inclusionary zoning programs by themselves (for example,
density bonuses to developers willing to construct lower-income housing) may not be enough to open up exclusionary communities for lower-
income households, especially if federal support for lower-income housing continues to be minimal. Moreover, inclusionary zoning laws will
not result in production of lower-income housing if private developers
simply will not build in the community. (Indeed, passing overly strin-
gent inclusionary zoning laws can be a method by which an exclusionary
suburb remains exclusionary, while appearing to comply with inclusionary zoning requirements, by making the inclusionary requirements
so burdensome that no developer wishes to build in the suburb.) Thus
mandatory inclusionary devices, such as laws requiring mandatory set-
asides of a minimum percentage of lower-priced units, will be necessary
in most cases.[57] To insure that lower-income housing produced will
remain affordable to lower-income households, all inclusionary zoning
programs (whether voluntary or mandatory) should require that such
housing be sold to entities in the Social Housing Sector, with deed
restrictions prohibiting their resale outside the Social Housing Sector,
so that the property would never be resold into the private for-profit
sector.

Where inclusionary zoning programs are non-existent, or do not result

in the construction of lower-income housing, production by the municipality or the federal government, or by various social housing developers with the support of the local, state, or federal government, will
be necessary.

Handicapped Accessibility

The 1988 Amendments to the Fair Housing Act included an important
first step in attacking the problem of housing discrimination against the
handicapped. As of March 1989, the act prohibits discrimination based
on handicap in the sale or rental of housing and requires new multifamily
dwelling units of four or more units to meet wheelchair-accessibility
requirements. The act also requires landlords to allow tenants to modify
apartments to make them handicapped-accessible, although the landlord
may require the tenant to agree to pay the cost of restoring certain
portions of the premises to its original condition after leaving, if the
request for restoration is "reasonable."[58] HUD's regulations imple-
menting the new law make it clear that the prohibition against discrimination against the handicapped extends to persons who have diseases
or are treated as if they have a disease. Thus, those with AIDS or HIV-
infection or who are regarded as having AIDS or HIV-infection (because
of antigay or racist attitudes) are covered by the act.[59]

The act should be further strengthened by eliminating the requirement
that a handicapped tenant pay for the cost of restoring the premises to
its original condition if the tenant has modified it to make it handicapped-
accessible, unless such modification would make the unit less functional
for able-bodied persons. Other handicapped tenants can benefit from
the unit having been made handicapped-accessible, and there is no
reason in most cases why a unit should be made handicapped-*in*accessible when the tenant moves out—virtually all modifications that make
a unit accessible do not diminish the value of the unit for able-bodied
individuals.

In addition, federal or state financial assistance should be provided to
handicapped tenants who need to modify a unit to make it handicapped-
accessible. Otherwise, a disabled individual bears the full cost of improving a housing unit, even though future tenants may also benefit from the
improvement.

Household Composition Discrimination

Many localities have taken an exceedingly narrow view of what con-
stitutes a family. The zoning laws of many jurisdictions limit occupancy
of a housing unit to those who are related to each other by blood or
marriage, or permit "unrelated" people to live together only if the number of such persons does not exceed two or three. Courts generally have

upheld such zoning restrictions. In 1974, the Supreme Court upheld a zoning law that limited occupancy to persons related by blood, marriage, or adoption (except that two persons not so related could live together). Although in 1977, the Court held that a zoning ordinance could not exclude grandparents, uncles, aunts, and cousins from the definition of family, the decision was only 5–4.[60] In 1986, the Missouri Court of Appeals upheld a municipality's zoning law that prevented *any* persons in single family residential zones who were not related by blood or marriage from living together (except for domestic servants residing in homes). In that case, a heterosexual couple who were not married to each other had purchased a house jointly in the single-family zone. The City of Ladue demanded that the couple vacate their home because they were not a "family"; when they failed to do so, the city sought an injunction against the couple to prevent them from violating the zoning law. The court held that the couple was not a family, and that the city could adopt such a restrictive ordinance as part of its power to promote health, safety, morals, and general welfare.[61]

As in the *City of Ladue* case, such laws usually are based on the premise that only those who are blood relatives or married to each other are family. Such an approach ignores the fact that there are a variety of other types of families: those with foster children, those with step-children, nonmarried heterosexual couples, gay and lesbian families (with or without children), and those who choose to live together for economic or emotional support (e.g., poorer families, elderly people). Such laws violate First Amendment rights to free association, and important privacy rights. While municipalities may have a legitimate interest in regulating the *number* of persons in a housing unit to avoid over-crowding, or in regulating the number of cars associated with any one household (to avoid street congestion), such an interest is totally independent of the blood or marriage relationship of the persons in the household. Accordingly, laws restricting occupancy of housing units based on the blood or marriage relationship of the parties should be repealed or struck down by the courts. In addition, the federal Fair Housing Act should be amended to prohibit discrimination based on marital status or sexual orientation.

Racial and class segregation are still widespread in our urban areas. Although the Fair Housing Act was passed in 1968, vigorous enforcement of that law has been lacking. Therefore, it is impossible to know how far down the road we can expect to go in eliminating racial and ethnic discrimination until we first try whole-heartedly to attack the problem. With regard to class discrimination, there are no federal laws preventing suburban exclusion based on class, and only recently have states and state court systems begun to address the problem. There again, we cannot expect to open up the suburbs to poorer households until we at least try to do so. In 1988, Congress took important steps toward dealing with the problems of handicapped discrimination and discrimination against children. We will see over the next few years whether or not those changes in the law result in significant change in the problems that handicapped persons and families with children face when seeking housing. Finally, steps must be taken to eliminate discrimination based on marital status, sexual orientation or family composition.

Chapter 7 _____

Displacement

Coming up with systems to finance and produce adequate units of affordable housing will not be enough to end the housing crisis. We also must minimize displacement. Those proposals made in Chapter 4 that make housing affordable will, of course, reduce displacement. Those proposals made in Chapter 5 to retain public and subsidized housing as housing for lower-income persons will also reduce displacement, as will the proposal to end FHA's practice of requiring foreclosed property to be vacated. This chapter therefore discusses other types of displacement: displacement caused by failure to maintain property, by government-sponsored redevelopment, and by invasions of middle- and upper-class yuppies. The focus of this chapter is on the history of legal developments pertaining to urban renewal and redevelopment, proposals for laws to protect households from displacement, and proposals for adequate provision for the displaced household (where displacement is absolutely necessary).[1]

HISTORICAL BACKGROUND

In 1931 President Hoover established a Conference on Home Building and Home Ownership. Out of the report of this conference came many of the seed ideas that later gave rise to urban renewal and redevelopment. The conference developed the concept of district replanning, recommending that communities develop master plans and comprehensive zoning laws designed to eliminate low-income neighborhoods, which the conference saw as detrimental to the health and character of urban citizens. It recommended that governments use eminent domain powers to reduce the cost of acquiring property and to eliminate hold-outs, reselling the property acquired to private developers. It further proposed that local government should pay for the cost of infrastructure improvements, such as streets, lights, and sewers. The conference opposed any relocation assistance to those who would be displaced by the building projects.[2]

Before district replanning could become a reality, legal barriers had to be overcome. While the Fifth Amendment to the United States Constitution implicitly recognizes the power of eminent domain, by providing that private property can not be taken for public use unless just compensation is paid, eminent domain is supposed to be used only when the taking of private property is for a public use, and not when it is for the benefit of a private person or company.[3] Prior to the 1930s, courts had not approved of the use of eminent domain for the acquisition of property to rebuild urban areas. Indeed, in 1935, the Sixth Circuit Court of Appeals held unconstitutional that portion of the National Industrial Recovery Act that authorized the federal government to acquire property by eminent domain for the construction of low-cost housing or for slum clearance, finding it to be beyond the scope of federal power.[4]

Not until 1936 was the first favorable ruling issued, in a case involving the constitutionality of the exercise of eminent domain by a local government body. The New York Court of Appeals held that the acquisition of private property by the New York City Housing Authority for the purpose of eliminating slums and providing housing at low cost was a public purpose and therefore a proper use of eminent domain.[5] This broke the ice, and other state courts quickly followed suit with favorable rulings upholding the use of eminent domain by local government bodies for slum clearance and public housing purposes.[6] This paved the way for urban renewal.

The Urban Land Institute (ULI), the research arm of the National Association of Real Estate Boards (NAREB), began developing its master vision of redevelopment in urban areas. In the early 1940s, it published studies on proposed downtown redevelopment in major cities. It called for the establishment of local redevelopment commissions, which would use federal money to acquire land in blighted areas and then sell or lease the land to private businesses for redevelopment. It urged adoption of state laws that would allow the reuse of cleared slum areas in accordance with a comprehensive plan, and opposed limiting land use to housing development. It also opposed any limitation on the profits of developers and any requirements that displaced tenants be rehoused. To assist this redevelopment effort, it recommended that the federal government provide money to local planning agencies to draft master plans.[7] Finally, the ULI's parent organization, NAREB, proposed in 1944 that local governments give tax breaks for redevelopment.[8]

The New York Court of Appeals in 1943 had given its legal blessing for the ULI/NAREB type of redevelopment strategy by upholding a New York law that permitted local governments to use eminent domain to acquire property in blighted areas, and then to convey that property to limited profit corporations for redevelopment. At the time of the ruling, eight other states had similar laws allowing for the condemnation of blighted areas so that nonprofit entities could redevelop them. Within a year following the decision, eleven more states passed such laws.[9] Moreover, Missouri went even further than other states, authorizing cities to give the power of eminent domain directly to private urban redevelopers, thereby by-passing the necessity of having the city acquire property for the redevelopers.[10]

The definition of "blight" in such redevelopment laws often was extremely broad. For example, the Missouri law defined it as follows:

"Blighted area" shall mean that portion of the city within which the legislative authority of the city determines that by reason of age, obsolescence, inadequate or outmoded design or physical deterioration, have become economic and social liabilities, and that such conditions are conducive to ill health, transmission of disease, crime or inability to pay reasonable taxes.[11]

Thus, merely "outmoded design" or "obsolescence" could target an area for a designation of blight.

After the war, publicly supported urban redevelopment began in earnest, following the recommendations of the Urban Land Institute. However, it was not until the passage of the 1949 Housing Act,[12] which provided for the first major federal involvement in urban redevelopment since the war, that government-assisted redevelopment significantly accelerated across the nation. The 1949 act represented a victory for the ULI's vision of state-supported capitalism, by incorporating almost all of the model federal legislation for urban redevelopment that had been drafted by the ULI in 1943.[13] The act authorized the federal government to provide federal loans to local planning agencies to survey and buy land for redevelopment projects. The federal government could provide grants as well, for up to two-thirds of the losses associated with acquiring property and preparing the site for an urban redevelopment project, so long as a local government body covered the remaining one-third of the loss. The act, with minor exceptions, specifically prohibited using federal money for any construction on the acquired land.[14] After the local agency had acquired and cleared land, it then sold the land at a loss to private investors for redevelopment.[15]

While the ULI had wanted the law to allow for federal subsidies in any type of urban area, commercial or residential, the 1949 act limited the areas eligible for federal assistance to those that were predominantly residential either before *or* after redevelopment. Thus, a residential neighborhood could be torn down to make way for business development. Furthermore, this "restriction" on urban renewal was weakened in later years when Congress allowed certain exemptions from the "predominantly residential" requirement.[16]

Urban redevelopment projects could not be successful unless they were profitable to private real estate interests, since local redevelopment agencies would only be able to sell those lands that would be profitable for private real estate concerns to redevelop. Therefore, agencies tended to acquire land in areas that would be attractive to private realtors, often in or near the central business districts that were desirable to private redevelopers and investors. Cities often provided "sweeteners" to private developers to increase further the attractiveness of renewal areas to private enterprise, including one or more of the following: partial abatement of real estate taxes, low assessment on redeveloped property, and provision of community facilities in the area of the renewal project. Thus, business leaders used urban renewal to increase the value of downtown real estate.[17]

Urban redevelopment that benefited private interests received its legal stamp of approval from the United States Supreme Court in a landmark unanimous decision in 1954, written by Justice William O. Douglas. The case, *Berman v Parker*,[18] involved a challenge to the Washington, D.C., redevelopment law. Patterned on the ULI/NAREB scheme of redevelopment, the law allowed the D.C. Redevelopment Land Agency to acquire property by eminent domain in "blighted" areas, and then to resell the property to private redevelopers or public agencies, with preference being given for sale to private developers. The law was challenged on the grounds that it allowed the taking of private property from one business for the benefit of another, and therefore violated the Fifth Amendment prohibition against the taking of private property for private use. The Supreme Court upheld the redevelopment statute, on the grounds that it was within the proper scope of the police power of the government, since Congress had declared the redevelopment to be in the public interest; once Congress had decided that redevelopment was in the public interest, it was up to Congress to decide the means of executing the redevelopment.

Urban renewal provided a useful weapon for those in power to remove those who were unpopular and less powerful. The people who had input into urban renewal plans generally were those who controlled political power, credit, and building development, not the residents of the redevelopment areas. Often, urban renewal plans were developed in secret by those who had political power, to be announced to the public only when the mechanisms for approval were well in place. This withholding of information reduced the ability of opponents to mobilize and block urban renewal plans.[19]

While the 1949 act required urban renewal projects to contain a "feasible method" for relocating persons displaced into decent, safe, and sanitary housing within the family's financial means, there was no effective enforcement mechanism.[20] Urban renewal led to the demolition of 400,000 dwelling units, while only 107,000 were built. Of these new units, only 11,000 were public housing.[21] Moreover, not until 1956 was any moving expense payment to displaced families authorized, and that was limited to the paltry sum of $100. This was increased to $200 in 1959, and in 1964 an additional $500 displacement allowance was authorized for families and elderly individuals.[22] By contrast, private developers each got the equivalent of tens of thousands of dollars in financial assistance, since public development agencies usually sold the land they had acquired to private developers for about 30 percent of their costs in obtaining, clearing, and improving the land.[23]

The enormous displacement of persons caused by urban renewal did lead eventually to the passage of the Uniform Relocation Assistance and Real Property Acquisition Act of 1970 (URA).[24] Under this legislation as it originally passed, no federally assisted project was to be undertaken unless there were satisfactory assurances that there would be relocation housing available, *prior to displacement*, to persons to be displaced owing to acquisition of property for the project. The relocation housing had to be decent, safe, and sanitary, in a neighborhood as desirable with regard to public utilities and facilities as the prior neighborhood, reasonably accessible to employment, and within the financial means of the displaced persons. Relocation advisory services had to be set up to assist persons in finding relocation housing. Any person who moved as a result of the acquisition of property for the project was entitled to certain monetary relocation benefits. A homeowner whose property was acquired for the project was entitled to receive not only the fair market value of the property but also an amount, up to a maximum of $15,000, to cover the increased mortgage and interest costs of a replacement dwelling, as well as money for closing costs. A tenant displaced by a federally funded project was entitled to receive money toward the increased rent of another apartment, up to $1,000 per year for four years. The key to coverage under the URA was that the displacement had to occur as a result of a federally funded project. Displacement because of private redevelopment was not covered in the act.

The URA was passed at the tail end of the heavy federal government involvement in urban renewal that occurred from 1949 to 1974. In 1974, Congress replaced the urban renewal program with the Community

Development Block Grant (CDBG) program, which reduced significantly direct federal involvement in central city redevelopment. Private redevelopment (albeit often with the assistance of local governments, using CDBG funds) became the primary vehicle of central city redevelopment.[25] Under the CDBG program, cities apply for federal funds to carry out community development projects. A city does not have to get each particular project approved by the federal government, as had been required under the urban renewal program. Instead, the city only has to show that its projects either principally benefit low- or moderate-income persons, aid in the prevention or elimination of slums or blight, or meet other urgent community needs. As with urban renewal, CDBG funds not infrequently have been used to aid redevelopment for the middle and upper classes, under the posture of preventing or eliminating slums or blight.

This change in the federal laws pertaining to urban redevelopment, together with court interpretations of the URA, rendered the URA inapplicable to most displacement. The Supreme Court held unanimously in 1979 that the URA applied only to displacement caused directly by acquisition of property for a project undertaken and funded by the federal government that is intended to benefit the public as a whole.[26] Thus, the Court held that displacement of tenants from a federally managed housing project was not covered by the URA. Because the displacement was not for a federal project but instead was an incidental occurrence after acquisition by HUD of the apartment building owing to default on the mortgage payments by an owner with a government-insured mortgage, the Court ruled that the URA did not apply. Other court decisions held that no URA benefits had to be given to persons displaced when a public housing project was demolished,[27] or to persons displaced by private developers rather than state agencies, even though the private developers received federal financial assistance for their redevelopment project.[28] Thus, under the CDBG program, cities could provide millions of federal dollars of aid to private redevelopment efforts that cause displacement, yet none of the persons displaced by the redevelopment would be entitled to relocation assistance under the URA, so long as a private developer was doing the displacement.

The experience of residents of the Pershing-Waterman Redevelopment area in St. Louis in the late 1970s illustrates this gap in the URA. This area of St. Louis had at least 500 families in 1976, when the city approved a redevelopment plan for the area, proposed by the Pershing Redevelopment Corporation (PRC), a private corporation organized under the Missouri statute that allows cities to grant eminent domain powers and tax abatements to limited-profit urban redevelopment corporations.[29] The ordinance approving the redevelopment plan authorized the PRC to use the Land Clearance for Redevelopment Authority of the City of

St. Louis to acquire property for the PRC; the ordinance further required the Land Reutilization Authority of the city to assemble land and buildings in the area and sell them to the PRC for a nominal price. The city also agreed to cooperate with the developer to obtain all improvements in municipal services and facilities that were consistent with the development plan, to complete all public improvements for the project, to rezone as necessary, to perform all building demolitions for the developer, and to provide park improvements requested by the developer, all at city expense. The PRC's development proposal to the city noted that the economic feasibility of the project was dependent on these steps being taken by the city for the developer. The PRC also requested, and received, twenty-five-year tax abatements from the city; an economic analysis of the proposal estimated the value of the tax abatements at $5.8 million. To aid the development project, the city not only sold 106 parcels of land held by the Land Reutilization Authority to the PRC for less than $122 per parcel and demolished nine buildings at city expense for the PRC, but it also applied for and received $1.4 million dollars in federal CDBG funds within the first three years of the project, in order to carry out the public improvements that it had agreed to do in support of the project.

The redevelopment plan called for the rehabilitation of numerous large apartment buildings, resulting in the eviction of a large number of residents. Various tactics were used to evict tenants: issuance of notices to vacate; according to trial testimony, turning off heat and other utilities; and including clauses in PRC's contracts to buy buildings that the seller-landlord would deliver the building vacant at the closing, or that the seller-landlord would issue notices to vacate to the remaining tenants and would disconnect the utilities before closing.

When residents of the Pershing-Waterman area filed suit challenging their displacement, on the grounds that they were not being provided with the relocation benefits required under the URA, the Eighth Circuit Court of Appeals held that the URA did not apply to the redevelopment project. Although the PRC had been given the city's power of eminent domain, and millions of dollars of federal CDBG money were being and would be spent in the Pershing-Waterman area to assure the success of the redevelopment project, the court held that a private redevelopment project undertaken with federal assistance was not required to follow the provisions of the URA. It held that the activities of the city and the PRC were not sufficiently intertwined to make the redevelopment project one that was covered by the URA.[30]

By interpreting the URA in such a way, the court gave the green light to cities and states to give tax breaks, powers of eminent domain, and other advantages to private redevelopers without the government or the redevelopers having to concern themselves with the requirements of the

URA. Because most displacement since 1974 has resulted from rising rents, private redevelopment projects, gentrification, and demolition/ abandonment, none of this displacement was covered by the URA— such displacement is not the direct result of a federal acquisition of property.

In 1987, in response to the problems that had surfaced with regard to the URA, Congress made some changes in the law. Now all federally assisted rehabilitation and demolition activities, as well as federally assisted acquisition, are covered by the act. While this is an improvement in the law, the law still requires that the displacement must be a "direct" result of the federally funded activity. Thus, where federal CDBG funds are used to support a private redevelopment project (as in the case of the Pershing-Waterman Redevelopment project in St. Louis), it is doubtful that persons displaced as a result of such redevelopment projects will be provided benefits under the 1987 amendments to the URA, if federal funds are not involved in that part of the project that involves displacement. Moreover, with the cutback that has taken place in federal funding for urban areas, there is much redevelopment activity that is occurring without any federal involvement. Thus, it is quite likely that the amendments to the URA will not aid those being displaced by private redevelopment activities, even if those activities are supported by local, state, and federal authorities.

The Depression years gave birth to the widespread urban renewal projects that began after World War II. After federally funded urban renewal programs had got the ball rolling in the 1950s and 1960s, displacing many residents from the central business districts, private redevelopment and gentrification continued on in the 1970s and 1980s in portions of some central cities, particularly near central business districts. Where private redevelopment is proceeding, portions of the central cities are being slowly transformed to havens for the middle- and upper-class professionals and managers who work in the administrative, executive, and financial centers that are increasingly concentrated in the central business districts of central cities. In areas of gentrification, poor and working-class residents are being forced out.[31]

PROPOSALS

Displacement is a broad concept that can refer to virtually any type of involuntary removal of persons from their homes, whether due to natural disasters, government action, or private action.[32] The immediate cause of displacement can be, as noted by Peter Marcuse, physical, economic, and/or "displacement pressure."[33] Physical displacement is displacement caused by such things as lack of one or more essential utilities, building deterioration or demolition, or displacement caused by eviction as the result of the sale of the building to a new owner who displaces the occupants. Economic displacement is that which is caused by such things as rent increases, foreclosures, and condominium conversions. Displacement pressure is the pressure to move that occurs as a neighborhood becomes less livable (because of deterioration and abandonment), less affordable, or loses social support services (through gentrification). As residents see the neighborhood going down, becoming gentrified, or friends leaving, they may move rather than wait for what they know to be the inevitable displacement to come.

Marcuse proposes that the concept of displacement, for public policy purposes, be narrowed by deleting causes that are beyond public control (e.g., natural disasters); he also proposes that it be broadened to encompass three additional categories: exclusionary displacement, chain displacement, and blocked displacement.[34] He defines exclusionary displacement as the exclusion from a housing unit of a household that previously could have moved in, due to factors beyond that household's control. For example, if rents jump in a particular area, making an area formerly affordable to lower-income persons now unaffordable, then lower-income households are the victims of exclusionary displacement. Chain displacement is the recurrent displacement of households from a single housing unit over time, for example, by recurrent rent increases. Blocked displacement is the prevention of displacement from a unit that a household would otherwise have vacated because there is no place else to move. Marcuse proposes that the definition of displacement, for public policy purposes, include not merely the direct displacement of households from property due to physical and economic factors but also off-site displacement, which he defines as displacement that occurs "when, as a result of private or public action affecting housing but not targeting the particular unit, the continued or new occupancy of that unit is made impossible, hazardous, unaffordable, or socially untenable, for a household which, but for that action, would occupy that unit."[35]

To adequately combat displacement, all of these types of displacement must be addressed by public policy: physical, economic, and "displacement pressure" displacement, exclusionary displacement, chain displacement, blocked displacement, and off-site displacement. Prior chapters of this book have made proposals that will address some of this displacement. Antidemolition laws, taking absentee-owned deteriorated housing by eminent domain, rehabilitation of public housing, and preservation of foreclosed and subsidized housing as low-income housing (see Chapter 5) will help to end physical displacement. The Social Housing Sector (Chapter 3), rent control (Chapter 4), subsidies and low-interest loan programs for low-income homeowners (Chapters 4 and 5), and resale price controls (Chapter 4) will combat economic and off-site displacement. The Housing Bank and other finance and production proposals made in Chapters 4 and 5, which will help to reduce the price of housing and increase its production, will decrease blocked displacement.

This chapter proposes several additional measures that will reduce physical displacement: strengthening of property maintenance laws, security of tenure laws, restrictions on condominium conversions, elimination of eminent domain powers for private entities, and strengthening of relocation assistance laws. Antidisplacement zoning, also proposed in this chapter, will help to combat exclusionary and off-site displacement, as well as displacement pressure.

Strengthen Property Maintenance Laws

All dwelling units should be deemed to have an implied warranty that the unit is habitable, defined as one that is in compliance with minimum housing code standards. Tenants should have the right to "repair and deduct," if a landlord refuses to repair property defects within a reasonable time after the tenants notify the landlord of the defects. That is, the tenants should have the right to proceed to repair the defects themselves, and then to deduct the cost of the repairs from their rent payments. The length of time that is reasonable for a landlord to repair defects after receiving notice would depend on the circumstances. For example, it would not be reasonable to wait a week during a heat wave before calling a repair person to fix an air-conditioning system, while it might not be unreasonable to take a month to repair some chipping paint, unless the tenant had children that might eat the paint. Should the landlord persist in refusing to do necessary repairs and the tenants be unable to afford to do the repairs, the city should have the right to do the work, and then bill the landlord for the cost, with the bill being a tax lien on the property. Failure of the landlord to pay the lien within a one-year period of time would give the municipality the right to acquire the landlord's property by eminent domain.

Security of Tenure

While security of tenure is a standard feature of most rent control laws, security of tenure laws should be enacted even where there is no rent control, to provide *all* tenants with security that they cannot be evicted except for cause. Evictions should be restricted to the following situations: (1) failure to pay rent; (2) damage or destruction of property; (3) interference with or threats to the peace, comfort, or safety of others living in the building; or (4) refusal to allow the landlord reasonable access to do repairs. In addition, the landlord should be able to recover possession of the property in two additional situations: (5) when the landlord wishes to use the unit for himself or herself or members of his or her immediate or extended family (family defined to include non-married cohabitants); or (6) when repairs necessary to maintain the property at minimum housing code standards or at its previous standard require the temporary vacation of the unit. In this last circumstance, the tenant should have the first right to rent the repaired dwelling unit at the prior rent level. This would prevent repairs from being used as a way to evict tenants in order to rehabilitate the building for a higher-income population.

Moreover, security of tenure laws should extend to members of the tenant's household upon the death of the tenant. Persons who lived with the tenant for a certain minimum period of time as part of the tenant's household should have the right to continue remaining as tenants of the apartment even after the named tenant on the lease dies. This will prevent spouses, children, lovers, and roommates from being displaced merely because the tenant listed on the lease dies.

Elimination of Eminent Domain Powers for Private Entities

Missouri is one of the few states that permit municipalities to grant the power of eminent domain to private developers. The experiences of residents in St. Louis with this grant of eminent domain power to private entities demonstrates the reason that such powers should never be delegated by the state or municipality to other entities, whether nonprofit or for-profit.

In 1978, the Midtown Medical Center Redevelopment Corporation (MMCRC), a limited-profit corporation, obtained eminent domain powers over a segment of the City of St. Louis surrounding St. Louis University's medical center. The ordinance approving the redevelopment plan provided that MMCRC could not use its eminent domain powers against those owner-occupants who were willing to rehabilitate their property, and provided for certain relocation assistance to displaced households. The residents of the development area quickly found that MMCRC used its power to make unreasonable demands for rehabilitation, requiring property owners to agree to an extensive set of restrictive covenants on the title to their property. The result of these arbitrary demands by the developer was that many owners who wished to rehabilitate their property and remain in the area would not sign a rehabilitation agreement. This then exposed the property owner to having his or her property taken by MMCRC through its power of eminent domain. The experience of the Williams family graphically illustrates this abuse.

Carl and Delores Williams were black homeowners who had purchased a twelve-room, three-story house in the Tiffany portion of the development area.[36] The house contained eight bedrooms, a living room, a dining room, a kitchen, an entertainment room, and two-and-a-half baths. In December 1980, MMCRC wrote to the Williamses, asking them to sign a letter of intent to rehabilitate their home; the Williamses signed this in February 1981. In July 1981 the Williamses entered into a $6,500 contract with a local contractor for tuckpointing, new guttering, painting, new siding in the back of their home, and several other repairs. In November 1981 MMCRC sent the Williamses a rehabilitation agreement for their signature. This rehabilitation agreement contained the following provisions that were part of all rehabilitation agreements that MMCRC sent to property owners in the development area:

3. Prior to the commencement of the contemplated rehabilitation work and in no event later than ———, 19—, the owner shall convey the Property to MMCRC by Special Warranty Deed. During the time MMCRC holds title to the property it is agreed that the Property shall be subjected to the provisions of the Tiffany Neighborhood Declaration of Covenants and Restrictions dated January 15, 1981. . . .

4. The Owner hereby agrees to indemnify and hold harmless MMCRC against any and all loss, cost or expense (including reasonable attorney's fees) occasioned by any claim arising in whole or in part out of the holding of title to the Property by MMCRC pursuant to the provisions of this Agreement or as a result of the failure of the Owner to carry out any or all of its obligations hereunder.

8. Provided that the Owner complies with all of the provisions of this Agreement and the aforementioned Declaration of Covenants and Restrictions, MMCRC agrees that it will not institute condemnation proceedings with respect to the Property.

Once the rehabilitation work was done, MMCRC would then reconvey the title to the property to the property owner, along with the twenty-five-page Declaration of Covenants and Restrictions, which then became restrictive covenants on the property.

The Declaration of Covenants and Restrictions established a Tiffany Community Association that would have control over any improvements made to property-owners' homes, even after the property owners had rehabilitated their homes. The neighborhood association created by this deed restriction was controlled by the developer: until January 1, 1983, the developer was to have two votes for every vote that property owners in the area held. The covenants also created an Architectural Control Committee, which had to approve all exterior work or changes in property in the Tiffany area, including color, height, materials, nature, and kind of work. The Tiffany Community Association was given the authority to enter the property of an owner at any time without being deemed guilty of trespass, and had the power to do exterior improvements to property and assess the costs against the property owner. The covenants further contained restrictions on pets, on the types of fences and shrubbery that property owners could install, and prohibitions against hanging laundry outside and against parking any motor vehicles on one's own property unless the vehicles were in a garage. Thus, the rehabilitation agreement that was offered to the Williamses would have placed them under the control of a neighborhood committee and allowed their property to be invaded at any time by the committee.

The rehabilitation agreement contained a work write-up detailing the rehabilitation work that MMCRC would require of the Williamses before it would be willing to release the Williamses from the threat of eminent domain. This write-up included numerous interior and aesthetic requirements in excess of the property maintenance code of the City of St. Louis: installation of new switches, plugs, and light fixtures; insulation of all duct work running through unheated spaces; privacy locks on all bathrooms; deadbolt locks on basement doors; specification as to the gloss of paint to be used for interior paint work; use of carpeting rather than any other floor covering in the interior of the Williamses' home; prior approval from MMCRC as to all exterior colors, details, materials, and scope of work; replacement of the Williamses' existing new aluminum storm windows with brown enamel storm windows (an expense itself of almost $1,000); installation of a six-foot privacy fence; installation of a colonial style solid core wood or insulated steel door, with brass kickplate and hardware, at the front of their house; use of 6'-high gold-leaf lettering to paint the Williamses' address on the transom above their front door; installation of a new six-panel colonial full light or French door with a brass lockset on the second floor front porch; and prior approval from MMCRC as to the Williamses' design plans for their porch and porch ceiling light.

The Williamses refused to sign the rehabilitation agreement unless substantial modifications were made. MMCRC refused to make any significant changes in the rehabilitation agreement.

In September 1982, MMCRC filed a petition for condemnation against the Williamses' property, which was located just a few houses away from the developer's office. In November 1982, the court granted MMCRC's petition for condemnation. In December 1982 the Williamses, who still wished to rehabilitate their home, entered into another contract for $7,600 for a new roof, a new water stack, new wood steps to the basement, and remodeling of the first- and second-floor bathrooms. In January 1983, the City of St. Louis issued the Williamses an inspection certificate certifying that the house met the property maintenance codes of the City of St. Louis. Despite the fact that the Williamses had brought their house up to at least minimum property code standards, MMCRC kept pressing forward to seize the Williamses' house from them.

In September 1983, court hearings were held on a legal challenge filed by the Williamses with regard to the condemnation order that had been entered in November 1982. After several days of court hearings on various motions, the judge ruled on December 30, 1983 that the rehabilitation agreement that MMCRC had proposed to the Williamses was proper under the redevelopment ordinance, that the condemnation of the Williamses' home was proper, and that the developer had made the requisite attempts to relocate the Williamses as required by the ordinance. The judge gave the Williamses 21 days to accept MMCRC's relocation offer, or else the judge would issue a Writ of Possession on January 31, 1984, ordering the sheriff to evict the Williamses and all their property from their home.

Refusing to cave in to the pressure, the Williamses continued to reject the relocation offer, and community organizing succeeded where legal challenges had failed: on January 30, 1984, MMCRC agreed to stop all proceedings against the Williamses and to enter into negotiations with them over the rehabilitation agreement, which is what the Williamses had been seeking for well over a year. The negotiations between the Williamses and MMCRC took five months, and final settlement was not reached until June 1984, more than two-and-a-half years after the first rehabilitation agreement had been submitted to the Williamses by MMCRC. As a result of continuing pressure from the neighborhood due to the organizing efforts of the community groups, the developer made significant concessions. The work write-up for rehabilitation deleted many of the most objectionable features, including the requirements pertaining to the interior of the house. Furthermore, the developer agreed that the Williamses did not have to make their property subject to the Declaration of Covenants and Restrictions, but only to covenants that would be established in the future that would not contain an Architectural Control Committee, or the right of access to property owners' homes. Furthermore, the Williamses would only be required to maintain their home after rehabilitation in accordance with the minimum housing code standards of the City of St. Louis, and would not be subject to higher standards set by the developer.

While the Williams family eventually won their fight, it was only after considerable stress, expense, and community organizing, and the victory occurred despite, rather than because of, the judicial system. While limiting the grant of eminent domain powers to governmental bodies does not ensure that eminent domain power will not be abused, government bodies are, at least, more subject to democratic control than are nongovernmental developers. Therefore, laws granting eminent domain powers to private or nonprofit developers should be repealed.

Restrictions on Condominium Conversions

There should be restrictions or prohibitions on condominium conversions to prevent tenants from being displaced by landlords who wish to convert their properties to for-sale units. A landowner wishing to convert rental property should be required to notify the local government, and to apply for a permit. The local government and other entities that are part of the Social Housing Sector then should have the first right to buy the property from the landlord, for an amount equal to the original investment that the landlord made in the property, payments made on the mortgage principal, and the value of improvements, plus a small return on the original investment. Only if the option were not exercised would a landowner be able to convert. Alternatively, conversion of rental units to condominiums should be prohibited, unless at least two-thirds of the tenants in the building consent to such conversion, and unless all tenants in the building who cannot buy a condominium are given the alternative of either receiving the relocation assistance detailed in the following section or being allowed to remain in the unit as a tenant at the previous rent.

Strengthening of Relocation Assistance Laws

A relocation assistance law needs to be in place to provide a disincentive for displacement, by making those who displace others bear the full cost of such displacement. If developers and cities had to pay all the costs associated with displacement and had to ensure that redevelopment plans included relocation dwelling units, it is likely that redevelopment plans would change substantially and would result in plans that require much less, if any, displacement.

In addition, since there will be situations where necessary public works will require that some people be displaced, relocation assistance needs to be in place for those occasions. Displacement should not be allowed as part of a public works project, however, unless four conditions are met:

1. The public works project is essential for the welfare of the community;
2. Members of the neighborhood facing dislocation were involved in the development of the public works project;
3. There is no way to accomplish the public project without displacement; and
4. All the provisions of the relocation law proposed here are complied with.

The federal Uniform Relocation Act should be amended to add the protections listed below to the provisions of the existing law. All relocation laws, whether state or local, should contain at least these protections, as well as those in the current law.

Definition of Displaced Person. A displaced person entitled to protection under the URA should be any person who moves as a result of redevelopment, rehabilitation, demolition, or code-enforcement activities carried out by any federal, state, or local agency (including a private entity with power of eminent domain), by any entity receiving financial assistance from any governmental unit, or by any entity operating under an order or agreement of any government unit. Thus, any entity receiving any type of government assistance, operating in accordance with a government-approved redevelopment, rehabilitation, demolition, or code-enforcement plan, or having the power of eminent domain, would be obligated to follow the requirements of the relocation law, regardless of the source of funds used for displacement.

This definition of displaced person will prevent courts from refusing to apply the relocation law to developers simply because government funds were not used in the displacement, or on the basis that the federally funded project is separate from the displacing project. It will also extend relocation protections to those threatened with displacement by state- or locally funded or supported activities.

Infirm Persons. No displacement of those who are likely to deteriorate physically as a result of a move (for example, an elderly person likely to experience "transfer trauma" from a move) should be permitted, unless the dwelling unit has been declared unhealthy or unsafe by local authorities.

Replacement Housing. Before anyone is displaced, decent, affordable, and accessible replacement housing should be required to be made available within the redevelopment area for those to be displaced. If there is not sufficient replacement housing in the area, then the government or developer will have to build such replacement housing before displacement occurs. For homeowners facing displacement, the developer should be required to ensure that there are replacement homes to buy within the redevelopment area that are decent, affordable, accessible, and comparable in size and amenities to the homeowner's prior home before any homeowner can be displaced.

Relocation Expenses. Developers should be required to pay for all the actual reasonable moving expenses of the displaced family, to ensure that persons being displaced are not required to bear any of the financial cost of moving. In addition to moving expenses, all displaced persons should receive a substantial dislocation allowance as partial compensation for the trauma of moving. Upon displacement, the developer also should have to pay for all the medical, nursing, and counseling services necessary for the household's relocation. For example, if a handicapped or elderly person is displaced, he or she may need special nursing or medical services during the displacement and adjustment to the new housing unit.

Homeowners' Compensation for Taking of Property. A homeowner whose property is taken by eminent domain should be entitled to receive as fair market value for the property the *greater* of the following: (a) the value of the property at the time that the government or developer first announced that the area in which the property is located is proposed for blighting or redevelopment, or (b) the value of the property on the date the property is acquired by eminent domain. This would prevent the developer from benefiting from the decrease in market values that often occurs after an area of a city is designated for blighting. Where a municipality has resale price controls in effect (see Chapter 4), the homeowner should, despite the resale price controls, be able to keep the entire fair market value of the property, as a type of further compensation to the displaced homeowner. In addition, a homeowner should be entitled to such further compensation as is necessary to keep the homeowner's monthly housing expenditures no higher than they were prior to displacement, as well as payment for all closing costs, points, and other costs associated with purchasing a decent replacement home comparable to the one taken.

Housing Bank Loans. Tenants and homeowners to be displaced should have first priority for the receipt of Housing Bank loans for the purchase of replacement homes.

Illegal Evictions of Tenants. Tenants evicted in violation of security of tenure laws, or forced out by utility service shut-offs by the landlord or by the unlivable condition of the building, should be entitled to moving expenses and dislocation allowances from the landlord. Because the landlord in such a situation may refuse to make these payments to the tenants, the municipality should be required to pay these sums to the displaced tenants, with the owner of the building then being liable to the municipality for the sums paid to the tenants. Such liability could be collected either by direct suit against the landlord or by lien on the property.

Displacement Compensation Not Income. Any payments received by a homeowner or tenant under the relocation act should not be considered income or resources for purposes of the Internal Revenue Code or any public assistance program. This would ensure that those displaced do not have to pay taxes on their compensation and that they would not lose, or be unable to qualify for, public assistance benefits because of the compensation.

Private Right of Action. Any displaced person or person about to be displaced (as defined under the act) should have a cause of action against the party responsible for the displacement, to enforce compliance with the law. Courts should have the obligation to issue not only injunctive relief and compensation where proper but also attorney's fees and court costs to the prevailing plaintiff, as well as prejudgment interest from the date the person became entitled to relocation benefits. If the party responsible for displacement is not a governmental body, then the displaced person should also have a cause of action against the municipal, state, or federal government that has approved or ordered the displacing activity. Making the government liable, even if the government is not the displacing entity, would give governments a vested interest in ensuring that redevelopment projects comply with all laws. It would also provide displaced persons with the assurance that they can get the protection and compensation to which they are entitled, in the event that a developer goes out of business or into bankruptcy.

Antidisplacement Zoning

While the proposed changes in the Uniform Relocation Act would impose certain responsibilities on those who directly cause displacement, the following proposal for an antidisplacement zoning law would attack the problem of exclusionary displacement, off-site displacement, and displacement pressure in gentrifying neighborhoods.

Under the antidisplacement zoning law, which is based on a model law developed by Peter Marcuse,[37] a municipality would designate certain neighborhoods as ones in which residents are likely to face displacement should new construction or rehabilitation occur in those neighborhoods without any controls. In such neighborhoods, before a contractor or builder could build or rehabilitate (other than rehabilitation necessary to maintain minimum property code standards), he or she would have to apply to the zoning commission for an antidisplacement construction permit. Such a permit would be issued only if the number of low- and moderate-income rental units in any structure affected by the construction would not be decreased by the construction project. Moreover, in areas that are already highly developed, a permit should be issued only if three additional conditions are met: (1) there will be an increase in the number of low- and moderate-income units after the construction; (2) there will be no displacement of existing residents (except if a structure is vacated because it is a safety hazard); and (3) there will be no demolition unless the structure has been declared unsafe by the city. Any persons displaced from a hazardous building should be entitled to the relocation assistance and financial benefits provided by the relocation act proposed above.

There should be procedures in such an ordinance for a neighborhood to be designated as an antidisplacement zone. The types of construction or rehabilitation permitted in different antidisplacement zones could vary depending on the extent of existing development in the zone, and the economic characteristics of persons living in the area.

Antidisplacement laws should be seen as a last layer of protection for tenants and homeowners. If many of the other proposals made in this book were adopted, the amount of displacement should decrease substantially. In that case, antidisplacement laws would be used rarely, not because they are irrelevant to the type of displacement occurring but because the amount of displacement would be negligible. Antidisplacement laws are not the panacea for the problem of displacement. Rather, they are a strong deterrent to displacement and a way of providing adequately for those who are displaced.

Chapter 8

Legal Issues and Financing Mechanisms

Two questions remain concerning the housing platform: are the proposals consistent with the Constitution and existing legal standards, and are there realistic methods of financing the proposals? The answer to both questions is Yes.

CONSTITUTIONAL CONSIDERATIONS

Taking of Property for a Public Purpose

The Fifth Amendment to the United States Constitution, made applicable to the states by the Fourteenth Amendment, prohibits the taking of private property for public use without just compensation. The purpose of the Fifth Amendment is to prevent the government from forcing some people to bear burdens that should be borne by the public as a whole. Thus, where a court finds that property has been taken for a public use, within the meaning of the Constitution, the court will require that compensation be paid to the property owner. If a court finds that a proposed taking of property is merely for a private purpose, it will hold the taking to be invalid. Ever since the courts found urban renewal projects to be constitutional in the 1930s (see Chapter 7), they have consistently upheld the constitutionality of laws that promote housing or urban development, as within the police power of the state, provided that owners were paid just compensation for property taken for the project.

Perhaps the broadest endorsement of governmental power to control property ownership in the interest of the public is the 1984 decision of the United States Supreme Court in *Hawaii Housing Authority v Midkiff*.[1] In that case, the Court considered the constitutionality of Hawaii's Land Reform Act of 1967, which provides for the redistribution of Hawaiian land from landlords to tenants. The act had been passed because only seventy-two private landowners controlled 47 percent of Hawaiian land, and the rest of the Hawaiian population controlled only 4 percent (the federal and state government controlled the remaining 49 percent of the land). The Hawaiian state legislature concluded that land redistribution was required in order to eliminate concentrated land ownership. The Land Reform Act allows tenants on single-family residential lots within development tracts of at least five acres to ask the Hawaiian Housing Authority to condemn the land. Once either 25 tenants or half the tenants on a tract, whichever is fewer, request condemnation, the Housing Authority is required to hold a public hearing to determine if condemnation would carry out the purpose of the Land Reform Act. If the Housing Authority finds acquisition to be appropriate, then the Housing Authority pays to the landowner the price that is set at a condemnation trial, or the price that is negotiated between the landlord and the tenants. The Housing Authority can then sell the land to the tenants, although it can not sell more than one lot to any one tenant.

The Court of Appeals held the Land Reform Act to be unconstitutional, on the grounds that the taking of land from the landowners was not for a public purpose but solely for the benefit of private tenants, in violation of the requirement that private property be taken only for public use. However, the United States Supreme Court reversed the appellate court and upheld the constitutionality of the Land Reform Act in an 8–0 decision. Justice O'Connor wrote:

To be sure, the Court's cases have repeatedly stated that "one person's property may not be taken for the benefit of another private person without a justifying public purpose, even though compensation be paid." . . . But where the exercise of eminent domain power is rationally related to a conceivable public purpose, the Court has never held a compensated taking to be proscribed by the Public Use Clause. . . .

On this basis, we have no trouble concluding that the Hawaii Act is constitutional. The people of Hawaii have attempted . . . to reduce the perceived social and economic evils of a land oligopoly. . . . The land oligopoly has, according to the Hawaii Legislature, created artificial deterrents to the normal functioning of the State's residential land market and forced thousands of individual homeowners to lease, rather than buy, the land underneath their homes. Regulating oligopoly and the evils associated with it is a classic exercise of a State's police powers. . . .

Nor can we condemn as irrational the Act's approach to correcting the land oligopoly problem. The Act presumes that when a sufficiently large number of persons declare that they are willing but unable to buy lots at fair prices the land market is malfunctioning. When such a malfunction is signalled, the Act authorizes HHA [Hawaiian Housing Authority] to condemn lots in the relevant tract. The Act limits the number of lots any one tenant can purchase and authorizes HHA to use public funds to ensure that the market dilution goals will be achieved. This is a comprehensive and rational approach to identifying and correcting market failure.[2]

Because it found that the Land Reform Act was not passed to benefit a particular class of people but rather to attack the evils of concentrated land ownership, the Supreme Court held that the act was constitutional.

Thus, the Hawaiian land reform case, together with the unanimous Supreme Court decision in *Berman v Parker* upholding Washington, D.C.'s redevelopment law that allowed the city's redevelopment authority to sell land acquired through eminent domain to private parties (discussed in Chapter 7), make it clear that there is no prohibition in the Federal Constitution against state or local governments taking private property where it is necessary to correct social injustice. There are just two constitutional requirements that must be met: (1) the taking must not be *solely* for the *purpose* of benefiting private persons (although private persons may in fact benefit from the taking); and (2) the property owner must be given "just compensation" for the property taken.[3]

Accordingly, the proposals made in this book to permit local or state governments to take property by eminent domain from landlords who fail to pay taxes or to maintain their property, or who discriminate, would pass constitutional muster, as would provisions that give priority for the resale of such property to entities in the Social Housing Sector.

Economic Regulation

While the Constitution requires compensation for the taking of private property for a public use, the Supreme Court has upheld *noncompensated* economic *regulation*, including zoning and land use regulation, when done for the general health, safety, morals, or welfare of the population. Such economic regulation falls within the police power of the state.[4] In general, so long as a public program is adopted to adjust the "benefits and burdens of economic life to promote the common good," land use regulation will be upheld by the courts. Such regulation will be upheld even if the regulation reduces the profits that a property owner could make from the property without regulation.[5] Thus, courts have upheld zoning laws that restrict the use of land and building height, requirements that certain parcels of land be left undeveloped, and historical landmark designations that impose certain requirements on the owners of buildings so designated. If, however, the economic regulation is so severe as to almost completely destroy the owner's right to an economically viable use of the property, or the regulation amounts to a permanent physical "occupation" of the property owner's property, then the courts will find that such regulation is, in fact, a taking of the property and will require that compensation be paid to the property owner.[6] Where the courts draw the line between permissible economic regulation (with no compensation) and an unlawful taking of property without just compensation depends on the type of attempted regulation, as well as the political climate of the country.

Landlord-Tenant Regulation. The application of these principles has been hotly contested in the area of regulation of the landlord-tenant relationship. In evaluating rent control laws, the key issue for the courts has been whether or not the laws amount to a taking of the landlord's property without compensation. This issue arises in several areas of rent control laws: standards for rent increases, security of tenure, and restrictions on condominium conversions and demolitions.

Rent control laws must provide mechanisms whereby landlords can receive a fair return on their *investment*, or else such laws will be held to be unconstitutional on the grounds that they constitute a taking of property without compensation. Rent control laws do not, however, have to provide for a return on the *value* of the property, nor do landlords have a right to recover for imprudent investments or inflated operating costs.[7]

In 1988, in *Pennell v City of San Jose*, the United States Supreme Court upheld a rent control law that included, in its factors to be considered in evaluating a request for a rent increase, the hardship to the tenant if an increase were granted.[8] The rent control law in that case allowed for automatic rent increases of up to 8 percent. If the landlord wished to raise rent more than 8 percent and the tenant objected, then a hearing officer of the rent control board had to determine if the landlord's request for a higher increase was "reasonable under the circumstances." The hearing officer was to use seven factors in determining whether or not the requested increase was warranted: (1) cost of debt service, (2) rent history of the unit, (3) physical condition, (4) changes in housing services provided, (5) other financial information provided by the landlord, (6) market value of rents for similar units, and (7) economic and financial hardship to the tenants. A landlord group challenged the requirement that tenant hardship be considered in determining whether or not to approve the rent increase. They argued that allowing the rent control board to reduce rent to below the level determined by the first six factors amounted to a transfer of the landlord's property involuntarily to hardship tenants, and thus constituted a taking of the landlord's property without compensation. The Supreme Court refused to strike down the tenant hardship provisions. It held that protection of tenants is a legitimate goal of rent control. Further, it held that, in this case, the tenant hardship provisions were a rational attempt to protect tenants from burdensome rent increases, while guaranteeing landlords a fair return on their investment.

Thus, under the present state of the law, hardship to tenants that would be caused by rent increases is a legitimate factor that can be used in determining rent increases, provided that the law allows for a reasonable return on the landlord's investment. If a rent control law would prevent landlords from earning a fair return on their investment, then such a law will almost certainly be struck down by the courts as an unlawful taking of the landlord's property.[9]

With regard to the question of security of tenure, restrictions on evictions of tenants by landlords generally do not raise any constitutional issues. Such laws must, however, allow for eviction when the owner wishes to recover the premises for occupancy by himself or herself or for family members. Such security of tenure legislation has been held to be within the police power of the states.[10]

Prohibitions of condominium conversions and demolitions are important adjuncts to rent control laws and are often necessary, as well, to preserve the stock of rental housing. As with rent control and security of tenure laws, these laws have been attacked on Fifth Amendment grounds by property owners, who claim that such prohibitions amount to a taking of property by the state without compensation, because the owner's ability to control and dispose of the property is restricted. Most courts that have considered these issues have upheld laws restricting condominium conversions and demolitions, on one or more of the following grounds: (1) that the laws do not deprive the owners of all beneficial use of the property and therefore do not amount to a taking, because they can still earn a return on their investment; (2) that the owners had notice of the restrictions before they bought their units and therefore the restrictions do not interfere with the owners' expectations as to the use of their property; (3) that the burden on the owners' liberty interests is indirect and minimal; or (4) by deferring to the legislature's balancing of the interests.[11]

In *Nash v City of Santa Monica*,[12] the California Supreme Court upheld the constitutionality of a Santa Monica ordinance that required a landlord to obtain a permit before converting or demolishing a housing unit. A permit could be granted only if three conditions were met: (1) the building were not occupied by low- or moderate-income households and could not be afforded by such households; (2) removal would not adversely affect the housing supply; and (3) the owner could not make a reasonable return on investment as a landlord. A speculator who wished to demolish his apartment building and hold the land vacant claimed that this law prohibited him from going out of business as a landlord and therefore restricted his rights. He claimed an absolute right to demolish the building, as owner of the building. The court disagreed. The court held that the law was constitutional as a valid land-use regulation, because the landlord was able to earn a fair return on his investment; alternatively, the owner could sell the property and reinvest the proceeds elsewhere.

Not all courts, however, have upheld restrictions on the disposition of property, some finding that such restrictions infringe on a fundamental right of ownership.[13] The proposal for first right of refusal to the Social Housing Sector when a landlord wishes to convert rental property therefore is likely to face a challenge from landlords, on the grounds that such a law appropriates the owner's right to sell property to persons of his or her own choice. The proposal for first right of refusal would, however, guarantee to the property owner a fair return on his or her investment; it merely would prevent profits from being made on increases in market value that were not the result of improvements by the property owner. Based on Supreme Court rulings, such laws should, in most cases, be found to be constitutional. The Supreme Court has long since upheld the right of the nation to regulate property owners in the use and disposition of their property. The Court has upheld antidiscrimination laws, fire regulations, rent control, and mortgage moratoria, all of which have been challenged on the grounds that they restrict owners' use and disposition of their property.[14] As the Court stated recently, " . . . States have broad power to regulate housing conditions in general and the landlord-tenant relationship in particular without paying compensation for all economic injuries that such regulation entails."[15] Moreover, since the property owner could not have predicted future changes in market value at the time of original purchase of the property, such a restriction on resale does not diminish the owner's original expectation of earnings. Some state courts may, however, strike down such laws on the grounds that they interfere with the owner's right to dispose of property. For example, in *Gregory v City of San Juan Capistrano*, a California appellate court struck down a city ordinance that gave mobile home park residents the first right of refusal to purchase the park, on the grounds that the law appropriated the owner's right to sell property to persons of his own choice.[16]

Thus, while the demolition and condominium conversion restrictions proposed in Chapters 5 and 7 should be constitutional in most states, it would be important to study the laws in the particular state where such legislation is proposed, to ensure that the courts would not strike down the laws. In states where such restrictions would be struck down as an unconstitutional restriction on the property owner's right to dispose of his or her property, state legislatures may need to pass laws authorizing municipalities to take property sought to be demolished or converted by property owners by eminent domain (in which case the city would have to pay full fair market value) and then resell the property into the Social Housing Sector.

With regard to proposals to allow tenants to withhold rent if the apartment needs repairs, such laws would face no viable legal challenge. In some states, in the absence of legislation from the legislature, courts have found an implied warranty that urban rental housing units are fit for occupancy, and have judicially allowed tenants to sue for damages or cancellation of the lease, or to withhold rent, where the premises did not meet minimum code. Some courts also have prohibited eviction where the tenant was able to prove that the eviction suit was brought in retaliation for the tenant complaining to public authorities concerning the condition of the building.[17]

Those drafting rent control, condominium conversion, demolition conversion, or security of tenure legislation will need to study carefully the law and court decisions in their own states before determining how to formulate the law. Moreover, since some state laws preempt local rent control and condominium conversion regulation, state laws need to be examined if a campaign is planned for a municipality, to ensure that the local laws would not be preempted by state laws.[18] It is apparent, however, that most legislative enactments proposed in the area of restriction on landlords' rights will be upheld if carefully drafted, provided municipal regulation is not preempted by state law. If municipal regulation is preempted, then the state legislature would be the only body that could adopt laws to regulate the issue that is preempted.

Antispeculation Laws. Several proposals in this book have the purpose of reducing or eliminating speculative profits in real estate, so that housing prices and rents will stabilize. These proposals include resale price controls (Chapter 4), antispeculation capital gains taxes (Chapter 4), and requirements that owners of subsidized housing sell their property to the Social Housing Sector if they wish to terminate their subsidy contracts (Chapter 5).

The determination by the courts as to whether or not such laws are valid will depend on how the laws are characterized by the courts—as a taking of property, or as a regulation of property. The antispeculation tax is least likely to be struck down, as there is a long tradition of taxing long-term and short-term capital gains differently, and of taxing different types of property differently. Resale price control laws also should be upheld, just as rent control laws have been upheld, for they allow the property owner to obtain a fair return on his or her initial down payment and to recover the cost of any improvements (less depreciation) made to the land or property. Moreover, since property owners would buy property with full knowledge of the controls, such controls do not interfere with the property owner's reasonable expectations as to their return on investment.

The third antispeculation proposal is that owners of subsidized housing who wish to terminate their contracts with the government be required to sell their property for a fair return on their investment to the Social Housing Sector. The Emergency Low Income Housing Preservation Act of 1987, which imposed a virtual two-year moratorium on the termination of subsidized housing contracts in the Section 8 New Construction, Section 221(d)(3), and Section 236 programs, has already been subjected to challenge by a property owner. The owner asserted that the law impaired the federal government's contract with the property owner and that the law amounted to a taking of property without compensation. In December 1988, the District Court for the Eastern District of Illinois rejected these contentions.[19] It held that the Contract Clause of the Constitution, which prohibits states from impairing the obligation of contracts, applies only to state governments, not to the federal government. It further held that congressional legislation designed to adjust the burdens and benefits of economic life is presumed to be constitutional. With regard to the argument that the law amounted to a taking of property without compensation, the court held that the federal government has the sovereign power to enact legislation affecting its contracts, and that such regulation of contracts does not amount to a taking. Thus, *federal* laws restricting the disposition of subsidized housing should not be found to be unconstitutional. State laws restricting property owners' ability to terminate their contracts or restricting their disposition of the property might be found to violate the Contracts Clause or state constitutions. Therefore, federal legislation in this area is essential, in order to avoid such laws from being struck down by the courts.

Criminal Forfeiture

Chapter 5 proposes that landlords who discriminate should be subject to forfeiture of their property after conviction for discrimination. The federal criminal code has forfeiture provisions requiring the forfeiture of property used or acquired in racketeering activities, and the Supreme Court has upheld this law as a legitimate attack by Congress on the economic roots of organized crime.[20] Congressional passage of a criminal forfeiture law making forfeiture of the property involved in discrimination a consequence of conviction for housing discrimination should therefore be upheld. Since criminal statutes require proof of guilt beyond a reasonable doubt before there can be a conviction (and hence any forfeiture), the criminal forfeiture provisions probably would be rarely invoked. In those particularly egregious cases of misconduct by property owners, however, the criminal law should be used, in addition to any civil suits for discrimination, so that the state does not have to pay any compensation for the property acquired: the forfeiture would be part of the criminal penalty to which the property owner was subject.

FINANCING MECHANISMS

The funds to finance the production of low-income housing, as well as the subsidies that will be necessary for those families that cannot pay adequate rents, can come from several sources. At the federal level, there are two sources that could provide billions in dollars each year for housing programs: the military budget and the mortgage interest and property tax deductions. At the state and local level, revenue sources could include payments received from resale price controls, capital gains taxes, real estate transfer taxes, linkage programs, and requirements that tax-exempt organizations deposit part of their funds into the Housing Bank.

The Military Budget

The most obvious source of funding for low- and moderate-cost housing is the military budget, for military spending not only is far greater than conceivably necessary for defense of the country but itself contributes to the housing crisis. The United States already has sufficient nuclear weapons to destroy the Soviet Union (and the world) several times over and needs no further nuclear weapons.[21] While the 1977 military budget was $100 billion, eleven years later, the 1988 military budget totaled $292 billion. Even with inflation of almost 100 percent during that period, this was a substantial real increase in the military budget. This budget could be cut in half, by eliminating production of first-strike nuclear weapons and funding for the Strategic Defense Initiative (SDI) ($27 billion), reducing intervention in Third World countries ($72 billion), reducing forces for war in Europe ($44 billion), ending funding for biological and chemical weapons ($1 billion), and cutting the CIA budget ($2 billion).[22] Cutting the budget in half would still leave close to $150 billion for the military. Given the fact that the country has had an unprecedented amount of military spending in the past decade, the military budget could undoubtedly be cut even further.[23] However, assuming that the amount of reduction in the military budget were $146 billion and assuming that a substantial portion of the cut would be redirected to programs other than housing or to deficit reduction, the Women's International League has calculated that there still could be $28 billion to be directed to housing programs on an annual basis.[24] This would be in addition to the amounts of money that are already budgeted for housing.

Not only would transferring military money to housing production directly result in more housing being built for low- and moderate-income persons, or more direct subsidies being available for lower-income households, but a reduction in the military budget would have positive effects on the economy as a whole, with positive spin-off effects on housing. This is because military spending has had an adverse effect on the U.S. economy, contributing to a huge deficit, high interest rates, inflation, and unemployment.

The Deficit. The bloated deficit, caused in large part by the inflated military budget, requires that the federal government borrow money to finance its military budget. The government's demand for money causes interest rates to remain high,[25] resulting, in the case of housing, in reduced construction. In addition, as the national debt increases, a greater and greater proportion of the federal budget is spent paying interest on the debt rather than on socially productive programs.

Inflation. Not only does the military budget contribute to high interest rates, placing inflationary pressures on the economy, but the military payroll itself is inflationary. Persons hired in the military sector of the economy use their earnings to buy more consumer goods; since the military does not produce consumer goods, this increases the demand for consumer goods relative to supply, thereby increasing the price of consumer goods. Moreover, corporations that have military contracts have no incentive to keep their costs down, as they operate on a "cost-plus" basis with the Pentagon. Accordingly, they can outbid civilian corporations for raw materials, because they can pay almost any amount to acquire scarce materials. This, in turn, causes prices of these materials to rise for civilian industries.[26] Thus, military spending is inherently inflationary.

Unemployment. The shifting of federal dollars from social service to military expenditures results in a net *loss* of jobs in the economy. Ten billion dollars spent on the military creates 54,000 to 99,000 fewer jobs than $10 billion spent on civilian programs (depending on the type of military spending),[27] or, put another way, when $10 billion is switched from civilian to military spending, 54,000 to 99,000 jobs are lost. To take only construction as an example, in 1979 one billion dollars spent on construction created 42,718 jobs, whereas one billion dollars spent on the military created only 25,983 jobs.[28] Moreover, when one billion *more* dollars were spent on the military, $114 million *fewer* dollars were spent on residential construction. With fewer dollars spent on housing construction, fewer carpenters, bricklayers, plasterers, electricians, plumbers, and painters are hired, creating a negative ripple effect in the economy, as those persons have smaller disposable incomes to spend on other goods.[29]

In short, redirection of military spending to spending on housing not only will directly cause housing production to rise but will indirectly aid the construction industry by helping to reduce interest rate and inflationary pressures and by increasing employment in construction. Moreover, a redirection of the military budget toward social needs could be expected to generate billions of additional consumer dollars for housing.

Homeowner Tax Deductions

Should the redirection of the military budget not be a sufficient source of funds, Congress could also make reductions in the tax deductions currently allowed to homebuyers who itemize their deductions. Currently, each year, taxpayers pay about $50 billion in fewer federal taxes than they would otherwise owe, due to the mortgage interest and real estate tax deductions allowed to taxpayers who itemize, and the capital gains deferral and exclusion allowed to homeowners. Of these deductions, the mortgage interest tax deduction results in the largest amount of lost revenue, $32 to $35 billion per year. The property tax deduction accounts for an additional $10 to $11 billion in lost revenues each year.[30] While fewer than half of all taxpayers take the mortgage interest deduction, either because they can not itemize their deductions or because they have no mortgage interest to deduct, in 1984, 26.3 million taxpayers paid an average of $889 in lower taxes as a result of claiming the mortgage interest deduction.[31]

For starters, the real estate tax deduction could be eliminated, saving over $10 billion per year. Moreover, the mortgage interest deduction could be made both fairer and less costly to the government by allowing all those who pay mortgage interest to claim a tax credit equal to 28 percent of the mortgage interest paid, up to $200 maximum credit. (The 28 percent figure was used because this is the tax bracket of most working-class and middle-class homeowners.) This credit would be fairer, because it would not be limited to those who are able to itemize their deductions but would be available as a credit to all who pay mortgage interest. In addition, the proposed credit would result in less tax revenue lost due to the mortgage interest deduction, as no taxpayer could reduce his or her tax obligation through the mortgage interest deduction by more than $200. The tax loss each year from the mortgage interest deduction would be reduced by at least $20 billion, from over $32 billion at present to approximately $11 billion (56 million homeowning taxpayers times $200 per taxpayer = $11 billion).[32] In fact, the tax loss would probably be reduced by more than $20 billion, as not all taxpayers would be able to

156   The Urban Housing Crisis

take the maximum credit of $200. Moreover, if the Housing Bank were established as proposed in Chapter 4, with low-interest loans being made available to homebuyers, then the tax loss from the mortgage interest deduction would be even less, since the amount of interest payments on mortgages would decrease substantially. These tax savings from reduction or deletion of the real estate tax and mortgage interest tax deductions could be dedicated to the development and preservation of low- and moderate-income housing.[33]

Alternative but less substantial methods of reducing the amount of tax revenue lost as a result of homeowner tax deductions would result in the following savings annually: limiting the mortgage interest deduction to 15 percent of interest paid ($10.1 billion); taxing 30 percent of the capital gains from the sale of a home ($5.4 billion); taxing capital gains at death ($4 billion); or limiting the mortgage interest deduction to $12,000 for a single person or $20,000 for a couple ($2 billion).[34]

State and Local Sources

While federal funding must be the primary source of funding for housing, for the reason that the federal budget is far more able to pay for housing needs than state and local budgets, state and local governments can raise money for housing in a variety of ways. A key standard in selecting the method to raise money at a local and state level should be the criterion that the funding methods should not burden low- and moderate-income homeowners. Thus, the proposals made below have all been selected because they do not impose further economic hardship on low- and moderate-income households. By contrast, proposals to raise real estate rates generally, to increase recording fees for all real estate transactions, or to use interest earned on mortgage escrow accounts to help fund housing trust funds should all be rejected, because they would increase the financial burdens on low- and moderate-income homebuyers. Without increasing the burden on such households, state and local governments can raise money for housing.

Resale Price Controls. If resale price controls are adopted, the local government would receive funds from buyers upon the purchase of land under resale price controls, whenever the value of land had increased since the prior owner had purchased the land. The funds raised from this source would, presumably, diminish over the years, if housing and land prices stabilize as a result of the controls. In the early years of a Housing Bank, however, such funds could be an important source of capitalization for such a bank.

Capital Gains Tax. The antispeculation capital gains tax proposed in Chapter 4 would also generate income for a state and the revenues from such a tax could be ear-marked for housing.

Real Estate Transfer Tax. The state or local government could establish a percentage tax on all real estate transfers on the value of property transferred above a certain minimum, say $150,000, with the funds received from the tax earmarked for low- and moderate-income housing production. By limiting the transfer tax to higher-priced property, only upper-middle-class and upper-class taxpayers would be required to pay the transfer tax. State laws would need to be examined, however, to ensure that the local government has authority under state law to impose such a tax. Otherwise, a campaign would first have to be mounted to amend state law to grant such authority to local governments.

Linkage Programs. Local governments may be able to require developers of office and commercial space either to build housing or to contribute a fee to the Housing Bank, ear-marked for low- and moderate-income housing loans, as a condition of receiving approval for the development. This method of raising funds, normally referred to as "linkage programs," will only work in a municipality that has a strong real estate market; in municipalities lacking a strong demand for new commercial development, such a linkage program either will drive away developers, or will be irrelevant because there are no interested developers.[35]

In a city where such a linkage program is economically feasible, a legal evaluation will have to be made as to whether or not such a program would be struck down by the courts. If the court views the linkage program as simply a type of economic regulation, then normally a linkage program will be upheld, provided that the type of obligations imposed on the developer are not so burdensome as to make it impossible for the developer to make use of the land (in which case it would amount to an unconstitutional taking of property without compensation). If, as is more common, a court believes that the linkage program is an "exaction," that is, a contribution by the developer to obtain approval, then the issue becomes whether or not there is a rational or substantial relationship between the municipality's interest in affordable housing and the commercial development in question. Courts generally will allow fees to be imposed that bear a substantial relationship to improvements. For example, it is common for suburban developers to have to pay fees (exactions) to cover the costs of sewer and water system expansion that is required by a new development.

The legal issue in a linkage program becomes whether or not a commercial development has a clear relationship to the housing problem. The legal argument in support of linkage programs is that commercial development creates a need for affordable housing for the workers who will be employed by such a development. Therefore, the linkage program is substantially related to meeting the need for housing that is generated by the development. Opposition to linkage programs centers on the claim that such programs are not exactions at all but instead are

But Boston has enabling legal.

taxes. Since specific authority to tax must exist before a municipality can tax, linkage programs will be struck down if a court finds that it is neither legitimate economic regulation under the police power nor an exaction, but instead a tax, and that there is no specific legislative authority for such a tax.[36] Since linkage programs are very new, these legal issues have yet to be definitely resolved by the courts.

Deposit Requirements. Tax-exempt organizations and institutions could be required to deposit all or a certain percentage of their assets over $1 million in the Housing Bank. This would help to ensure adequate funds in the bank for housing loans.

This book has called for the establishment of a Housing Bank that would provide low-interest loans to persons buying homes and to home-builders, with the interest rates lower for those constructing housing in the Social Housing Sector. Resale price controls, antispeculation laws, and, where necessary, rent control would be used to stabilize housing prices. Absentee property owners who fail to maintain their property, who fail to pay their taxes, and who discriminate would all face loss of their property and transfer of ownership into the Social Housing Sector. Inclusionary housing programs are proposed to ensure the production of adequate quantities of lower-priced housing. Where such programs are insufficient to accomplish the task, production by local government should be mandated. Federal financing for such production programs is essential to guarantee their feasibility, as well as federal funds to train persons in development of the Social Housing Sector. Strengthening of antidiscrimination laws, stronger enforcement of such laws and broadening of the laws to prohibit discrimination based on family composition and sexual orientation are all essential to ensure the availability of adequate affordable housing to all people without regard to their membership in a minority group, or, in the case of women, without regard to their sex. To reduce the extensive displacement that is occurring in urban areas, the book proposes security of tenure laws, restrictions on demolitions and condominium conversions, restrictions on displacement for developments claimed to be for the benefit of the general public, and stronger relocation assistance laws.

The financial mechanisms exist to solve the housing crisis, and there are no serious federal constitutional impediments to adopting the housing platform proposed in this book. What is needed is the political will to adopt the legislation that will ensure that the housing problem will be solved. It is hoped that this book has been one step in the process of developing housing policies that will achieve true and lasting reforms.

Notes

CHAPTER 1

1. The U.S. Bureau of the Census (hereafter U.S. Census Bureau), "Selected Housing Costs—Renter Occupied Units," *American Housing Survey for the United States in 1985* (hereafter, *1985 American Housing Survey*), Current Housing Reports, No. H–150–85 (Washington D.C.: U.S. Government Printing Office, 1988) gives a figure of 8.16 million tenant households below the poverty line, with 5.46 million not receiving any subsidies; Cushing Dolbeare, *Low Income Housing Needs* (Washington, D.C.: National Low Income Housing Coalition, 1987), p.17, gives a figure of 7.5 million renter households below the poverty line in 1985, with 5.57 million not receiving any subsidies.

2. U.S. Census Bureau, "Income Characteristics—Owner Occupied Units," *1985 American Housing Survey*, Table 3–12. According to figures calculated by Cushing Dolbeare, only 200,000 owner-occupied housing units received direct housing subsidies in 1985; by 1988 the figure was expected to drop to 163,000. See Dolbeare, *Low Income Housing Needs*, pp. 20, 22. Some low-income homeowners do get indirect subsidies, through circuit breaker programs that give some property tax relief to the lower-income elderly, or through homeowner tax deductions. Since homeowner tax deductions can only be taken by those who itemize their deductions, however, this prevents most poor owners from being able to take advantage of the homeowner tax deductions.

3. Dolbeare, *Low Income Housing Needs*, p. 3.

4. AFL-CIO, "National Assisted Housing Needs, and Resources," in *A New National Housing Policy: Recommendations of Organizations and Individuals Concerned about Affordable Housing in America* (hereafter, *A New National Housing Policy*), printed for the use of the Committee on Banking, Housing, and Urban Affairs, United States Senate, and Committee on Banking, Finance and Urban Affairs,

House of Representatives, 100th Cong., 1st sess., 1987. Sen. Print 100–58, pp.103, 112; Council of Large Public Housing Authorities (hereafter CLPHA), *Public Housing Today* (1988), 9.

5. Nancy Reder, "The Search for Low-Cost Housing," *The National Voter* 38, no. 2 (August 1988): 6.

6. Low Income Housing Information Service (hereafter LIHIS), *Low Income Housing and Homelessness: Facts and Myths* (Washington, D.C.: Low Income Housing Information Service, 1989), p.15.

7. Andrew Scherer, "Is there Life after Abandonment? The Key Role of New York City's *In Rem* Housing in Establishing an Entitlement to Decent, Affordable Housing," *New York University Review of Law and Social Change* 13, no. 4 (1984–85): 954.

8. John I. Gilderbloom and Richard P. Appelbaum, *Rethinking Rental Housing* (Philadelphia: Temple University Press, 1988), Table 2.3 and 2.4, pp. 21–22. According to the *1985 American Housing Survey*, Tables 4–12 ("Income Characteristics—Renter Occupied Units") and 4–13 ("Selected Housing Costs—Renter Occupied Units"), this ratio decreased to 30 percent for central city renter households. It is not clear, however, if the figures developed by Gilderbloom and Appelbaum refer to total household income or to income of the primary family in the household.

9. U.S. Census Bureau, "Selected Housing Costs—Renter Occupied Units," *1985 American Housing Survey*, table 4–13.

10. Gilderbloom and Appelbaum, *Rethinking Rental Housing*, pp.127, 129–32, 139–42. Rent control is most common in California, New Jersey, and New York. Rent control is discussed in more detail in Chapter 4.

11. John Atlas and Peter Dreier, "Ingredients for a Housing Action Agenda in '88: Tenants Rights and Homelessness," *Shelterforce* 11, no. 2 (August/September, 1988): 9.

12. Chester Hartman, "Housing Policies under the Reagan Administration," in *Critical Perspectives on Housing*, eds. Rachel Bratt, Chester Hartman, and Ann Meyerson (Philadelphia: Temple University Press, 1986), p. 368.

13. Michael E. Stone, "Housing and the Economic Crisis: An Analysis and Emergency Program," in *America's Housing Crisis: What Is To Be Done?*, ed. Chester Hartman (Boston: Routledge & Kegan Paul, 1983), pp.103–5.

14. Calculated from Cushing Dolbeare, "The Low-Income Housing Crisis," in *America's Housing Crisis*, Table 2.4, p. 34.

15. Median income for all renters was $12,400. Gilderbloom and Appelbaum, *Rethinking Rental Housing*, p.24.

16. George Sternlieb and James W. Hughes, "Housing the Poor in a Post-shelter Society," *The Annals* 465 (January 1983): Table 4, 113.

17. "Homelessness in America," *Newsweek*, January 2, 1984, 23.

18. National Coalition for the Homeless (hereafter NCH), *Pushed Out: America's Homeless* (Washington, D.C.: unpublished report, 1987), p. 81.

19. Dolbeare, *Low Income Housing Needs*, Table 11, p.24; National Coalition for the Homeless, "Homelessness in America: A Summary" (Washington, D.C.: National Coalition for the Homeless, n.d., but apparently 1988).

20. Gilderbloom and Appelbaum, *Rethinking Rental Housing*, Table 2.1, p. 18.

21. U.S. Census Bureau, "Introductory Characteristics—Occupied Units,"

"Introductory Characteristics—In Cental Cities—Occupied Units" and "Introductory Characteristics—Suburbs—Occupied Units," *1985 American Housing Survey*, Tables 2–1, 8–1, and 9–1.

22. David C. Schwartz, Richard C. Ferlauto, and Daniel N. Hoffman, *A New Housing Policy for America: Recapturing the American Dream* (Philadelphia: Temple University Press, 1988), p. 122.

23. Mortgage Bankers Association of America, "A Report on National Housing Policy," in *A New National Housing Policy*, Exhibit IV–2, p. 386; U.S. Census Bureau, "Size of Unit and Lot—Renter Occupied Units," *1985 American Housing Survey*, Table 4–3.

24. AFL-CLO, "National Assisted Housing Needs," p.111.

25. CLPHA, "Recommendations," in *A New National Housing Policy*, p.180.

26. Not until 1988 was the 1968 Fair Housing Act amended to prohibit discrimination against children in housing, by prohibiting discrimination based on familial status. See 42 U.S.C., Secs. 3604 and 3605.

27. George Sternlieb and James W. Hughes, "Housing and Shelter Cost: The Schizoid Problem of the Central City," in *America's Housing, Prospects and Problems*, eds. George Sternlieb, James W. Hughes, and Robert W. Burchell (New Brunswick, N.J.: Center for Urban Policy Research, Rutgers University, 1980), p.112.

28. The information regarding child neglect is based on the author's experience as an attorney representing parties in child neglect cases in Juvenile Court in both Missouri and West Virginia.

29. "100,000 Children Are Homeless: Study Group Irate," St. Louis *Post-Dispatch*, September 21, 1988, 1A.

30. Reder, "The Search for Low-Cost Housing": 7.

31. NCH, *Pushed Out*, pp. iii, vi.

32. "Department of Education Finds 220,000 School-Aged Children without Homes," *Safety Network* 8, no. 4 (April 1989): 2.

33. Madeleine R. Stoner, "An Analysis of Public and Private Sector Provisions for Homeless People," pp. 3–4; Philip Kasinitz, "Gentrification and Homelessness: The Single Room Occupant and the Inner City Renewal," pp. 9–14; and Nancy K. Kaufman, "Homelessness: A Comprehensive Policy Approach," pp.21–22; all in *Tthe Urban and Social Change Review* 17, no. 1 (Winter 1984).

34. NCH, "Homelessness in America," p.2.

35. "100,000 Children Are Homeless."

36. Stoner, "Provisions for Homeless People," p. 4.

37. Mortgage Bankers, "A Report," pp. 352, 354, 356–57, 396.

38. Manuel Mariano Lopez, "Su casa no es mi casa: Hispanic Housing Conditions in Contemporary America, 1949–1980," in *Race, Ethnicity and Minority Housing in the United States*, ed. Jamshid A. Momeni (Westport, Ct.: Greenwood Press, 1986), p.130; U.S. Census Bureau, "Introductory Characteristics—Occupied Units with Hispanic Householder," *1985 American Housing Survey*, Table 6–1.

39. Kenneth T. Rosen, *Affordable Housing: New Policies for the Housing and Mortgage Markets* (Cambridge, Mass.: Ballinger Publishing Co., 1984), p. 5.

40. See Table entitled "Historical Listing of HUD/FHA Maximum Allowable Interest Rates," *Housing and Development Reporter*, August 19, 1985, 10:0021; "Adjusting: Interest Rate Climb Pinches Homeowners," St. Louis *Post-Dispatch*,

March 20, 1989, 14 BP; "Rising Mortgage Rates Lower the Boom," St. Louis *Post-Dispatch* April 19, 1987, lE. While rates on FHA-insured loans are usually slightly below rates on conventional loans, the record of FHA rates gives a good indication of the change in interest rates in general for mortgage loans since World War II. In 1983, FHA regulation of interest rates on insured loans was abolished.

41. AFL-CIO, "National Assisted Housing Needs," p.113.

42. Calculated from James W. Hughes and George Sternlieb, *The Dynamics of American Housing* (New Brunswick, N.J.: Rutgers, State University of New Jersey, 1987), Exhibits 10–1 to 10–3, and 10–5, pp.139, 143, and 146; "Mortgage Rates," St. Louis *Post Dispatch* April 12, 1987, lJ; "Adjusting: Interest-Rate Climb Pinches Homeowners," St. Louis *Post Dispatch* March 20, 1989, 14 BP.

43. Stone, "Housing and the Dynamics of U.S. Capitalism," in *Critical Perspectives*, p. 55–56.

44. Stone, "Housing and the Economic Crisis," p.129.

45. Emily Paradise Achtenberg and Peter Marcuse, "Toward the Decommodification of Housing," in *America's Housing Crisis*, p.205.

46. Calculated from Mortgage Bankers, "A Report," Exhibit II–5, p. 357.

47. After tax cost are the costs of mortgage and property tax payments, utilities, maintenance, repairs, insurance and transaction costs, after subtracting tax deductions for mortgage interest and real estate tax payments.

48. Mortgage Bankers, "A Report," Exhibits II–7 and II–8, p. 360 and 362.

49. "Jobless Americans Going without Benefits," *Safety Network* 7, no. 6 (September 1988): 4.

50. Calculated from Hughes and Sternlieb, *The Dynamics of American Housing*, Exhibit 10–1, p.139.

51. "Mortgage Delinquency Rate Rising Again," St. Louis *Post Dispatch*, March 18, 1989, 11A.

52. "Revitalization" is a value-laden word, as it implies that working-class neighborhoods that are undergoing an invasion by middle- and upper-income persons were not vital neighborhoods before the middle and upper classes arrived. See Bruce London and J. John Palen, "Introduction: Some Theoretical and Practical Issues Regarding Inner-City Revitalization," in *Gentrification, Displacement and Neighborhood Revitalization*, eds. J. John Palen and Bruce London (Albany: State University of New York Press, 1984), p.10.

53. Richard T. LeGates and Chester Hartman, "Displacement," *Clearinghouse Review* 15, no. 3 (July 1981): 229–31.

54. The term *gentrification* is something of a misnomer, since the term *gentry* means a member of the landed aristocracy. Those moving into certain neighborhoods of the central cities are not moving in from rural areas, nor are they members of the aristocracy. See London and Palen, "Introduction," pp. 7–8.

55. Richard T. LeGates and Chester Hartman, "The Anatomy of Displacement in the United States," in *Gentrification of the City*, eds., Neil Smith and Peter Williams (Boston: Allen & Unwin, 1986), pp.178–200.

56. LeGates and Hartman, "Displacement," pp.213, 220.

57. U.S. Census Bureau, "Reasons for Move and Choice of Current Residence—Occupied Units," *1985 American Housing Survey*, Table 2–11.

58. Calculated from U.S. Census Bureau, "Household Composition—Occupied Units," *1985 American Housing Survey*, Table 2–9.

59. Calculated from U.S. Census Bureau, "Reasons for Move and Choice of Current Residence—Renter Occupied Units," *1985 American Housing Survey*, Table 4–11. The average size of central city tenant households, calculated from Table 4.9, "Household Composition—Renter—Occupied Units," is 2.3 persons.

60. Mortgage Bankers, "A Report," Exhibits III–3, III–4, and III–9, pp. 372, 374, and 379.

61. Schwartz, Ferlauto, and Hoffman, *A New Housing Policy*, pp. 4–5.

62. Calculated from U.S. Census Bureau, "Introductory Characteristics—Occupied Units," *1985 American Housing Survey*, Table 2–1.

63. Douglas S. Massey and Nancy A. Denton, "Suburbanization and Segregation in U.S. Metropolitan Areas," *American Journal of Sociology* 94, no. 3 (November 1988): 592–626.

64. See *Race, Ethnicity, and Minority Housing*, ed. Jamshid A. Momeni (Westport, Ct.: Greenwood Press, 1986).

65. John F. Kain, "The Influence of Race and Income on Racial Segregation and Housing Policy," in *Housing Desegregation and Federal Policy*, ed. John M. Goering (Chapel Hill, N.C.: University of North Carolina Press, 1986), pp.102–10.

66. Lawrence Bobo, Howard Schuman, and Charlotte Steeh, "Changing Racial Attitudes toward Residential Integration," in *Housing Desegregation*, pp.153–54, 156.

67. Kain, "The Influence of Race and Income," in *Housing Desegregation*, p.114.

68. John M. Goering, "Minority Housing Needs and Civil Rights Enforcement," in *Race, Ethnicity, and Minority Housing*, p.203.

69. The Atlanta Journal and The Atlanta Constitution, *The Color of Money: Home Mortgage Lending Practices Discriminate against Blacks* (Atlanta, Ga.: The Atlanta Journal, 1988).

70. Franklin J. James and Eileen A. Tynan, "Segregation and Discrimination of Hispanic Americans: An Exploratory Analysis," in *Housing Desegregation*, pp. 83–98.

71. Lopez, "Su casa no es mi casa," pp. 133–34.

72. LIHIS, *Special Memorandum: The Fiscal Year 1990 Budget and Low-Income Housing* (Washington, D.C.: Low Income Housing Information Service, 1989), Tables 1 to 3.

73. "Administration Violated McKinney Act, Judge Says," *Safety Network* 7, no. 8 (November 1988): 1; "Administration Violated Court Order in Surplus Property Case," *Safety Network* 7, no. 9 (December 1988): 3.

74. LIHIS, *Special Memorandum: The Fiscal Year 1990 Budget*, Table 7.

75. Marshall W. Dennis, *Mortgage Lending Fundamentals and Practice* (Reston, Va.: Reston Publishing Co., 1981), p. 115.

76. John A. Tuccillo and John L. Goodman, Jr., *Housing Finance: A Changing System in the Reagan Era* (Washington, D.C.: The Urban Institute Press, 1983), p. 43; Ann Meyerson, "Deregulation and the Restructuring of the Housing Finance System," in *Critical Perspectives*, p. 86.

77. Schwartz, Ferlauto, and Hoffman, *A New Housing Policy*, p.10.

78. Meyerson, "Deregulation," p. 88.

79. Jane Bryant Quinn, "If Lender Sells Your Mortgage, It May Cause Problems," St. Louis *Post Dispatch*, August 1, 1986, 8C.

80. Tuccillo, *Housing Finance*, p. 54.

81. Meyerson, "Deregulation," p. 73.

82. "Once-Sleepy Savings and Loan Industry under Siege," St. Louis *Post Dispatch*, February 5, 1989, 1B.

83. Rosen, *Affordable Housing*, p. 74.

84. Tuccillo, *Housing Finance*, p. 57.

85. Rosen, *Affordable Housing*, p.164.

86. "Adjusting: Interest Rate Climb Pinches Homeowners," St. Louis *Post Dispatch*, March 20, 1989, 14–15 BP.

87. Schwartz, Ferlauto, and Hoffman, *A New Housing Policy*, pp.129–30.

88. Stone, "Housing and the Dynamics of U.S. Capitalism," pp. 57–58; Meyerson, "Deregulation" pp. 91–92.

89. Meyerson, "Deregulation," pp. 69–70, 79–81, 88.

90. Schwartz, Ferlauto, and Hoffman, *A New Housing Policy*, pp. 77–80.

91. Kenneth Harney, "Eleventh Hour Housing Candy," St. Louis *Post-Dispatch*, November 6, 1988, 1H.

92. Gilderbloom and Appelbaum, *Rethinking Rental Housing*, pp. 80–82; Schwartz, Ferlauto, and Hoffman, *A New Housing Policy*, pp. 52–54.

CHAPTER 2

1. John I. Gilderbloom and Richard P. Appelbaum, *Rethinking Rental Housing* (Philadelphia: Temple University Press, 1988), p. 112.

2. See the excellent critique of the traditional supply and demand analysis of rent in Gilderbloom and Appelbaum, *Rethinking Rental Housing*, chaps. 3–6.

3. The 1986 Tax Reform Act lengthened the period for depreciation, reducing the profit available to speculators.

4. In the worst cases, in the absence of building code enforcement, as each speculator increases the profits made on the initial investment by cutting back or eliminating building maintenance, the building eventually becomes unfit for human occupancy.

5. Jim Kemeny, *The Myth of Home Ownership: Private versus Public Choices in Housing Tenure* (London: Routledge & Kegan Paul, 1981), pp. 36–37.

6. See, for example, George Sternlieb and James W. Hughes, "Housing and Shelter Costs: The Schizoid Problem of the Central City," in *America's Housing: Problems and Prospects*, eds. George Sternlieb, James W. Hughes, and Robert W. Burchell (New Brunswick, N.J.: Center for Urban Policy Research, Rutgers University, 1980), pp.103–4.

7. See data on annual housing starts for 1950 to 1985 in George Sternlieb and David Listokin, "A Review of National Housing Policy," in *Housing America's Poor*, ed. Peter D. Salins (Chapel Hill, N.C.: University of North Carolina Press, 1987), p.29.

8. Michael Sumichrast and Maury Seldin, *Housing Markets: The Complete Guide to Analysis and Strategy for Builders, Lenders, and Other Investors* (Homewood, Ill.: Dow Jones Irwin, 1977), pp. 42, 59.

9. Charles Abrams, *The Future of Housing* (New York: Harper & Row, 1946), p.116.

10. "Historical Listing of HUD/FHA Maximum Allowable Interest Rates," *Housing and Development Reporter*, August 19, 1985, 10:0021.

11. Ivan Szelenyi, *Urban Inequalities under State Socialism* (London: Oxford University Press, 1983), pp.23–24. At the same time, it is important to note that a certain level of industrial development is a necessary precondition to the development of an adequate housing production industry in urban areas.

12. Szelenyi, *Urban Inequalities*, pp. 74–75.

13. Szelenyi, *Urban Inequalities*, pp. 5–7, 33–34, 52–63; Zsuzsa Dániel, "The Effect of Housing Allocation on Social Inequality in Hungary," *Journal of Comparative Economics* 9 (1985): 391–409.

14. People in socialist countries that tie housing to employment may have an advantage over workers in capitalist countries because unemployment rates generally are much lower there than in the United States.

15. Jill Hamburg, "The Dynamics of Cuban Housing Policy," in *Critical Perspectives on Housing*, eds. Rachel Bratt, Chester Hartman, and Ann Meyerson (Philadelphia: Temple University Press, 1986), p. 601.

16. See *Otero v New York City Housing Authority*, 484 F.2d 1122 (2d Cir. 1973) for an example of the tipping point argument that was successfully argued in the courts. See also Anthony Downs, *Opening up the Suburbs: An Urban Strategy for America* (New Haven, Conn.: Yale University Press, 1973).

CHAPTER 3

1. Many if the ideas for a Social Housing Sector are based on proposals made by the Institute for Policy Studies. See Working Group on Housing, *A Progressive Housing Program for America* (Washington, D.C.: Institute for Policy Studies, 1987).

2. Institute for Community Economics (hereafter ICE), *Community Land Trust Handbook* (Emmaus, Pa.: Rodale Press, 1982), chap. 2. See also ICE's Model Ground Lease, Prepared 9/88.

3. ICE, *The Community Land Trust Handbook*, pp. 31–32.

4. For information about limited equity cooperatives and community land trusts, see Chuck Matthei, "Land Reform Begins at Home," *Building Economic Alternatives* (Winter 1986), pp. 7–8; ICE, *The Community Land Trust Handbook*, pp.18–35. This discussion is taken from these two publications, as well as from a conversation with Chuck Matthei, November 1988.

CHAPTER 4

1. Sam Bass Warner, Jr., *The Urban Wilderness: A History of the American City* (New York: Harper & Row, 1972), p.239; Michael E. Stone, "Housing and the American Economy: A Marxist Analysis," in *Urban and Regional Planning in an Age of Austerity*, eds. Pierre Clavel, John Forester, and William W. Goldsmith (New York: Pergamon Press, 1980), p. 89.

2. John A. Tuccillo, et al., *Housing Finance: A Changing System in the Reagan Era* (Washington, D.C.: The Urban Institute Press, 1983), p. 36; Kenneth T. Rosen, *Affordable Housing: New Policies for the Housing and Mortgage Markets* (Cambridge, Mass.: Ballinger Press, 1983), pp.109, 111.

3. Barry G. Jacobs, et al., *Guide to Federal Housing Programs* (Washington, D.C.:

Bureau of National Affairs, 1982), 1st ed., pp. 7–8; American Enterprise Institute, *Proposals for Reform of the Deposit Insurance System* (Washington, D.C.: American Enterprise Institute, 1985), p. 3.

4. About 3.35 million public housing and subsidized housing units have been constructed, of which 840,000 were constructed under the Section 8 program, which is a rent supplement rather than a finance subsidy program. National Low Income Housing Preservation Commission, *Preventing the Disappearance of Low-Income Housing* (Washington, D.C.: Balmar Printing and Graphics, 1988), p.17. Figure for total housing starts calculated from George Sternlieb and David Listokin, "A Review of National Housing Policy," in *Housing America's Poor*, ed. Peter D. Salins (Chapel Hill, N.C.: University of North Carolina Press, 1987), p.29.

5. Cedric Pugh, *Housing in Capitalist Societies* (Westmead, Eng.: Gower Publishing Co., Ltd., 1980), pp. 39–40, 76, 175–77, 206–8.

6. Bruce Headey, *Housing Policy in the Developed Economy* (New York: St. Martin's Press, 1978), pp. 71, 76, 88–89; Richard P. Appelbaum, "Swedish Housing in the Postwar Period: Some Lessons for American Housing Policy," in *Critical Perspectives on Housing*, eds. Rachel G. Bratt, Chester Hartman, and Ann Meyerson (Philadelphia: Temple University Press, 1986), pp. 545–46; Jim Kemeny, *The Myth of Home-Ownership: Private versus Public Choices in Housing Tenure* (London: Routledge & Kegan Paul, 1981), p. 95.

7. Headey, *Housing Policy*, p. 80; Martin Schnitzer, *The Economy of Sweden* (New York: Praeger Publishers, 1970), pp.185–86.

8. The housing bank could, of course, be federal, or even municipal. The principles discussed for a housing bank would be applicable to a federal or municipal housing bank. Simply the scope, and sources of capitalization, would be different.

9. E. Jay Howenstine, *Attacking Housing Costs: Foreign Policies and Strategies* (New Brunswick: Rutgers State University of New Jersey, 1983), p.119.

10. Comments by Calvin Bradford at "Initiatives for Affordable Housing," a conference sponsored by the National Training and Information Center in Chicago in November 1988.

11. David C. Schwartz, Richard C. Ferlauto, and Daniel N. Hoffman, *A New Housing Policy for America: Recapturing the American Dream* (Philadelphia: Temple University Press, 1988), p.10.

12. Howenstine, *Attacking Housing Costs*, p.119.

13. Pierre Clavel, *The Progressive City* (New Brunswick, N.J.: Rutgers University Press, 1986), p.109; Chuck Matthei, "Land Reform Begins at Home," *Building Economic Alternatives* (Winter 1986): 6.

14. Jill Hamburg, "The Dynamics of Cuban Housing Policy," in *Critical Perspectives*, pp. 589, 591–92, 610–11; Tony Schuman, "Housing: A Challenge Met," *Cuba Review* 5 (March 1975): p. 7.

15. Alan Mallach, *Inclusionary Housing Programs: Policies and Practices* (New Brunswick, N.J.: Center for Urban Policy Research, 1984), pp.156–58.

16. Kenneth K. Baar, "Guidelines for Drafting Rent Control Laws: Lessons a of Decade," *Rutgers Law Review* 35 (Summer 1983): 740.

17. See Mallach, *Inclusionary Housing Programs*, p.155.

18. The City of Palo Alto ties appreciation in home prices in its inclusionary

zoning program to one-third of the CPI. Mallach, *Inclusionary Housing Programs*, p. 155.

19. Mallach, *Inclusionary Housing Programs*, pp.146–47.

20. Headey, *Housing Policy*, pp. 75, 85–86; Appelbaum, "Swedish Housing," p. 545.

21. 32 Vt. Stat. Ann. Secs. 10001–10010.

22. Gregory D. Andrusz, *Housing Urban Development in the USSR* (Albany: State University of New York Press, 1984), pp.28, 132–33, 144–45, 148; Vic George and Nick Manning, *Socialism, Social Welfare, and the Soviet Union* (London: Routledge & Kegan Paul, 1980, pp.137–38; Alfred John DiMaio, Jr., *Soviet Urban Housing: Problems and Policies* (New York: Praeger Publishers, 1974), p.144; Mervyn Matthews, "Social Dimensions in Soviet Urban Housing," in *The Socialist City: Spatial Structure and Urban Policy*, eds. R. A. French and F. E. Ian Hamilton (Chichester: John Wiley & Sons, 1979), pp.109–10.

23. Kemeny, *The Myth of Home-ownership*, pp. 95–96.

24. Kemeny, *The Myth*, pp. 99–100.

25. Kemeny, *The Myth*, p.100; Headey, *Housing Policy*, pp. 71–72, 85; Appelbaum, "Swedish Housing," p. 543.

26. Hamburg, "The Dynamics of Cuban Housing Policy," pp. 589–92, 621 (footnote 13); Schuman, "Housing: A Challenge Met," p. 7.

27. Baar, "Guidelines for Drafting Rent Control Laws," pp. 723, 725, 736–37, 784–85, 809–17. This article provides a detailed and excellent analysis of the pros and cons of each of the different types of rent control ordinances in use in the United States.

28. Gilderbloom and Appelbaum, *Rethinking Rental Housing*, pp.129, 131.

29. Baar, "Guidelines for Drafting Rent Control Laws," pp. 723, 725, 736–37, 784–85, 809–17.

30. Gilderbloom and Appelbaum, *Rethinking Rental Housing*, p.132.

31. Gilderbloom and Appelbaum, *Rethinking Rental Housing*; p.131.

32. Baar, "Guidelines for Drafting Rental Control Laws," pp. 784–85.

33. Baar, "Guidelines for Drafting Rental Control Laws," pp. 766–67. Due to the constitutional prohibition on impairing contracts, the rent control law probably could not require landlords to *reduce* their rents to a predetermined level set by the rent control board. Thus, a rollback in rent to the rent that was charged on a particular base date is probably the most that could be done constitutionally in a rent control law.

34. Cushing N. Dolbeare and Judith A. Canales, *The Hispanic Housing Crisis* (Washington, D.C.: National Council of La Raza, 1988), p. 52.

35. Cushing Dolbeare, "How the Income Tax System Subsidizes Housing for the Affluent," in *Critical Perspectives*, pp.266, 268. Calculation of average amount of reduced taxes are this author's.

36. John Atlas and Peter Dreier, "Ingredients for a Housing Action Agenda: Assisting First-Time Homebuyers," *Shelterforce* 45 (October/November 1988): 7.

37. Dolbeare and Canales, *The Hispanic Housing Crisis*, p. 52.

38. Pugh, *Housing in Capitalist Societies*, p.207.

39. Headey, *Housing Policy*, p. 85; Appelbaum, "Swedish Housing," p. 536.

40. Woody Widrow, "Dispelling the Myths of Housing Vouchers," *Shelterforce* 10, no. 4 (September/October 1987): 15.

CHAPTER 5

1. The following discussion of Soviet planning principles is taken from Michael Ellman, *Socialist Planning* (Cambridge: Cambridge University Press, 1979), pp.17–19, 203.

2. Alfred John DiMaio, Jr., *Soviet Urban Housing: Problems and Policies* (New York: Praeger Publishers, 1974), p.21; Adam Andrzejewski, "Postwar Housing Development in Poland," *City and Regional Planning in Poland*, ed. Jack Fisher (Ithaca, N.Y.: Cornell University Press, 1966), pp.160–61, 172–73; Michael Ball and Michael Harloe, *Housing Policy in a Socialist Country: The Case of Poland* (London: Center for Environmental Studies, CES Research Paper 8, 1974), pp.27–28, 39–40; D. V. Donnison, "Housing Policies in Eastern Europe," *Transactions of the Bartlett Society* 3 (1964–65): 103–4.

3. Andrzejewski, "Postwar Housing Development in Poland," pp.161, 166, 173–74; Ball and Harloe, *Housing Policy*, pp. 39–40; Donnison, "Housing Policies in Eastern Europe," pp.103–4.

4. Bruce Headey, *Housing Policy in the Developed Economy* (New York: St. Martin's Press, 1978), pp. 44–45, 75.

5. Headey, *Housing Policy*, pp. 75, 85–86, 89–90; Richard P. Appelbaum, "Swedish Housing in the Postwar Period: Some Lessons for American Housing Policy," in *Critical Perspectives on Housing*, eds. Rachel G. Bratt, Chester Hartman, and Ann Meyerson (Philadelphia: Temple University Press, 1986), p. 540.

6. Martin Schrenk, *Yugoslavia: Self-Management Socialism and the Challenge of Development* (Baltimore: Johns Hopkins University Press, 1979), pp. 45–47; J. M. Simmie and D. J. Hale, "Urban Self-Management in Yugoslavia," *Regional Studies* 12 (1978): 703.

7. Schrenk, *Yugoslavia: Self-Management Socialism*, pp. 59–60, 69–70; Daniel R. Mandelker, "Planning and Housing in the Yugoslav Republic of Slovenia," *Urban Law and Policy* 4 (1981): 357, 360–63, 365–67; Peter Bassin, "Yugoslavia," in *Housing in Europe*, ed. Martin Wynn (London: Croom Helm, 1984). p.163.

8. Mandelker, "Planning and Housing in Slovenia," p. 360.

9. Schrenk, *Yugoslavia: Self-Management Socialism*, pp. 43–44, 74–77.

10. See *West's Cal. Gov't. Code* Secs. 65302(c), 65580 to 65589.5 and 65913.1 (St. Paul, MN: West, 1983).

11. Mandelker, "Planning and Housing in Slovenia," p. 368; Simmie and Hale, "Urban Self-Management in Yugoslavia," p. 710.

12. Robert Goodman, *After the Planners* (New York: Simon & Schuster, 1971), pp.147–51; Sam Bass Warner, Jr., *The Urban Wilderness*, pp.28, 222–23; Roy Lubove, *The Progressives and the Slums* (Pittsburgh: The University of Pittsburgh Press, 1962), pp.244–45; Charles Abrams, *The Future of Housing* (New York: Harper & Row, 1946), p.211; and Blake McKelvey, *The Emergence of Metropolitan America: 1915–1966* (New Brunswick, N.J.: Rutgers University Press, 1968), p. 49.

13. Steve Schifferes, "The Dilemmas of British Housing Policy," in *Critical Perspectives*, p. 515.

14. Peter Marcuse, "The Beginnings of Public Housing in New York," *Journal of Urban History* 12, no. 4 (August 1986), pp. 354, 363–64.

15. Eugene J. Meehan, *The Quality of Federal Policymaking: Programmed Failure in Public Housing* (Columbia, Mo.: University of Missouri Press, 1978), p.21.

16. Abrams, *The Future of Housing*, p.216; 42 U.S.C.A. Sec. 1524.

17. Meehan, *The Quality of Federal Policymaking*, pp.20–21; figures on public housing construction calculated from Table 20.1 in Rachel Bratt, "Public Housing: The Controversy and Contribution," in *Critical Perspectives*, p. 338.

18. Meehan, *The Quality of Federal Policymaking*, pp.24–28; Bratt, "Public Housing," p. 339.

19. Alvin Schorr, "Slums and Social Security," in *Urban Renewal: People, Politics, and Planning*, eds. Jewell Bellush and Murray Hausknecht (Garden City, N.Y.: Anchor Books, 1967), p. 417.

20. Leonard Freedman, *Public Housing: The Politics of Poverty* (New York: Holt, Rinehart & Winston, 1969), p.104.

21. This naturally led local authorities to focus on providing housing for the elderly, at the expense of other groups. Meehan, *The Quality of Federal Policymaking*, pp. 36–38.

22. Figure calculated from Bratt, "Public Housing," p. 338, and Low Income Housing Information Service, *The Fiscal Year 1990 Budget and Low Income Housing* (Washington, D.C.: Low Income Housing Information Service, 1989), Table 3.

23. The Report of the National Low Income Housing Preservation Commission (hereafter "Housing Preservation Commission"), *Preventing the Disappearance of Low-Income Housing* (Washington, D.C.: Balmar Printing & Graphics, 1986), pp.15–17.

24. Vic George and Nick Manning, *Socialism, Social Welfare, and the Soviet Union* (London: Routledge & Kegan Paul, 1980), p.151.

25. Gregory D. Andrusz, *Housing and Urban Development in the USSR* (Albany: State University of New York Press, 1984), pp. 83–87; *Poland: A Handbook* (Warsaw: Interpress Publishers, 1977), p. 305.

26. Andrusz, *Housing and Urban Development in the USSR*, pp.159–60, 162–63; DiMaio, Jr., *Soviet Urban Housing*, p.24; Henry W. Morton, "Housing Problems and Policies in Eastern Europe and the Soviet Union," *Studies in Comparative Communism* 12, no. 4 (Winter 1979): 318–19.

27. Andrusz, *Housing and Urban Development in the USSR*, pp. 83–87.

28. Andrusz, *Housing and Urban Development in the USSR*, pp. 33, 36–37, 45, 47–49, 69–70; George and Manning, *Socialism*, p.141.

29. Ball and Harloe, *Housing Policy in a Socialist Country*, p.28; Andrzejewski, "Postwar Housing Development in Poland," p.165; Donnison, "Housing Policies in Eastern Europe," pp.100, 104.

30. Schifferes, "The Dilemmas of British Housing Policy," p. 520.

31. Roger H. Duclad-Williams, *The Politics of Housing in Britain and France* (London: Heinemann, 1978), p.155–57; Headey, *Housing Policy*, pp.136–37; Schifferes, "The Dilemmas of British Housing Policy," p. 519.

32. Stephen Merrett, *State Housing in Britain* (London: Routledge & Kegan Paul, 1979), pp. 93–95, 98, 166.

33. Headey, *Housing Policy*, p. 72.

34. Alan Mallach, *Inclusionary Housing Programs: Policies and Practices* (New Brunswick, N.J.: Rutgers, the State University of New Jersey, 1984), pp. 60–62, 75–76. Mallach estimates a 24 percent reduction in site costs by increases in net density.

35. Robert W. Burchell, W. Patrick Beaton, and David Listokin, *Mount Laurel*

II: Challenge and Delivery of Low-Cost Housing (New Brunswick, N.J.: Rutgers University, 1983), p. 337.

36. Mallach, *Inclusionary Housing Programs*, pp. 65–69.

37. National Coalition for the Homeless, *Precious Resources: Government-Owned Housing and the Needs of the Homeless, A Survey of 32 Cities* (September 1988), pp.20–21, 51.

38. Currently, 44 percent of units under the Section 221(d)(3) and Section 236 programs receive rent subsidies. Housing Preservation Commission, *Preventing the Disappearance of Low-Income Housing*, pp.16, 77.

39. Housing Preservation Commission, *Preventing*, pp.15–19, 24–25, 44, 77.

40. Housing Preservation Commission, *Preventing*, pp.19–20.

41. Emergency Low Income Housing Preservation Act of 1987, P.L. 100–424, 12 U.S.C. Sec. 1715L, notes.

42. The following description is based on Gill Burke, *Housing and Social Justice: The Role of Policy in British Housing* (London: Longman, 1981), pp.16, 27–28; and Merrett, *State Housing in Britain*, pp.215–17, 227.

43. 24 C.F.R. Sec. 960.204.

44. Andrusz, *Housing and Urban Development in the USSR*, pp. 83–87.

45. The following discussion is based on Jon Pynoos, *Breaking the Rules: Bureaucracy and Reform in Public Housing* (New York: Plenum Press, 1986).

46. Pynoos, *Breaking the Rules*, pp.203–4.

CHAPTER 6

1. Cushing N. Dolbeare and Judith A. Canales, *The Hispanic Housing Crisis* (Washington, D.C.: Council of La Raza, 1988), pp. 48–49.

2. 42 U.S.C. Secs. 3602(k) and 3604–3606.

3. Rose Helper, *Racial Policies and Practices of Real Estate Brokers* (Minneapolis: University of Minnesota Press, 1969), pp. 3–4, and 224–26.

4. Article 34 of the Code, quoted in Helper, *Racial Policies and Practices*, p.201.

5. Helper, *Racial Policies and Practices*, p.201.

6. *Buchanan v. Warley*, 245 U.S. 60 (1917);. *Harmon v. Taylor*, 273 U.S. 668 (1927); *City of Richmond v Deans*, 281 U.S. 704 (1930).

7. 334 U.S. 1 (1948); Robert G. Schwemm, *Housing Discrimination Law* (Washington, D.C.: The Bureau of National Affairs, Inc., 1983), pp.19–21.

8. Helper, *Racial Policies and Practices*, pp.202–3.

9. Gary Orfield, *Must We Bus?* (Washington, D.C.: Brookings Institute, 1978), pp. 80–81; David Harvey, "The Political Economy of Urbanization in Advanced Capitalist Societies: The Case of the United States," in *The Social Economy of Cities*, eds. Gary Gapper and Harold M. Rose (Beverly Hills: Sage Publications, Ltd., 1975), pp.147–51. The Veterans Administration, which offered mortgage guarantees on loans of veterans, had a record as dismal as the Federal Housing Administration. In 1950, nonwhites held only 2 percent of the VA's guaranteed mortgages. See Orfield, *Must We Bus?*, p. 83.

10. Peter Kivisto, "A Historical Review of Changes in Public Housing Policies and their Impact on Minorities," in *Race, Ethnicity and Minority Housing in the United States*, ed. Jamshid A. Momeni (Westport, Ct.: Greenwood Press, 1986), pp. 4, 6–7.

11. Michael N. Danielson, *The Politics of Exclusion* (New York: Columbia University Press, 1976), pp. 52–60, 70–73, 98–99.

12. John O. Calmore, "Fair Housing and the Black Poor: An Advocacy Guide," *Clearinghouse Review* 18, no. 6 (November 1984): 639.

13. Robert W. Burchell, W. Patrick Beaton, and David Listokin, *Mount Laurel II: Challenge and Delivery of Low-Cost Housing* (New Brunswick, N.J.: Rutgers-University, 1983), p. 3.

14. See Luigi Laurenti, *Property Values and Race: Studies in Seven Cities* (Berkeley: University of California Press, 1960), and Helper, *Racial Policies and Practices*, p. 319.

15. Robert C. Art, "Social Responsibility in Bank Credit Decisions: The Community Reinvestment Act One Decade Later," *Pacific Law Journal* 18, no. 4 (July 1978): 1078, n. 26.

16. David Harvey, "The Political Economy of Urbanization," in *The Social Economy of Cities*, pp.144–47; and Lynne Beyer Sagalyn, "Mortgage Lending in Older Urban Neighborhoods: Lessons from Past Experience," *The Annals* 465 (January 1983): 99–101. See also *Clark v Universal Builders, Inc.*, 501 F.2d 324 (7th Cir. 1974), cert. den. 419 U.S. 1970 (1974), 706 F.2d 204 (7th Cir. 1983).

17. Robert Weaver, "The Urban Complex," in *Urban Renewal: People, Politics, and Planning*, eds. Jewel Bellush and Murray Hausknecht (Garden City, N.Y.: Anchor Books, 1967), p. 94; Robert Goodman, *After the Planners* (New York: Simon and Schuster, 1971), p. 69.

18. Orfield, *Must We Bus?*, pp. 81–82.

19. Orfield, *Must We Bus?*, pp. 32–33.

20. Orfield, *Must We Bus?*, pp. 83–84; Sam Bass Warner, Jr., *The Urban Wilderness* (New York: Harper & Row, 1972), p.234.

21. 1968 Fair Housing Law: 42 U.S.C. Secs. 3601–3619; *Jones v Alfred H. Mayer Co.*, 392 U.S. 409 (1968).

22. Robert W. Lake, *The New Suburbanites: Race and Housing in the Suburbs* (New Brunswick, N.J.: Rutgers—The State University of New Jersey, 1981), pp.213–33, 244–47; Morris Milgram, *Good Neighborhood: The Challenge of Open Housing* (New York: W.W. Norton & Co., 1977), pp.25–26.

23. Lake, *The New Suburbanites*, p.241.

24. 42 U.S.C. Sec. 3608(d)(5).

25. *Shannon v HUD*, 436 F.2d 809 (3d Cir. 1970).

26. John O. Calmore, "Fair Housing v Fair Housing," *Housing Law Bulletin* 9, no. 6 (November/December 1979): 3–4, 7.

27. *Otero v New York City Housing Authority*, 484 F.2d 1122 (2d Cir. 1973).

28. Michael J. Vernarelli, "Where Should HUD Locate Assisted Housing? The Evolution of Fair Housing Policy," in *Housing Desegregation and Federal Policy*, ed. John M. Goering (Chapel Hill, N.C.: University of North Carolina Press, 1986), pp.214–34.

29. *U.S. v Starrett City Associates*, 840 F.2d 1096 (2d Cir. 1988), cert. den. 109 S.Ct. 376 (1988). A United States District Court had, several years previously, struck down an integration maintenance program, but the *Starrett City* decision was the first Appeals Court decision to do so. See *Burney v Housing Authority of County of Beaver*, 551 F.Supp. 746 (W.D.Pa. 1982).

30. Franklin J. James, Betty I. McCummings, and Eileen A. Tynan, *Minorities*

in the Sunbelt (New Brunswick, N.J.: Center for Urban Policy Research, 1984), p.128.

31. Robert W. Lake, "Postscript: Unresolved Themes in the Evolution of Fair Housing," in *Housing Desegregation*, p. 324.

32. Pub.L. 100–430, Sept. 13, 1988.

33. 12 U.S.C. Sec. 2801 *et seq.*

34. See *National State Bank, Elizabeth, N.J. v Long*, 630 F.2d 981 (3rd Cir. 1980); *Glen Ellyn Savings and Loan Assn. v Tsoumas*, 377 N.E.2d 1 (Ill. 1978), *cert. den.* 99 S.Ct. 311 (1978).

35. 12 U.S.C. Sec. 2901 *et seq.*

36. Art, "Social Responsibility," pp.1105–06.

37. 12 U.S.C. Sec. 2903(1).

38. *Northeast Bank Corp. v Board of Governors of the Federal Reserve System*, 105 S.Ct. 2545 (1985).

39. Florence Wagman Roisman, "Preventing or Ameliorating Displacement in Connection with Section 8" (Unpublished paper, n.d.), p.29.

40. *National State Bank v Long*, 630 F. 2d 981 (3rd Cir. 1980).

41. *Corning Savings and Loan Association v Federal Home Loan Bank Board*, 571 F. Supp. 396 (E.D.Ark. 1983), *aff'd* 736 F.2d 479 (8th Cir. 1984).

42. Art, "Social Responsibility," pp.1101, 1110–34.

43. Danielson, *The Politics of Exclusion*, pp. 79–82.

44. *Village of Arlington Heights v Metropolitan Housing Development Corporation*, 429 U.S. 252 (1977).

45. There are exceptions, of course, notably the City of Yonkers. See *U.S. v Yonkers Board of Education*, 837 F.2d 1181 (2nd Cir. 1987), *cert. den.* 108 S.Ct. 2821 (1988).

46. *James v Valtierra*, 402 U.S. 137 (1971).

47. *City of Eastlake v Forest City Enterprises, Inc.*, 426 U.S. 668 (1976).

48. Burchell, Beaton, and Listokin, *Mount Laurel II*, pp.1–2.

49. *Southern Burlington County NAACP v Township of Mount Laurel*, 336 A.2d 713 (N.J. 1975).

50. *Southern Burlington County NAACP v Township of Mount Laurel*, 456 A.2d 390, 410 (N.J. 1983).

51. *Southern Burlington County NAACP v Township of Mount Laurel*, 456 A.2d 390, 441–452 (N.J. 1983).

52. Alan Mallach, "Opening the Suburbs: New Jersey's Mount Laurel Experience," *Shelterforce* 11, no. 2 (August/September 1988): 12–15.

53. Dolbeare and Canales, *The Hispanic Housing Crisis*, p. 49.

54. Lake, *The New Suburbanites*, pp.247–48, proposed many of ideas in this section.

55. See Milgram, *Good Neighborhood*, p. 76, for an example of a previously all-black slum being changed in a relatively short period of time to an integrated community through a combination of aggressive marketing and market factors.

56. See *West Cal. Gov't. Code* Secs. 65302(c), 65580 to 65589.5, 65913.1, and 65915 (West 1983), for an example of this type of law.

57. See Alan Mallach, *Inclusionary Housing Programs: Policies and Programs* (New Brunswick, N.J.: Rutgers—The State University of New Jersey, 1984), pp.2, 13–14, 106–29, for an excellent discussion of these issues. For a proposed model

mandatory inclusionary zoning law, see Carolyn Burton, "California Legislature Prohibits Exclusionary Zoning, Mandates Fair Share: Inclusionary Housing Programs a Likely Response," *San Fernando Valley Law Review* 9 (1981): 38–46.

58. 42 U.S.C. Secs. 3604–3606; Robert G. Schwemm, "Handicap Discrimination Under the New Fair Housing Act," *Trends* 27, no. 5 (February/March 1989): 6.

59. Sec. 100.201, 54 *Fed. Reg.* 3288 (1989).

60. *Village of Belle Terre v Boraas*, 416 U.S. 1 (1974); *Moore v City of East Cleveland*, 431 U.S. 494 (1977).

61. *City of Ladue v Horn*, 720 S.W.2d 745 (Mo. App. 1986).

CHAPTER 7

1. A detailed discussion of the causes of redevelopment and gentrification, and of the neighborhoods most likely to be targeted for such efforts, is beyond the scope of this chapter. The interested reader is referred to the following recent anthologies on this issue: *Gentrification, Displacement and Neighborhood Revitalization*, eds. J. John Palen and Bruce London (Albany: State University of New York Press, 1984); and *Gentrification of the City*, eds. Neil Smith and Peter Williams (Boston: Allen & Unwin, 1986).

2. See Charles Abrams, *The Future of Housing* (New York: Harper & Row, 1946), pp.211–12; Marc Weiss, "The Origins and Legacy of Urban Renewal," in *Urban and Regional Planning in an Age of Austerity*, eds. Pierre Clavel, John Forester, and William W. Goldsmith (New York: Pergamon Press, 1980), pp. 55–58; Robert Goodman, *After the Planners* (New York: Simon and Schuster, 1971), pp. 56–57.

3. See *United States v Jones*, 109 U.S. 513 (1883). See also Chapter 8.

4. *United States v Certain Lands in City of Louisville*, 9 F.Supp. 137 (D.C. Ky 1935), 78 F.2d 684 (6th Cir. 1935).

5. *New York City Housing Authority v Muller, et al.*, 1 N.E. 2d 153 (N.Y.Ct. App. 1936).

6. Abrams, *The Future of Housing*, p.200.

7. Weiss, "The Origins and Legacy," pp. 60–62.

8. Blake McKelvey, *The Emergence of Metropolitan America: 1915–1966* (New Brunswick, N.J.: Rutgers University Press, 1968), p.129.

9. McKelvey, *The Emergence of Metropolitan America*, pp.128 and 130; *Murray v LaGuardia*, 52 N.E. 2d 884 (N.Y. Ct. App. 1943).

10. Chapter 353 R.S.Mo.

11. Sec. 353.020(3) R.S.Mo.

12. 42 U.S.C. Sec. 1441 *et seq.*

13. Weiss, "The Origins and Legacy," pp. 58–62.

14. 42 U.S.C. Secs. 1452–1454, 1460(c). The "net project loss" was the difference between the value of the property acquired and the cost of acquiring and clearing the property (which generally exceeded the prerenewal market value of the property).

15. Robert Goodman, *After the Planners* (New York: Simon & Schuster, 1971), p. 59.

16. 42 U.S.C. Sec. 1460(c); Weiss, "The Origins and Legacy," pp. 58–62, 67.

17. Raymond Vernon, "The Myth and Reality of Our Urban Problems," in *Urban Renewal: People, Politics, and Planning*, eds. Jewell Bellush and Murray Hausknecht (Garden City, N.Y.: Anchor Books, 1967), pp.172–174; Wilton S. Sogg and Warren Wertheimer, "Legal and Governmental Issues in Urban Renewal," in *Urban Renewal: The Record and the Controversy*, ed. James Q. Wilson (Cambridge, Mass.: The MIT Press, 1966), pp.163–64; Nancy Klieniewski, "From Industrial to Corporate City: The Role of Urban Renewal," in *Marxism and the Metropolis*, 2d ed., eds. William K. Tabb and Larry Sawers (New York: Oxford University Press, 1984), p.205.

18. *Berman v Parker*, 75 S.Ct. 98 (1954).

19. Scott Greer, "Urban Renewal and American Cities," in *Urban Renewal: People, Politics, and Planning*, p. 87; Jewell Bellush and Murray Hausknecht, "Entrepreneurs and Urban Renewal: The New Men of Power," in *Urban Renewal: People, Politics and Planning*, p.221; Peter Rossi and Robert Dentler, *The Politics of Urban Renewal—the Chicago Findings* (New York: Free Press of Glencoe, 1961); Klieniewski, "From Industrial to Corporate City," pp.209–11.

20. 42 U.S.C. Sec. 1455(c).

21. Goodman, *After the Planners*, p. 64.

22. Foard and Fefferman, "Federal Urban Renewal Legislation," in *Urban Renewal: The Record*, p.101; William L. Slayton, "The Operation and Achievements of the Urban Renewal Program," in *Urban Renewal: The Record*, p.211; Sec. 305 of the Housing Act of 1956; Sec. 409 of the Housing Act of 1959; and Sec. 310 of the Housing Act of 1964.

23. Martin Anderson, *The Federal Bulldozer* (Cambridge, Mass.: The MIT Press, 1964), pp.2–3, 56–57.

24. 42 U.S.C. Sec. 4601 *et seq.*

25. See Peter Williams and Neil Smith, "From 'Renaissance' to Restructuring: The Dynamics of Contemporary Urban Development," in *Gentrification of the City*, pp.214–15.

26. *Alexander v HUD*, 441 U.S. 39 (1979).

27. *Harris v Hill*, 555 F.2d 1357 (8th Cir. 1977).

28. *Moorer v HUD*, 561 F.2d 175 (8th Cir. 1975), *cert. den.* 436 U.S. 919 (1978); *Young v Harris*, 599 F.2d 870 (8th Cir. 1979).

29. The information on the Pershing-Waterman redevelopment project is based on the briefs by appellants and appellees in the case of *Young v Harris*, 599 F.2d 870 (8th Cir. 1979), a class action suit filed in 1978 by the author and Margaret Zonia Morrison when they were staff attorneys at Legal Services of Eastern Missouri. The suit, among other claims, challenged the displacement of residents of the Pershing-Waterman area, without relocation assistance and benefits being given under the URA.

30. *Young v Harris*, 599 F.2d 870 (8th Cir. 1979).

31. Neil Smith, "Gentrification, the Frontier, and the Restructuring of Urban Space," in *Gentrification of the City*, pp.15–34; Kathryn P. Nelson, *Gentrification and Distressed Cities: An Assessment of Trends in Intrametropolitan Migration* (Madison: The University of Wisconsin Press, 1988). As Nelson's study shows, redevelopment and gentrification are not, by any means, universal phenomena. In fact, most cities continue to show a new out-migration of upper-income

residents. Redevelopment more typically is centered on a few areas of central cities. In some cities, it is virtually nonexistent.

32. See, for example, the well-known definition of displacement devised by George and Eunice Grier in 1978, quoted by Richard T. LeGates and Chester Hartman in "Displacement," *Clearinghouse Review* 15, no. 3 (July 1981): 214: "Displacement occurs when any household is forced to move from its residence by conditions which affect the dwelling or its immediate surroundings, and which: 1. are beyond the household's reasonable ability to control or prevent; 2. occur despite the household's having met all previously imposed conditions of occupancy; and 3. make continued occupancy by that household impossible, hazardous, or unaffordable."

33. Peter Marcuse, "Abandonment, Gentrification, and Displacement: The Linkages in New York City," in *Gentrification of the City*, pp.153–77. The following discussion uses the concepts developed by Marcuse in this article.

34. Peter Marcuse, "Off-Site Displacement" (Testimony for the House Sub-committee on Housing and Community Development, Committee on Banking, Financing, and Urban Affairs, United States House of Representatives, October 1, 1988), pp. 7–9.

35. Marcuse, "Off-Site Displacement," p. 9. See *Munoz-Mendoza v Pierce*, 711 F.2d. 421 (1st Cir. 1983), and *Chinese Staff and Workers Association v City of New York*, 509 N.Y.S. 2d 499 (N.Y.Ct.App. 1986), for two examples of off-site displacement that would result from redevelopment projects.

36. The information on the Williams family is based on the evidence that was presented in court in 1983 when the Williamses retained the author to represent them in their efforts to save their home, as well as the author's attendance at community meetings in the Tiffany area during 1983 and 1984.

37. Peter Marcuse, "To Control Gentrification: Anti-Displacement Zoning and Planning for Stable Residential Districts," *New York University Review of Law and Social Change* 13, no. 4 (1984–85): 931–52. Marcuse's article contains a detailed model anti-displacement zoning ordinance, which is the basis for this author's proposal.

CHAPTER 8

1. *Hawaii Housing Authority v Midkiff, et al.*, 104 S.Ct. 2321 (1984).

2. *Hawaii Housing Authority v Midkiff, et al.*, at 2329–30.

3. While most state constitutions are written in a similar fashion to the federal Constitution with regard to eminent domain, those drafting legislation that authorizes the taking of property would need to research the state constitution and court decisions in their own states to ensure that such legislation would not violate state constitutional provisions.

4. *Village of Euclid v Ambler Realty Co.*, 272 U.S. 365 (1926) is the landmark Supreme Court case upholding the constitutionality of zoning laws, against a claim that such laws amount to a taking of property for a public purpose without just compensation.

5. *Penn Central Transportation Co. v City of New York*, 438 U.S. 121, 124 (1978); *Agins v City of Tiburon*, 447 U.S. 261 (1980).

6. *Loretto v Teleprompter Manhattan CATV Corp.*, 458 U.S. 419 (1982); *Penn Central* at 125–28; *Tiburon* at 260.

7. *Fisher v City of Berkeley*, 693 P.2d 261 (Cal. 1984), *aff'd* 106 S.Ct. 1045 (1986); John N. Drobak, "Constitutional Limits on Price and Rent Control: The Lessons of Utility Regulation," *Washington University Law Quarterly* 64, no. 1 (1986): 142–43. Kenneth K. Baar, "Guidelines for Drafting Rent Control Laws: Lessons of a Decade," *Rutgers Law Review* 35, no. 4 (Summer 1983): 723–885 provides an excellent summary of the economic, legal, and practical issues in rent control laws.

8. *Pennell v City of San Jose*, 108 S.Ct. 849 (1988).

9. See, for example, *Property Owners Association v Township of North Bergen*, 378 A.2d 25 (1977), in which the New Jersey Supreme Court struck down a rent control law that prevented rent increases for poor elderly tenants on the grounds that such a prohibition could result in rent levels that were insufficient to provide a fair return on the landlord's investment.

10. *Block v Hirsh*, 256 U.S. 135, 41 S.Ct. 458 (1921). Baar, "Guidelines for Drafting Rent Control Laws," pp. 834–35; Note, "Constitutionality of Rent Control Restrictions on Property Owners' Dominion Interests," *Harvard Law Review* 100, no. 5 (March 1987): 1072–73.

11. Note, "Constitutionality of Rent Control Restrictions," pp.1072–73.

12. 688 P.2d 894 (Ca. 1984), appeal dismissed for lack of a substantial federal question, 470 U.S. 1046 (1985).

13. Note, "Constitutionality of Rent Control Restrictions," pp.1072–73; Baar, "Guidelines for Drafting Rent Control Laws," pp. 835–40.

14. *Heart of Atlanta Motel, Inc. v United States*, 379 U.S. 241 (1964) (public accommodation); *Queenside Hills Realty Co. v Saxl*, 328 U.S. 80 (1946) (fire regulation); *Pennell v City of San Jose*, 108 S.Ct. 849 (1988) (rent control); and *Home Building & Loan Assn. v Blaisdell*, 290 U.S. 398 (1934) (mortgage moratorium).

15. *Loretto v Teleprompter Manhattan CATV Corp.*, 458 U.S. 419, 440 (1982).

16. 191 Cal. Rptr. 47 (Cal. App. 1983).

17. Jonathan M. Purver, "Modern Status of Rules as to Existence of Implied Warranty of Habitability or Fitness for Use of Leased Premises," *ALR 3d* 40: 646–58; Jonathan M. Purver, "Retaliatory Eviction of Tenant for Reporting Landlord's Violation of Law," *ALR 3d* 40: 753–59.

18. Janet Boeth Jones, "Validity and Construction of Law Regulating Conversion of Rental Housing to Condominiums," *ALR 4th* 21: 1083–1102.

19. *Orrego v Department of Housing and Urban Development*, 701 F.Supp. 1384 (N.D. Ill. 1988).

20. See, for example, the Racketeer Influenced and Corrupt Organizations Act (RICO), 18 U.S.C. Sec. 1963; *Russello v United States*, 104 S.Ct. 296 (1983).

21. Ronald V. Dellums, "Introduction," in *Defense Sense: The Search for a Rational Military Policy*, ed. Ronald W. Dellums (Cambridge, Mass.: Ballinger Publishing Co., 1983), pp. xvii–xviii, 3–4; Rear Adm. Gene R. LaRocque, "Preparing to Fight a Nuclear War . . . The Reagan Arms Budget," in *Defense Sense*, pp.109–11.

22. Dellums, "Introduction," pp. xxv–xxvi; Jane Midgley, *The Women's Budget: Third Edition* (Philadelphia: The Jane Addams Peace Association, 1989), pp. 6–10. Ninety percent of the U.S. military budget is for foreign intervention and

nuclear war; only ten percent is for actual defense of the country. LaRocque, "Preparing to Fight a Nuclear War," pp.113–14.

23. From 1946 to 1980, the Department of Defense budgets totaled $2 trillion; the military budget for just the eight years of the Reagan administration was $2 trillion, a substantial increase in the average annual military budget, even accounting for inflation. Midgley, *The Women's Budget*, p. 6; Seymour Melman, "Military Spending and Domestic Bankruptcy," in *Defense Sense*, p.163.

24. See Midgley, *The Women's Budget*, p. 5, where the figure of $28 billion for housing is proposed.

25. Gordon Adams, "The 'Iron Triangle' and the American Economy," in *Defense Sense*, pp.173–74; Anderson, "The Empty Pork Barrel," in *Defense Sense*, p.194.

26. Melman, "Military Spending," p.166; Anderson, "The Empty Pork Barrel," pp.193–94; Adams, "The 'Iron Triangle,' " p.173.

27. Midgley, *The Women's Budget*, p. 7.

28. Christina Willemsen and William Ramsey, *The St. Louis Peace Budget* (St. Louis: American Friends Service Committee, 1986), p. 9. According to the chart on p. 9, $1 billion spent on education creates 71,550 jobs, $1 billion spent on health care creates 54,267 jobs, and $1 billion spent on mass transit creates 39,532 jobs.

29. Anderson, "The Empty Pork Barrel," pp.185, 188, and 193.

30. Low Income Housing Information Service (hereafter LIHIS), *Special Memorandum: The Fiscal Year 1990 Budget and Low Income Housing* (Washington, D.C.: LIHIS, 1989), Table 6.

31. Cushing Dolbeare, "How the Income Tax System Subsidizes Housing for the Affluent," in *Critical Perspectives on Housing*, eds. Rachel Bratt, Chester Hartman, and Ann Meyerson (Philadelphia: Temple University Press, 1986), pp.266, 268. Calculation of average amount of reduced taxes are this author's.

32. Number of homeowning taxpayers in 1985, from U.S. Bureau of the Census, "Introductory Characteristics—Occupied Units," *American Housing Survey for the United States in 1985*, Current Housing Reports, No. H–150–85 (Washington, D.C.: U.S. Government Printing Office, 1988), Table 2–1.

33. To make the tax deductions fair for tenants, who presently cannot deduct that portion of their rent that goes to mortgage interest, tenants should also be allowed a tax credit of up to $200 for that portion of their rent that helps to pay the landlord's mortgage interest. To make this proposal revenue neutral, the expense deductions allowed to a landlord should be reduced by the amount of credit allowed the tenants in the landlord's building.

34. Jim Luther, " 'No New Taxes' Aside, Here is What Some Would Generate," St. Louis *Post-Dispatch*, December 27, 1988, 1B.

35. For more detailed discussion of the practical and legal issues involved in linkage programs, see Mary E. Brooks, *A Guide to Developing a Housing Trust Fund* (Washington, D.C.: Center for Community Change, 1989); Philip D. Tegeler, "Developer Payments and Downtown Housing Trust Funds," *Clearinghouse Review* 18, no. 6 (November 1984): 678–96; and Alan Mallach, *Inclusionary Housing Programs: Policies and Practices* (New Brunswick, N.J.: Center for Urban Policy Research, 1984), pp.166–92.

36. See, for example, *San Telmo Associates v City of Seattle*, 735 P.2d 673 (Wash.

1987), in which the Washington Supreme Court struck down a Seattle ordinance that required property owners that wished to convert property to nonresidential use either to provide relocation benefits to tenants and replace a percentage of the low-income housing with other housing, or else pay a fee into a low-income housing replacement fund. The court overruled the city's argument that this ordinance was economic regulation within its police powers and found, instead, that the ordinance was a tax that the city had no legal authority to impose under state law. In *Terminal Plaza Corp. v City and County of San Francisco*, 223 Cal. Rptr 3d 379 (Cal. 1986), by contrast, the California Supreme Court upheld a single-room occupancy preservation ordinance that required owners of residential hotels, before converting or demolishing such units, to provide relocation assistance to hotel residents and to construct or rehabilitate an equal number of residential hotel units or to pay a fee to the city of 40 percent of the units, stating that it was valid as part of general police power regulation and was not a tax.

Glossary

Administrative allocation. Allocation by a bureaucracy, using criteria established by law or regulation, rather than allocation by the market.

Block-busting. To block-bust, realtors spread rumors in a predominantly white neighborhood that minorities are moving in, causing panic selling at bargain prices; realtors can then sell these houses at a mark-up to minorities moving in, netting a substantial profit.

Crowded. A household with more than one person per room.

Dissimilarity index. This is a measure of the distribution of minority and majority groups in a metropolitan area. A dissimilarity index of 0 would mean that all tracts in the metropolitan area have the same percentage of minorities as exist in the total metropolitan area, while an index of 1.0 would mean that no minority and majority members share any tract in common.

Exclusionary zoning. These are zoning laws that have the purpose or effect of excluding lower-income housing from a municipality or an area of a municipality.

Federal Home Loan Mortgage Corporation (FHLMC). This is a secondary mortgage institution, created in 1970, with a primary focus on the purchase of conventional mortgages, although it is also allowed to purchase VA- and FHA-insured mortgages.

Federal National Mortgage Association (FNMA). This was created in 1938 to buy federally insured mortgages, so that mortgage lenders were assured a market on which they could sell their mortgage loans. In 1968, FNMA was converted to a privately owned but publicly sponsored agency.

Fair Plan. An inferior insurance plan established by state governments throughout the United States after the 1968 riots to provide insurance coverage when homeowners cannot obtain coverage on the private market.

Government National Mortgage Association (GNMA). This agency, created in 1968, took over FNMA's portfolio of government-insured mortgages.

Housing vouchers. Housing vouchers are payments to tenants of the difference between 30 percent of the tenant's income and the fair market rent of the unit.

Inadequate housing unit. One that has plumbing, heating, electrical, sewage, maintenance, or public hall defects.

Inclusionary zoning. These are zoning devices designed to ensure that lower-income housing is built as part of a housing development. Inclusionary zoning devices can include granting partial exemptions from density limitations or giving developers bonuses for each unit of lower-priced housing built.

Infrastructure. This refers to the facilities, services, and installations necessary for a community, for example, streets, sewers, lights, or electrical lines.

Low-income household. A household with income equal to or less than 50 percent of the area's median income, adjusted for household size. In federal housing law, this is referred to as a very-low-income household.

Lower-income household. A household with income below 80 percent of an area's median income, adjusted for household size.

Macroeconomics. The study of the national economy and the size and composition of the aggregate production of goods and services. Thus, it is concerned with factors influencing the Gross National Product and composition of the GNP.

Microeconomics. The study of individual transactions in the market place, and how prices and quantities of particular goods are determined.

Moderate-income household. A household with income between 50 and 80 percent of an area's median income, adjusted for household size.

Moderate physical problems. A housing unit is defined in the 1985 American Housing Survey as having moderate physical problems if it had problems with the plumbing at least three times in three months, had unvented heating units as the primary heating equipment, had three maintenance problems, had three hallway problems, or lacked certain kitchen appliances, but none of these problems was severe.

Nonnuclear families. Families that contain members other than parents and their children.

Nominal mortgage interest rate. The interest rate listed on mortgage loan.

Point. One percent of the loan amount. Lenders charge points on mortgage loans as part of the closing costs to increase the return on the loan. The points charged are in addition to the interest rate charged on the loan.

Racially restrictive covenants. These were agreements that were made part of the real estate deed to a piece of property and that provided that the property could not be sold to various minorities, such as blacks, Jews, Indians, Orientals, or Puerto Ricans.

Real mortgage interest rate. The nominal interest rate adjusted for inflation.

Redlining. The practice of refusing to make mortgage loans or provide homeowners' insurance to certain parts of a metropolitan area, because of the racial or economic composition of the area.

Secondary mortgage market. Mortgages are bought and sold by various institutions in the secondary mortgage market, thereby increasing the flow of credit into housing finance.

Section 8 program. This housing program, established in 1974, had three different components: existing housing, new construction, and substantial rehabilitation. Under the existing housing program, a low- or moderate-income household that has a Section 8 certificate pays between 10 and 30 percent of household income for rent, and the government pays the difference between the rent paid by the tenant and the market rate for the unit. The new construction program guaranteed to developers, for 20 to 40 years, depending on the type of financing for the project, that Section 8 rental assistance would be provided. The substantial rehabilitation program guaranteed housing assistance for 15 to 40 years.

Section 202 program. This program, established in 1959, provided federal loans at low interest rates to nonprofit developers of housing for the elderly and handicapped; in 1974, interest rates on the loans rose to market levels.

Section 221(d)(3) program. This program, established in 1961, provided below-market-rate financing to developers for low- and moderate-income rental housing. In return, the developers had to guarantee that they would maintain the units as affordable housing for low- and moderate-income households for 20 to 40 years.

Section 235 program. Under this program, established in 1968, the federal government made payments to lenders to reduce the interest rate for low- and moderate-income homebuyers to as low as 1 percent, in order to reduce mortgage payments for such homebuyers.

Section 236 program. The precursor to the Section 8 program, the Section 236 program, established in 1968, subsidized the interest rates on mortgages for private developers of rental housing projects that would be rented to lower-income tenants.

Section 312 program. The Section 312 program, established in 1964, provided low-interest loans to owners and tenants in urban areas to pay for rehabilitation to conform to urban renewal plans or insurance underwriting requirements of the Fair Plan.

Severe physical problems. A unit with severe physical problems is defined in the 1985 American Housing Survey as one that lacks certain plumbing, lacked adequate heating at least three times during the winter, has no electricity or has serious electrical problems, has five maintenance problems, or has four designated problems in the hallways.

Severely inadequate housing unit. One in which defects in plumbing, heating, electrical service, sewage, maintenance, or public hall are serious in terms of health, safety, and repair costs.

Steering. Steering is the practice of encouraging a prospective purchaser to look in some neighborhoods and not in others, based on the race of the purchaser or renter and the racial composition of neighborhoods.

Subsidized housing. For purposes of this book, this refers to housing (other than public housing) in which the owner or occupant receives direct government subsidies. It does not refer to housing that is indirectly subsidized through tax deductions for mortgage interest or real estate taxes.

Testers/testing. Testing for housing discrimination typically involves sending out a white and a minority person of the same race as the person seeking housing to the firm or person selling or renting real estate and recording the responses that are received. These testers can then testify in court to help the plaintiff prove that discrimination occurred.

Thrift institutions. Savings and loan associations and mutual savings banks.

Selected Bibliography

Abrams, Charles. *The Future of Housing*. New York: Harper & Row, 1946.

Andrusz, Gregory D. *Housing and Urban Development in the USSR*. Albany: State University of New York Press, 1984.

Art, Robert C. "Social Responsibility in Bank Credit Decisions: The Community Reinvestment Act One Decade Later." *Pacific Law Journal* 18, no. 4 (July 1987): 1071–1139.

Baar, Kenneth K. "Guidelines for Drafting Rent Control Laws: Lessons of a Decade." *Rutgers Law Review* 35 (Summer 1983): 723–885.

Bellush, Jewell, and Murray Hausknecht, eds. *Urban Renewal: People, Politics, and Planning*. Garden City, N.Y.: Anchor Books, 1967.

Bratt, Rachel, Chester Hartman, and Ann Meyerson, eds. *Critical Perspectives on Housing*. Philadelphia: Temple University Press, 1986.

Burchell, Robert W., W. Patrick Beaton, and David Listokin. *Mount Laurel II: Challenge and Delivery of Low-Cost Housing*. New Brunswick, N.J.: Rutgers University, 1983.

Burke, Gil. *Housing and Social Justice: The Role of Policy in British Housing*. London: Longman, 1981.

Calmore, John O. "Fair Housing and the Black Poor: An Advocacy Guide." *Clearinghouse Review* 18, no. 6 (November 1984): 606–73.

Clavel, Pierre, John Forester, and William W. Goldsmith, eds. *Urban and Regional Planning in an Age of Austerity*. New York: Pergamon Press, 1980.

Cowley, John. *Housing for People or for Profit?* London: Stage 1, 1979.

Danielson, Michael N. *The Politics of Exclusion*. New York: Columbia University Press, 1976.

DiMaio, Alfred John, Jr. *Soviet Urban Housing: Problems and Policies.* New York: Praeger Publishers, 1974.

Duclad-Williams, Roger H. *The Politics of Housing in Britain and France.* London: Heineman, 1978.

Ellman, Michael. *Socialist Planning.* Cambridge: Cambridge University Press, 1979.

French, R.A., and F.E. Ian Hamilton. *The Socialist City: Spatial Structure and Urban Policy.* Chichester: John Wiley & Sons, 1979.

George, Vic, and Nick Manning. *Socialism, Social Welfare, and the Soviet Union.* London: Routledge & Kegan Paul, 1980.

Gilderbloom, John I., and Richard P. Appelbaum. *Rethinking Rental Housing.* Philadelphia: Temple University Press, 1988.

Goering, John M. *Housing Desegregation and Federal Policy.* Chapel Hill, N.C.: University of North Carolina Press, 1986.

Goetze, Rolf. *Rescuing the American Dream: Public Policy and the Crisis in Housing.* New York: Holmes & Meier Publishers, 1983.

Goodman, Robert. *After the Planners.* New York: Simon & Schuster, 1971.

Harloe, Michael. *Private Rented Housing in the United States and Europe.* London: Croom Helm, 1985.

Hartman, Chester, ed. *America's Housing Crisis: What Is To Be Done?* Boston: Routledge & Kegan Paul, 1983.

Hawley, Peter K. *Housing in the Public Domain.* New York: Metropolitan Housing Council, 1978.

Headey, Bruce. *Housing Policy in the Developed Economy.* New York: St. Martin's Press, 1978.

Helper, Rose. *Racial Policies and Practices of Real Estate Brokers.* Minneapolis: University of Minnesota Press, 1969.

Horvat, Branko. *The Political Economy of Socialism: A Marxist Social Theory.* Armonk, N.Y.: M.E. Sharpe, Inc., 1982.

Institute for Community Economics. *The Community Land Trust Handbook.* Emmaus, Pa.: Rodale Press, 1982.

Jacobs, Barry, G. Kenneth R. Harney, Charles L. Edson, and Bruce S. Lane. *Guide to Federal Housing Programs.* 1st ed. Washington, D.C.: Bureau of National Affairs, 1982.

Keith, Nathaniel S. *Politics and the Housing Crisis since 1930.* New York: Universe Books, 1973.

Kemeny, Jim. *The Myth of Home Ownership: Private versus Public Choices in Housing Tenure.* London: Routledge & Kegan Paul, 1981.

Lake, Robert W. *The New Suburbanites: Race and Housing in the Suburbs.* New Brunswick, N.J.: Rutgers University, 1981.

LeGates, Richard T., and Chester Hartman. "Displacement." *Clearinghouse Review* 15, no. 3 (July 1981): 207–49.

London, Bruce, and J. John Palen, eds. *Gentrification, Displacement and Neighborhood Revitalization.* Albany: State University of New York Press, 1984.

Mallach, Alan. *Inclusionary Housing Programs: Policies and Practices.* New Brunswick, N.J.: Center for Urban Policy Research, 1984.

Marcuse, Peter. "To Control Gentrification: Anti-Displacement Zoning and Planning for Stable Residential Districts." *New York University Review of Law and Social Change* 13, no. 4 (1984–85): 931–52.

Massey, Douglas S., and Nancy A. Denton. "Suburbanization and Segregation in U.S. Metropolitan Areas." *American Journal of Sociology* 94, no. 3 (November 1988): 592–626.

Meehan, Eugene J. *The Quality of Federal Policymaking: Programmed Failure in Public Housing*. Columbia, Mo.: University of Missouri Press, 1978.

Merrett, Stephen. *State Housing in Britain*. London: Routledge & Kegan Paul, 1979.

Momeni, Jamshid A., ed. *Race, Ethnicity and Minority Housing in the United States*. New York: Greenwood Press, 1986.

Nelson, Kathryn P. *Gentrification and Distressed Cities: An Assessment of Trends in Intrametropolitan Migration*. Madison: The University of Wisconsin Press, 1988.

Nove, Alec. *The Economics of Feasible Socialism*. London: George Allen & Unwin, 1983.

Orfield, Gary. *Must We Bus*? Washington, D.C.: Brookings Institute, 1978.

Pugh, Cedric. *Housing in Capitalist Societies*. Westmead, Eng.: Gower Publishing Co., Ltd., 1980.

Pynoos, Jon. *Breaking the Rules: Bureaucracy and Reform in Public Housing*. New York: Plenum Press, 1986.

Rosen, Kenneth T. *Affordable Housing: New Policies for the Housing and Mortgage Markets*. Cambridge, Mass.: Ballinger Publishing Co., 1984.

Schrenk, Martin. *Yugoslavia: Self-Management Socialism and the Challenge of Development*. Baltimore: Johns Hopkins University Press, 1979.

Schwartz, David C., Richard C. Ferlauto, and Daniel N. Hoffman. *A New Housing Policy for America: Recapturing the American Dream*. Philadelphia: Temple University Press, 1988.

Smith, Neil, and Peter Williams. *Gentrification of the City*. Boston: Allen & Unwin, 1986.

Szelenyi, Ivan. *Urban Inequalities under State Socialism*. London: Oxford University Press, 1983.

Tabb, William K., and Larry Sawers, eds. *Marxism and the Metropolis*. 2d ed. New York: Oxford University Press, 1984.

Tuccillo, John A., and John J. Goodman, Jr. *Housing Finance: A Changing System in the Reagan Era*. Washington, D.C.: The Urban Institute Press, 1983.

U.S. Bureau of the Census. *American Housing Survey for the United States in 1985*. Current Housing Reports, No. H–150–85. Washington, D.C.: U.S. Government Printing Office, 1988.

U.S. Congress. Senate Committee on Banking, Housing, and Urban Affairs and House Committee on Banking, Finance, and Urban Affairs. *A New National Housing Policy: Recommendations of Organizations and Individuals Concerned about Affordable Housing in America*. 100th Cong., 1st sess., 1987, S. Print 100–58.

Wilson, James Q. *Urban Renewal: The Record and the Controversy*. Cambridge, Mass.: The MIT Press, 1966.

Working Group on Housing. *A Progressive Housing Program for America*. Washington, D.C.: Institute for Policy Studies, 1987.

Wynn, Martin, ed. *Housing in Europe*. London: Croom Helm, 1984.

Index

About the Author

ARLENE ZAREMBKA is an attorney in private practice in St. Louis, Missouri. From 1976 to 1980 she was an attorney in the Housing Unit at Legal Services of Eastern Missouri, where she handled both individual and class action suits opposing displacement by urban redevelopment corporations and challenging racial discrimination in housing. She also helped to develop and carry out a community education program that focused on the causes of the housing crisis.

Since leaving Legal Services, she has continued her involvement in housing rights work through teaching, legal representation of persons facing displacement, and work with local housing rights groups. Ms. Zarembka is also active in a broad range of other civil rights activities as a member of the National Lawyers Guild and the Program Committee of the American Friends Service Committee in St. Louis, and as a co-operating attorney for Lambda Legal Defense and Education Fund. Her articles on housing and civil rights have appeared in a variety of publications, including the *Housing Law Bulletin, St. Louis Post-Dispatch, Missouri Law Review, Barrister, Saint Louis University Public Law Review, ACLU Liberties,* and *Reproductive Rights Newsletter.*

She graduated Phi Beta Kappa with honors in economics from Swarthmore College in 1970, and received her law degree *cum laude* from St. Louis University Law School in 1974. She has taught as an adjunct faculty member at the St. Louis University and Washington University law schools, and in the Sociology and Women's Studies Departments of Washington University.